THE VALLEY
of the
SHADOW *of* DEATH

THE VALLEY

of the

SHADOW *of* DEATH

A TALE OF
TRAGEDY AND REDEMPTION

Kermit Alexander,
Alex Gerould, and Jeff Snipes

ATRIA BOOKS

NEW YORK   LONDON   TORONTO   SYDNEY   NEW DELHI

ATRIA BOOKS

An Imprint of Simon & Schuster, Inc.
1230 Avenue of the Americas
New York, NY 10020

First Atria Books hardcover edition September 2015

ATRIA B O O K S and colophon are trademarks of Simon & Schuster, Inc.

For information about special discounts for bulk purchases, please contact Simon & Schuster Special Sales at 1-866-506-1949 or business@simonandschuster.com.

The Simon & Schuster Speakers Bureau can bring authors to your live event. For more information or to book an event, contact the Simon & Schuster Speakers Bureau at 1-866-248-3049 or visit our website at www.simonspeakers.com.

Interior design by Kyoko Watanabe

Manufactured in the United States of America

10 9 8 7 6 5 4 3 2 1

Library of Congress Cataloging-in-Publication Data is available.

ISBN 978-1-4767-6576-1
ISBN 978-1-4767-6578-5 (ebook)

This book is dedicated to the memory of my mother, Ebora;
my sister, Dietra; and my nephews, Damon and Damani.

Psalm 23

The Lord is my shepherd; I shall not want.

He maketh me to lie down in green pastures; he leadeth me
beside the still waters.

He restoreth my soul; he leadeth me in the paths of righteousness
for his name's sake.

Even though I walk through the valley of the shadow of death,
I will fear no evil; for thou art with me; thy rod and thy staff
they comfort me.

Thou preparest a table before me in the presence of mine enemies:
thou anointest my head with oil; my cup runneth over.

Surely goodness and mercy shall follow me all the days of my life;
and I will dwell in the house of the Lord forever.

CONTENTS

AUTHOR'S NOTE

My name is Kermit Alexander, and this is my life story. The events in this book are based upon my own recollections. As to episodes for which I was not personally present, the narrative relies upon discussions with other family members, interviews with law enforcement and prison personnel, the newspaper coverage of the case, trial transcripts and legal documents, as well as the historical record. Source references are included at the back of the book.

THE VALLEY
of the
SHADOW *of* DEATH

PRELUDE

THE INCIDENT THAT gave rise to the events set forth in this book took place on the evening of October 4, 1983, in a now-defunct nightclub on the corner of Vermont and Gage in South Central Los Angeles. A young woman was dancing inside the tavern when a fight broke out involving fists, knives, furniture, and a .38-caliber revolver. After the altercation the young woman lay paralyzed. It was her twenty-first birthday. The events launched by this incident would devastate a family, haunt the community, and find their way to the heart of California's death penalty wars three decades later.

1

AN EMPTY HOUSE

I<small>T IS ONE</small> month since my family was massacred inside their home. The quadruple homicide remains unsolved. The police have no suspects.

Last week, the landlord told me to clean out the house. He wants to rent it as soon as possible. So along with movers and a cleaning crew, I return to the scene, 126 West Fifty-Ninth Street in South Central Los Angeles.

No one else in the family could bear to join me. It is the first time I have been back since my mother, sister, and two nephews were killed.

It is a hot September afternoon, the Santa Ana winds driving the desert air off the Mojave and into the valley.

As I walk the pathway to the one-story bungalow, the lawn on either side is scorched. My mother would have been ashamed.

Instinctively I pat my hip. Reassured that the pistol is secure at my side, I continue up the walkway.

Overhead, tall palms rustle in the dry wind.

I take the two broad stairs onto the porch, where I am met with more signs of disorder, as dirt, dead leaves, and uncollected papers litter the entryway.

I am already sweating. I exhale, brace myself, and open the front door into the living room. It stands frozen at 8 a.m. on August 31, 1984. The TV with outstretched rabbit-ear antennas still sits in the corner. Trophies crowd the mantel. Only the plants show the effects of time, the greenery by the front window dried and wilted, the poinsettia on the coffee table dead.

I direct the movers, and continue into the dining room.

It too remains unchanged. A white lace tablecloth lies undisturbed. Place mats, salt and pepper shakers, and a bottle of hot sauce stand in place, awaiting the next meal. A pair of reading glasses sits atop a stack of unopened mail. All the signs of everyday life are intact. I wait for family members to come rushing in at any moment, to restore the house to its rightful din. I listen, but only the shuffling of the movers breaks the silence.

On a credenza, beneath the dishware, rows of family photos line a shelf, graduations, football games, proms, weddings, reunions, and picnics. I stare at the pictures of brothers and sisters, nieces, nephews, grandchildren, grandchildren, grandchildren, my freshman picture with the UCLA Bruins, my rookie shot with the 49ers, another on the Rams, more grandchildren. The photos are stacked as thickly as LPs in a record store.

Finally I look away, break the trance. For the first time I notice how hot it is inside. I open a window.

I start boxing the photos.

In the breeze a tiny felt Santa dangles from the chandelier above the dining room table, a fugitive from last year's holidays. I reach up, remove it, and toss it into a box, then head for the kitchen.

Nothing in either the living or dining room hints at what occurred. The killers walked through both rooms, but left no trace.

The kitchen is a different matter. Though previously cleaned of blood, the smell lingers in the heat. Gnats swarm the spot where my mother was slain.

I push open more windows to drive away the stench.

I pat the weapon at my side.

In the kitchen, a kettle of burned beans remains on the stove. A half-finished cup of coffee sits upon the counter. An overturned frying pan lies on the floor. Bullet holes riddle the east wall.

After clearing the kitchen, I move on to the front bedroom. It defies house norms. Even my mother, with her iron rules of order, was no match for her visiting grandsons. Heaps of clothes bury the furniture. Boyish clutter squeezes the room small. Fingerprint powder coats smooth surfaces. Gnats cluster to the kill sites where my sister and nephews slept.

I direct the movers to pack the room, then head to the rear of the house. I pass by the back door where the killers fled.

I put off the rear bedroom closet until last. As I remove the clothes, I try, but fail, to block out my nephew's nightmare. The boy had saved his life by hiding in the closet, as the sound of gunfire, screams, and shattered glass tore through the house.

Otherwise, the room is untouched. The beds lie unmade. A desk is covered with books. Against the wall sits a couch with one arm singed by fire.

Now, as the movers pack the final pieces of furniture into the truck, I watch the house empty. The absence of long-familiar items drives home the finality. Gone are my mother's clothes laid out for the day ahead, her favorite armchair, the crucifix and rosary that hung above her bed, the couch where siblings once elbowed for space.

After the movers finish, I conduct a final walk-through.

The cleaning crew then goes to work, erasing all signs of crime. Soon the home will be ready for its new tenants. For the first time in seventeen years it stands bare.

My mother's familiar refrain rattles about my head.

Forever surrounded by a large family and constant company, she would always say, "There's nothing worse than an empty house."

For the moment, and for the first time in weeks, sorrow has drowned out rage. But I feel it stirring, clawing for release. With the house packed, the hunt can continue.

As we load the final boxes into the truck, I grab the one with the family photographs and place it in my car. I turn the ignition, but cannot make myself drive.

Before me, the movers' truck pulls away. Still I sit. I unroll the window. With a nervous tic I again feel for the gun.

From above, the palms shake in a harsh gust of desert air. A frond falls to the side of my car.

Still unable to drive, I begin rummaging through the box of pictures.

From inside the house the cleaning equipment hums and whirs, to my left, the sound of a passing car, then another. Across the street a man grabs a hose and waters his lawn. The wind drives the hundred-degree heat into my face. A plane drones overhead.

I am alone. The movers and cleaners are just doing their job. The cars, the man, the plane, all indifferent.

I pull out a photo of each of the departed and place them on the passenger seat beside me. My mother, just short of her sixtieth birthday, smiles from behind big round glasses. Her name is Ebora, but we all call her Madee (pronounced muh-DEE), short for mother dear. She wears a powder-blue dress and matching earrings, the colors of my alma mater, the University of California, Los Angeles. My youngest sister, Dietra, "the baby," is twenty-four years old and awaits her wedding day. My nephews, Damani, thirteen, and Damon, eight, grin from school yearbook pictures.

I cannot stop staring at the photos.

The car motor continues to run.

They are the last pictures taken of them in life, a portal to the other side, my window into their final hours.

I want to drive, floor the car, get as far away from that house as possible. But I just sit there, immobilized.

To leave is to concede defeat.

Over and over, I replay that morning, hoping somehow to will a new outcome, desperately trying to unwind time.

I dwell on that date. I curse it. August 31, 1984. The day the light went out of my life.

2

THERE WERE NO STRANGERS

On Friday, august 31, 1984, as she did every morning, Madee arose by five. She got into her bathrobe and slippers, put on her glasses, and made her way across the dark hallway. In the kitchen she turned on the lights and began making a pot of coffee.

She then walked through her dining room and living room to the entrance, opened the front door, and collected her morning paper.

As always, she swept the low, wide stairs and front porch.

Ritual and routine were important; cleanliness and appearance vital. She was proud of her home and things had to be just so.

Next she watered the flowers and plants surrounding the porch. The stream from the hose gleamed silver beneath the streetlamp.

With daybreak still an hour away, it already felt hot. The last day of August would be another scorcher in South Central, with the temperature once again hitting one hundred. As she reentered, she left the front door open to cool the house. The screen door rattled closed behind her. She left it unlocked.

Madee's home at 126 West Fifty-Ninth Street was known to all as an open house, where family, neighbors, and local kids were always welcome. She loved to play the hostess, and her home represented a community resource, a sanctuary where the residents of South Central could gather informally, and talk about family, the church, local politics, or neighborhood goings-on. At Madee's it was always "community time," a place where the private and public were one, where the word *stranger* was unknown, and the word *family* meant everyone who walked in the door. As usual she expected people to come and go throughout the day. Madee had raised eleven children. She liked it best when the house was full.

Lately, however, many of us had quarreled with her over the house. We stressed that the neighborhood had changed. East-side problems kept creeping west. She'd been there seventeen years. It was time to move on, somewhere nice, farther west, like Ladera Heights.

She would listen and tell us that she'd think about it. But we all knew she was in no rush. I'd even gone so far as to make a down payment on a house in a better part of town. But even that didn't convince her. Yes, she admitted she'd seen changes over the years. Her neighborhood of Florence had become blacker, poorer, and though she tried not to think about it, more dangerous. Gunshots and drive-bys were frequent, the police helicopter a constant. Just over a year ago, Madee herself was mugged, her purse ripped from her hands.

But despite the encroaching disorder, she remained. The robbery was a fluke, she insisted. The media exaggerated the decline. She resented her community being labeled "a ghetto." A tour of her neighborhood revealed mostly good people going about their lives, caring for their properties. Certainly it bore no resemblance to the burned-out Bronx, or Chicago's high-rise hells. It was mostly single-family bungalows, small yards, and palm-lined streets.

Now, in the early morning, as she made her way onto the porch and looked about at her plants and yard, the thought of leaving made her sad. She was loyal to her home and neighborhood, and she felt a sense of duty. She provided a service. She reached out to the community and literally brought it into her home. She was doing God's work, playing a part in *His* plan. She brought stability. She was one of the few remaining role models. Why should the good people, like her, move—forfeit what they had worked for, dreamed of—and abandon the neighborhood?

She wanted the community to "stick together," and she wasn't going to be the one to leave the kids behind. "If I left," she asked, "then who would give them hugs and make them peanut butter sandwiches?" She always said that little acts made for big differences: hug a kid, save a block, then a neighborhood, and so on. And no one could deny it, she had presence, a way about her that made kids listen.

And besides, Madee was tough. She had survived eleven childbirths, eleven children, Jim Crow segregation, a cross-country migration, a marital split, public housing, and the Watts Riots. Surely another tough neighborhood was just another hurdle, another one of *His* tests. And as always she would pass, she would muscle through. We all told her she was stubborn, but she just took it as a compliment. There was nothing wrong with a little stubbornness, she'd say; it showed heart, it helped you hold on. And besides, it was her home, she liked it, and she did not feel like moving. And that was that, she harrumphed to herself as she walked from the porch back into the house.

As she returned to her kitchen, carrying the morning paper, she passed the front bedroom where my sister Dietra slept. She would soon move out of the house for the first time, following her upcoming wedding. My nephews Damani and Damon also slept in the bedroom. Damani, as he did every year, came south from the San Francisco Bay Area to spend the summer with his grandmother, while Damon, an L.A. native, was visiting for the weekend. Both boys would return to school following Labor Day. Madee would miss them. She said the kids "made it a true home again."

In the kitchen she poured her first cup of coffee and made some toast. She then put a kettle of beans on the stove to simmer. They took hours to cook. She planned to serve them for dinner. Madee's red beans and rice were legendary.

The house was quiet save for the hum of the Harbor Freeway to the west. In the back bedroom two other family members slept: my brother, Neal, thirty-three, and nephew Ivan, fourteen. Madee knew she would be the only one awake for hours to come. She enjoyed this predawn solitude; it gave her time to reflect, plan her day, and prepare for all the activity soon to come.

As she sipped her coffee, she reflected on another fulfilling week at St. Vincent's Hospital, where she worked in food services, always arriving an hour early to pray in the chapel. She also looked forward to her upcoming activities at the nearby St. Columbkille Catholic Church. Madee sewed and ironed the vestments for the clergy, helped the parish principal manage the children, and then let loose with multiple rounds of bingo.

But as she pondered her pleasant week, she wasn't able to shake a negative feeling that continued to intrude. The previous evening when my sister Daphine dropped off her boys, Damon and Ivan, she told Madee that lately Damon seemed troubled and insecure. She said he would follow her around the house, refusing to be out of her presence. He had requested that she read him reassuring Bible stories, and even mused as to what a wonderful place Heaven must be. He cried uncharacteristically and insisted on sleeping in his mother's bed. When asked what was wrong, he was unable to say, simply answering with an unconvincing "nothing."

Madee had tried to push the thoughts aside. Like most childhood fears, she would have assured herself, Damon's insecurities would soon pass. The cause was probably just sadness over summer's end, anxiety over entering a new grade.

Boosted by the coffee and the first signs of the sun, her mood brightened. Nothing would better cheer the boy than a weekend filled with family and friends at Grandma's house. After all, he had begged his mother to let him stay the weekend at Madee's with his cousins. And as he went to bed last night he at least seemed happy, smiling, joking. He specifically said how excited he was about the plans to go by the Coliseum the following day, where they would search for remaindered souvenir pins on South Flower Street, and take in the afterglow of the recently concluded Olympic Games.

Madee too had caught Olympic fever, especially after she had attended the Games, where Mayor Tom Bradley, a longtime family friend, recognized her and greeted her warmly before a large crowd.

Afterward, she was so thrilled she said she had floated home. She couldn't wait to tell her family and friends.

————

The 1984 Los Angeles Summer Olympics were a magical time for my family and community, and marked a turning point for the city. Securing L.A. as the host represented a major coup for Mayor Bradley.

Tom Bradley, the city's first black mayor, had a long and path-breaking history in Los Angeles. After his family migrated from the Deep South in the 1920s, Bradley attended Polytechnic High School, and then received a track scholarship to UCLA. He next served for twenty years in the Los Angeles Police Department, becoming the first black lieutenant. Bradley then became the first black elected to the city council, before becoming mayor, where he would serve an unprecedented five terms.

For blacks throughout L.A., Tom Bradley was a hero and an inspiration: athlete, trailblazer, visionary. With the Olympic Games, he sought to establish Los Angeles as a true world city, a major node in a globalizing world.

As the Opening Ceremonies began, the Coliseum and South Central L.A. took center stage. Thousands of doves and streamers soared, Mayor Bradley waved the Olympic flag, President Ronald Reagan addressed the crowd. When he spoke, two and a half billion people around the world listened, making it "the largest audience in the history of mankind." More athletes and nations attended these games than any before. As each team was announced the Coliseum roared.

For Mayor Bradley, the event marked the end of a ten-year struggle to return the Games to Los Angeles, where they had last been held in 1932, and where a fourteen-year-old Tom Bradley peered through the fence. Four years later, his idol, track star Jesse Owens, shocked Hitler in the 1936 Berlin Olympics.

The 1984 Olympics were filled with hopes, and tensions. The Games focus the world's attention upon the host city. Success means glory, disaster an international black eye. Record security stood in place to counter rumored terrorist threats. While designed by the ancient Greeks to bring nations together in a spirit of competitive peace, it didn't always work out. The tragedy of Munich and the slaying of the Israeli wrestling team by the Palestinian terrorist organization Black September were just two Olympiads removed. And for Mayor Bradley, security concerns were particularly acute. In 1982 he lost a heartbreaking gubernatorial election to George Deukmejian, who got to the right of him on law and order, tarring Bradley as soft on crime.

Further, an eerie hypercharged mood marked the lead-up to the 1984 Games, as they signaled a final hot flash in the Cold War. On Christmas Day in 1979 the Soviet Union invaded Afghanistan, and despite international condemnation, refused to withdraw. In retaliation, the United States boycotted the 1980 Summer Olympics in Moscow. In return, the Soviets, along with thirteen communist allies, refused to attend the 1984 Summer Games. An electric patriotism surged through the city.

To everyone's relief, the Games ended in triumph. The United States took home a record eighty-three gold medals. The security stood sound. The Olympic Village remained safe. And, unlike many previous Olympiads, the Los Angeles Summer Games, under the leadership of U.S. Olympic Committee chairman Peter Ueberroth, proved a stunning financial success. One city councilman called the Games "a Super Bowl of all Super Bowls" and "a masterpiece," while Chairman Ueberroth said, "If I were giving out medals for leadership, Tom Bradley would get the gold."

Following the closing ceremonies, composer John Williams's epic "Olympic Fanfare and Theme" filled the Coliseum. Fireworks lit the night sky. The public address announcer's voice ended the evening: "The games are over, now the memories begin."

The memories included the University of Southern California's own O. J. Simpson, and Jesse Owens's granddaughter, serving as torchbearers; the 1960 decathlon winner and UCLA alum Rafer Johnson lighting the Olympic logo; the heroics of Carl Lewis equaling Jessie Owens's four gold medals in track and field; and gymnast Mary Lou Retton closing out her performances with two perfect tens.

America was always seen as a place to start a new life, California a place to chase a dream, and Los Angeles a land of hope. Sold as a place to restore health, with a Mediterranean climate akin to the Greek isles, it was the perfect site for a summer Olympic Games. And in the Olympics, as in a Hollywood script, small-town kids from the world over flocked to the land of make-believe and returned bearing gold. For a couple of weeks in the summer of '84 the dream was re-vived, flickering across the screen in a brief but brilliant instant. For as the crowds dispersed and the athletes returned home, Los Angeles had captured the global imagination. The city shone with the glow of renewal and arrival.

The triumph left us with a sense of collective pride. As the Coliseum was located in South Central, and as Mayor Bradley himself once walked a neighborhood beat, local residents took a stake in the Games. Our neighborhood hosted the Olympics and shined before the world. For just a moment, our community wasn't on the outside, for-gotten and left behind. Briefly, we stood at the center, and for once, for the right reasons—on the front page, but not because of drugs, riots, and murders. Triumph brought one large collective exhale.

For Madee, and my family, the communal victory was personal. We had lived in South Central for forty years and had known Mayor Bradley for almost as long. When he said the Olympic spirit brought "people together, making them forget their prejudices as they celebrated human excellence," we cheered, feeling a fresh sense of hope.

My brother Gordon recalled the Olympics as one of the most amazing things he'd ever seen, with the city coming together as one, without factions. I remember South Central at the time as exuberant, with residents taking a renewed pride in place, in their yards and lawns. Gordon said that Los Angeles in August 1984 "was a place in which there were no strangers."

———

Two miles south of the Coliseum, Madee replaced her coffee on the kitchen table and read the morning paper. She listened for signs of stirring. The younger boy, Damon, usually rose early, then woke his cousin to play. But she heard nothing. The house remained silent as her family slept.

————

Not far from her home a '75 Chevy van rolls east on Slauson.

The avenue is South Central's major east–west artery. It is named after land developer J. S. Slauson, a nineteenth-century L.A. booster, who sold the region as a land of orange groves and haciendas, a place where anyone could start anew. In the decades following the completion of the transcontinental railroad in the 1860s, millions traveled west, transforming L.A. from sleepy pueblo to modern metropolis. By 1920 Los Angeles surpassed San Francisco as the state's largest city. By midcentury, Slauson Avenue was a booming industrial center, the home of the Bethlehem Steel mill, where thousands were employed. Now, in 1984, a new global economics prevails. The plants have moved and the mill is closed. Postindustrial blight remains.

The van is driven by a black female. Her friend rides shotgun. Three black men sit in the back. The van is industrial with no rear side windows. The men sit in heavy shadows.

Just after dawn, the storefronts on Slauson remain gated. The van drives past auto body and muffler shops, wholesale carpeting, used furniture, barbecue joints, checks cashed, donuts, liquor stores, Episcopal and Baptist churches, old tires, vacant lots. The streets are ashen, dead to dreams.

The rising sun spreads through the smog on the horizon. Discarded furniture and abandoned cars litter the street. Folks walk about like zombies. Crack cocaine has just begun its tour of ruin.

The van continues east past barbershops, beauty salons, minimarts, a burger stand, a bar, a Methodist church, a chain-link fence, a shuttered store.

When it reaches the intersection of Slauson and Western, the gas gauge is pegged at empty. The driver turns into the Shell station, gets out, and pumps two dollars' worth.

Inside the van there is no talk.

The silence is broken as the driver returns, slams the door, and restarts the engine. She peers at the gas gauge. Two dollars barely budges the needle.

Pulling into the light early morning traffic, the driver continues east on Slauson. Passing beneath the Harbor Freeway, the van falls into shadows, then returns to face the rising sun. It makes a right turn onto Broadway and heads south until it reaches West Fifty-Ninth Street, where it turns left, then slows to a crawl in front of No. 126. It rolls to a stop a couple of doors down the street, just west of Main.

The sliding door on the van's right side opens. The three black men begin to exit curbside. One is told to stay with the women. He returns to the rear of the van. The other two leave the vehicle and begin walking westbound. The motor is kept running, the sliding door remains open.

The two men pass a blue bungalow on their left, No. 122. As they approach the next home, 126, they turn up the walkway and toward the low front porch. A small patch of lawn lies on either side of the path. The porch has two wide steps. It is set between brick columns and surrounded by plants. The porch is wet. Someone has recently watered. The front door is open, with only a screen door standing guard.

The house is silent.

As the two men approach, one pulls a small metal object from his waistband and holds it in his hand. The other clutches something wrapped within a light blue jacket.

––––––

From the kitchen in the rear of the house, Madee heard the front screen door open, then swing shut.

She figured it must be me. Every Friday morning I came over for coffee.

She glanced at the time. It was just before eight. I was running late.

From within the sleeping house she heard footsteps approaching through the living room, then into the dining room, but from inside the kitchen she could not see their source.

At any second she expected to hear me say, "Madee."
Hearing no greeting, she called out, "Kermit, is that you?"
She received no response.
Only continued footfalls.
"Kermit?" she repeated.
"Kermit?"

3

FROM JIM CROW
TO MUDTOWN

Look at me as a little boy, five years old, playing in the barn.

Look at my family on their farm in southern Louisiana, working the fields till the fingers bleed.

See my father sail for the South Seas to fight the Japanese.

Listen to the South sing "Dixie" as the crosses burn and the strange fruit swings.

And look at my mother as she holds my hand as we board the colored car of a westbound train, in search of the future.

And every time I tell this tale, someone says to me, that's *my* family you're talking about, that's *my* story: born of the South, flight from Jim Crow, California dreams, stark awakenings, struggle, injustice, violence, rage.

This is our story.

It's not about saints' lives, just ordinary folks striving for something better, and what they have been forced to endure.

It's about the decisions we make when shut in dark places.

This is my story.

———

I am the oldest of Ebora Alexander's eleven children, born in New Iberia, Louisiana, on January 4, 1941.

Located on the banks of Bayou Teche, southwest of Baton Rouge, New Iberia sits in the heart of Cajun country. Established by the Spanish in 1779 as Nueva Iberia, the town soon became known for a mix of Indian, Spanish, French, and African cultures. Its history marked by Union occupation, Mississippi floods, yellow fever, and nearly a century of Jim Crow segregation, today New Iberia is famous for its swamps, hot sauce, and jungle gardens. Antebellum estates with sprawling lawns, live oaks, and Spanish moss highlight the region.

Yearly, New Iberia hosts the World Championship Gumbo Cook-Off, the Cajun Hot Sauce Festival, and the Great Gator Race. In the Sugar Festival, representatives from all of Louisiana's parishes compete for the title of "Sugar Queen." Traditional dishes of New Iberia include jambalaya, corn maque choux, and sweet potato casserole with praline topping. The Tabasco sauce factory operates on nearby Avery Island. The town is home to the writer James Lee Burke's fictional detective Dave Robicheaux.

My first memories of the South involve the old farm. How my father tended to a pregnant mare, performed a C-section, delivered the colt, then stitched the mother back up with yarn, applying juice from chewing tobacco to help heal the wound. I also recall the slaughterhouses where cows and pigs were butchered, and how my relatives soaked their blistered hands in milk after picking peppers all day. Above all, I remember the fact that every year there were more and more babies. My father was one of sixteen children, each of whom in turn averaged another ten kids apiece. An Alexander family reunion was a town unto itself. I was also told tales of a legendary great-grandfather, a militant family guardian who was said to stalk his enemies deep into the Louisiana swamps.

My grandfather, King Alexander, owned the farm and was a pastor for the AME, or African Methodist Episcopal Church. King possessed that most valued African trait—he had *presence*. One simply felt his authority. He didn't need to say a word. And he was old-school, meaning Old Testament, sworn to take an eye for an eye, and a life for a life. Justice was simple, absolute, and inevitable. If someone did you wrong, you did them back, and the quicker the better. But if you had to wait, you did. There was no statute of limitations on vengeance. Sooner or later, the wrong would be righted. This code was rooted deep in our past, carried by ancestors from West Africa, from Haiti, through the Carolinas, passed from generation to generation, from King to my father, then down to me. In a culture of dueling and vengeance, the children were trained early in self-defense and in weapon use.

There was no misunderstanding the message: fight and never quit. It was imbued in me. "You will have to fight forever," my father said, "for the rest of your life." And with this message came a fire, a built-in sense of anger and rage. I felt cursed with the genetic family temper, and burdened by the duty to keep it under control. "Behave or we'll bury you," went another family saying.

My father, Kermit Sr., and my mother, Ebora, married in 1940. Kermit Sr. was a mechanic, a boxer, a horse trainer, and soon to be a serviceman. Ebora was fifteen and soon to be a mother. After the Japanese attack on Pearl Harbor, Kermit Sr. enlisted in the armed forces and traveled to Camp Montford Point, in Jacksonville, North Carolina. There he would become one of the legendary Montford Point Marines, the first blacks to join the Marine Corps. As with the famous Buffalo Soldiers of the Army, or the Tuskegee Airmen, the Montford Point Marines earned the Congressional Gold Medal, theirs for valor in battling the Japanese in the South Pacific.

My father joined the Marines for two reasons. The first was he wanted to fight. At the time, blacks joining the Army landed in support service roles, as janitors and cooks, in the Navy as stewards. And this didn't change even following Pearl Harbor. During the attack, Dorie Miller, a black sailor, sheltered his wounded captain, manned a machine gun, and defended the USS *West Virginia*. Miller received the Medal of Honor. He was the first American hero of World War II. But blacks were still denied combat. My father wanted action and refused to be "treated like a slave." His second reason for joining the military was that he had to leave town. He was wanted by the Klan.

During the war the Montford Point Marines gained a reputation for ruthlessness. As what were called tunnel rats, it was their job to clean out the underground mazes harboring Japanese soldiers who refused to surrender. On islands like Iwo Jima and Okinawa, defoliated graveyards with none left living aboveground, my father and his fellow Marines hunted the subterranean survivors. The few remaining Japanese, buried deep in the tunnels, finally raised their hands in forfeit when confronted by these dark-skinned Marines. Legend has it they thought them some kind of ghost or ghoul.

After the war, Kermit Sr. returned to Louisiana, where he sought to buy some land, build a home, and run an auto shop. When the local real estate agent left him waiting all day long, then told him there was no land for sale, he knew he had to move on. Overseas he had risked his life for his country. He felt like a hero. Back home he felt like he didn't exist. He was going to take control, and escape Jim Crow.

For a black, in the segregated South, the most routine task was made a degrading challenge. The constant dishonor drove him mad. Where can I go to the bathroom, buy lunch, get a drink of water? Everything was restricted, off-limits, blocked. Colored this, white that, waiting rooms, swimming pools, lunch counters, park benches. And if a white woman walked by, boy you better get off the sidewalk and stare at the ground—or else.

And after fighting for his country in its most brutal theater of war, in the epic battle against tyranny, his own hometown couldn't grant him a timely meeting—made him sit for hours, just to tell him, "No, we don't have any land for *you*." Fight for freedom abroad to get denied at home. An ancient traveler through Africa once said he had met no people with less tolerance for injustice. Justice makes a man. He'd had it.

Throughout the war black servicemen fought the double battle, "Double V" it was called, victory over the enemy abroad, victory over segregation at home. "Democracy at Home and Abroad" was the slogan. For the Montford Point Marines and other blacks in the military, the war provided an opportunity to demonstrate strength and patriotism. As one Marine put it, "sad you have to look forward to a war to prove your ability." But at the end, the indignities continued. Montford Point was mocked as "Monkey Point," and blacks returning in uniform were stopped in the South, charged with "impersonating a member of the U.S. military."

When there was no "V" to be had in the South, Kermit Sr. joined millions of blacks in the Great Migration, heading for the industrial centers of the North and West. In 1946 he left his new family—which now included me and my two baby sisters—back in Louisiana, as he caught a train west to California in search of a new life. His sudden departure had them talking back on the bayou. What was he running away from?

After less than a year, my father found work as a mechanic in Los Angeles, and sent for the family. Madee, my aunt Eldora, my sisters Barbara and Mary Ann, and I followed him west by train. Through the bayou, the cypress forests of Louisiana, and the vast stretches of Texas we rode the segregated car. Denied access to the dining room, we ate our packed lunches. I can still taste the homemade fried chicken, still feel the orange peel breaking apart beneath my fingers. To this day, my sister Mary talks about those oranges. The journey sparked for her a lifetime love of trains, and no trip could begin without a fresh bag of her favorite fruit. For me the cross-country train ride was like a party, as we ran around the car, played with the porters, and watched the plains speed by. It felt magical. I didn't quite get just where we were going, making the adventure all the more exciting. For my family, like many black migrants, trains would remain forever emotional: symbols of freedom, escape, and the future.

When we reached the Texas–New Mexico border, we waved goodbye to Jim Crow. The segregated cars of the South were abandoned as we continued west to California. Even as a little kid I remember sensing something special occurring, awaiting a moment of arrival. When the train reached downtown Los Angeles, it pulled into the new Union Station. I'd never seen anything like it, the high ceilings, the chandeliers, the shiny marble floors. I felt tiny. And when I looked around, all I saw were black people, families like ours reunited, children and wives rushing into the arms of fathers and husbands. No eyes stayed dry.

In California, opportunities for blacks were better than back in the South, and my father soon had steady work as both a mechanic and as a horse trainer at the Santa Anita racetrack. From the time my parents reunited in Los Angeles, they would have eight more children.

Like my family, most blacks found discrimination less oppressive in the West. One could vote without fear, and earn better wages. In L.A. blacks could shed what poet Paul Laurence Dunbar called "The Mask": "that veil of racial inferiority and servility mandated by Jim Crow society." So blacks from Texas and Louisiana, as well as other ex-Confederate states, flocked to Los Angeles in the years in and after World War II, greatly changing the city's makeup. In 1939 L.A.'s black population numbered less than 40,000; by 1960 it neared half a million.

As their numbers grew, so did tensions, and doubts. Some blacks began to wonder whether California could live up to its dream. Many of the problems they fled dogged them thousands of miles to the west, in particular, housing. Through the use of various tactics— redlining, blockbusting, and restrictive covenants—banks, lenders, real estate agents, and sellers managed to limit black access to real estate, confining them to certain parts of town.

Black resentment began to simmer. And the indignation was not just directed at whites, but increasingly turned inward, as the struggle for limited housing intensified. Black families established in Los Angeles for decades, considering themselves urban and sophisticated, resented the constant flood of newcomers, country come-latelys, and uncouth hicks. Thus within the broader racial dynamic emerged an internal competition, one focused upon the date of departure, with the earlier migrants looking down on later arrivals.

The initial housing destination for blacks in World War II was an area known as Little Tokyo, a Japanese enclave in downtown L.A. Following Pearl Harbor and internment, the area vacated overnight. Buddhist temples turned into Baptist storefronts. Japanese storefronts became squatters' havens. The black presence became so heavy the district was renamed "Bronzeville."

However, as the Great Migration accelerated during and after the war, more and more blacks settled on the east side of the city, south of downtown. Here, in a part of what would come to be known as South Central Los Angeles, called Watts, my father settled our family.

Originally called Mudtown, in 1900 the district was renamed after the Watts family that donated the land for a turn-of-the-century railroad station. In the twenties Watts was incorporated into L.A. Initially white, in the wake of the Great Migration Watts quickly turned into a black part of town. The large black population was why Los Angeles annexed Watts, as the city council feared that an independent Watts would elect a black mayor. Running through Watts is the Central Avenue corridor, a famous site of black culture known as the "Great Black Way," or "Harlem West."

When we first arrived, my father drove us down the Central Avenue strip. As a boy who had known only the rural South, it blew my mind: bright colored lights and the strange sounds, storefront churches with preachers barking salvation, dandies with shoes shined like mirrors, reflecting the neon above. And the music of Central Avenue, a new kind of jazz, changing from boogie-woogie and swing to bop, ever more dissonant, angular, angry. Those sounds, those lights, those voices: "Come and see . . ." "The end time is near." Flashes, screams, sirens, jarring chords, it was startling, alluring, a new and unknown world.

Later, as a teenager, I would ride my bicycle up to Central Avenue. Too young to get into the clubs, I'd steal a listen as the notes escaped through an open door, the sounds of Kid Ory, Dexter Gordon, Lionel Hampton, and Charles Mingus. At home my parents would spin their records on the phonograph, push all the furniture to the edges of the living room, and we would have our own Club Alexander, where family and friends danced late into the night.

4

CHARCOAL ALLEY

THROUGH THE 1950s we remained in Watts, moving from one house to another. However, the expenses of raising a growing family finally drove my father into debt, forcing him to move us into the newly built Jordan Downs housing project. Part of a New Deal housing plan, Jordan Downs and other projects in L.A. were meant to ease the housing crunch facing returning soldiers and the working poor. At first the projects struck me as gorgeous, resembling a manicured campus, green, tidy, organized, with parks and schools. The buildings fit in with the landscape, built just two stories high, with lots of space between. There were no restricted gang territories. It was open, and felt free. In the spring I'd walk up to the fence and watch the baseball games at Jordan High.

Initially, families had to qualify to gain entry, had to prove employment, and agree to residency standards. But over time the dual plague of gangs and drugs began to bring the projects down. Residents without jobs failed to keep up their property, people started destroying the grounds, litter and graffiti spread. My family did everything they could to keep out the riffraff, but it was sad to see the projects decay and our quality of life decline.

But, despite the worsening conditions, the strong hand of both parents held our growing brood in line. And as the oldest, I did my part as well. I looked after my siblings and helped my parents run the house. I stayed away from the gangs, even though they courted me, used all of the gang seductions, the girls, the money, the respect, the rep. They had their own way of walking, talking, dressing, and being. They were in, hip, and cool. My father talked to me about them, and put it straight up. If I chose to hang with the gang, then they'd be my family. "Run with them, and don't come back," he said.

Right there I knew the gangs were a dead end. And I had several advantages for keeping them at a distance. They gave me a pass because I was a dedicated athlete. They also didn't mess with me because I had lovely sisters they wanted to date. I never let them near my sisters, but they kept trying, and they knew if they messed with me they'd have no chance. But most important, the gangs knew I didn't want in, and knew I would fight to keep myself out.

As my mother matured she proved herself a natural leader, the head of the household who kept things under control. But as was the family way, when she ruled, she flashed a fierce temper. Discipline had the feel of the Old South.

If we crossed her, we knew that we would get "the shoe." Back in Louisiana, Madee was quite a softball player, strong, athletic. But when she threw a shoe, it was straight out of the major leagues, high and hard. Sometimes, I swear, she could throw a curve, the shoe hitting us long after we'd taken a corner on a dead run.

I still remember a time when my younger brother Kirk came home late, really late, making a mockery out of Madee's curfew. And she fixed him. She bolted the door and nailed every window in the house shut—except one. And when he tried to snake through that one, she was waiting for him. She slammed the window down on him so that his legs were outside, his chest and arms inside, and then she pummeled him with shoe after shoe. She never let any of us forget that she was the enforcer. Her motto: "Subdue the head and the body follows."

And it wasn't just shoes.

When my sister Barbara lagged in doing the dishes, engaging in a small act of passive resistance, Madee, her hands covered in flour, just stared at her and returned to kneading the dough. Then, whack, fast as a fired shoe, Madee struck out with her right hand. And there stood Barbara, stunned, a big white handprint across her black face.

When Gordon, fascinated with fire, set the couch ablaze, Madee made him sit there with a book of matches, light each one, and watch it burn down to the end. By the time the book was empty, Gordon's fingers looked like hot dogs blackened at a wiener roast.

But for certain wrongdoings, we Alexander children could only have hoped for Mama's wrath. If we really upset her, made her feel disrespected, she simply issued those most dreaded words, "wait till your father gets home." The hours were the slowest and most terrifying, sitting alone in our room and waiting, the fear as harsh as the pain to come. For the girls it would be the cord of an iron, or electrical wires, for the boys a cypress switch. The cords and wires he reused; the tree out back ran bare of low-hanging branches.

This was the violent code of the South, inflicted, generation after generation, upon all its sons and daughters. We were children of a harsh southern love. Justice wasn't gentle.

Besides demanding discipline and responsibility, my mother also stressed education. From her ancestors back home, Madee learned there were two ways for blacks to gain control over their lives: the church and education. They told her that after the Civil War ended and the slaves were freed, no government could protect southern black folk. Reconstruction, called the "glorious failure" for its grand dreams and broken hopes, ended just ten years after the war. At that point the forces of reaction, white "redeemers" and the Ku Klux Klan, did all they could to keep blacks in their place, making sure they couldn't vote or own land. Southern blacks held paper promises but saw few material gains. The chains of slavery gave way to the walls of Jim Crow.

For my family the worlds of the church and education provided the antidotes to the injustices of segregation. These two worlds were tightly linked. Several of my ancestors were preachers and they made sure their family got the message: our only peace the church, our only hope the grace of God, the only way to know Him to read His good word. Heeding these words, Madee took it as her mission that all eleven of us would attend private parochial schools, ensuring we received Catholic instruction. And whether it was through formal education or individual study, the power of knowledge stayed with all of the Alexander children for the rest of our lives. Books, we were told, contained knowledge, and knowledge translated to power. No wonder masters kept slaves illiterate, allowed only handpicked Bible stories about turning cheeks and the meek inheriting the earth. Thus we were taught to treasure books, to view them as keys to opportunity.

There was only one place I was free to go after school: the library. I remember looking at the rows of books on the shelves, setting a goal to complete a book, then a row, then a shelf. My favorites were stories of adventure and survival. From an early age I needed little sleep and became a night owl. Always last to bed, I read by a single lamp into the small hours of the night.

Finally, for Madee, it was always a world without excuses. You were responsible for controlling your own life. Booker T. Washington was the model, with his message of self-help, self-improvement, and the need to prove your own worth. And he didn't just say it, he did it. True to his code, he helped others improve through practical study at the Tuskegee Institute in Alabama. For what Booker T. preached was the truth. You can make all the speeches you want about education and human dignity, but if you aren't self-sufficient, you end up dependent. Without economic independence you can never be free. That was the lesson of history. So learn your history, she'd say. It makes you who you are. Just don't let it control where you go.

As I applied these lessons while growing up, I was constantly reminded of two things: I had exceptional athletic talent and if I didn't learn to control my temper, my talent was worthless.

Two incidents in my early life, both dealing with sports and anger, helped mold my future.

The first took place during a Catholic Youth Organization football game when I was twelve. When the referee blew the whistle, I lost control, yelling, throwing my helmet, and slamming the ball at his feet. My father, watching my meltdown from the sideline, stormed onto the field, grabbed me by the collar, and dragged me away, humiliating me in front of everyone. The five-foot-four ex-Marine then told the coach, a priest from my school, that I would not return to the game until I learned to control myself and stop embarrassing my family. There he was, short but looming, another man of presence. He projected himself, he cast a long shadow. "Do it, or else," he said. "Yes, sir."

The second incident occurred in the boxing ring. My father was a great boxer and taught me the art, knocking me out several times in the process. Once, when I was fifteen, an older, more seasoned fighter thrashed me in the ring. Embarrassed and enraged, I tracked the guy down and damn near beat him to death. Following this explosion, my father dressed down both my boxing coach and me. He told the coach he needed to help me, or all my talents would be wasted. Then he told me that unless I learned to channel my rage, I would "end up just another killer."

And he had been true to his words. When he was at the breaking point with Louisianan Kluxers, he channeled his violence into the armed services, took it out on our enemies. When he was ready to explode after being Jim Crowed, instead of getting thrown in jail or lynched he took his anger, packed his bags, and headed west.

Remember: "Behave, or we'll bury you."

I didn't forget. I vowed never to let rage control me again. And soon after, at Mount Carmel High School in South Central L.A., I found the release for my anger, as well as my passion: football. Prior to this time I considered baseball my most promising sport. I loved to play it and had magical memories of sitting around the radio with my family as we cheered for Jackie Robinson and the Brooklyn Dodgers. But baseball didn't free my anger like football.

On the gridiron you could go berserk, you could vent your hate in a way that few legitimate pursuits allowed. Knocking someone out was not only legal, it got you a standing O. In high school the rage remained; it was just better directed. It was violence condoned, and my adolescent fury lashed freely. During football season my whole family came out every Friday night to cheer their rising star.

In 1959 when I graduated from Mount Carmel I was recruited by universities with Division 1-A football programs. For me the choice came down to two schools: UCLA and USC. I loved Los Angeles and now considered it home. For despite its problems, the city still offered blacks better opportunities than just about anywhere else. It was no racial paradise, but it sure beat Dixie.

Ultimately, the decision was easy, UCLA. No white university had treated black athletes better. It was at UCLA that Tom Bradley excelled in track and field in the thirties, where Woody Strode and Kenny Washington starred in football before breaking the NFL's color barrier in 1946, and where Jackie Robinson was a four letterman, in baseball, basketball, football, and track, before becoming the first black major leaguer in 1947. Furthermore, in 1949, five years before the Supreme Court decision of *Brown v. Board of Education*, UCLA was the first primarily white college in America to elect an African American, Sherrill Luke, its student body president.

From 1959 to 1963 I played on both sides of the ball at UCLA, as a cornerback and safety on defense, and at running back on offense. I was honored as an All-American in both football and track, and won the NCAA triple-jump championship. While competing, I studied kinesiology and sociology. At the time my plan was to compete in the 1964 Summer Olympics in Tokyo, then go on to graduate school, earn a Ph.D., and become a professor.

However, during my senior year at UCLA, my coaches told me that I would go high in the upcoming draft and could be a professional football player. I was still skeptical, but when they told me I would start receiving an immediate paycheck instead of spending the next seven years in graduate school, that clinched it for me. For the first time since my family moved west, I could pay off their debt.

In 1963 I entered the draft. At the time there were two professional leagues, and I received offers from both the 49ers of the National Football League and the Broncos of the American Football League. The Niners picked me eighth overall, the Broncos fifth. I signed with San Francisco and moved up north.

When I left Los Angeles for the Bay Area, I swore I'd stay close with my family. The lessons were well ingrained—be responsible, take care of your own, don't expect anyone else to do it for you. Like

my legendary great-grandfather, I must be the family's guardian. As
the oldest son, and now a professional athlete, it was my job to provide for my mother and ten siblings. Once I started receiving NFL
paychecks, I made Madee's dream of sending all of her children to
private schools come true.

———

In the summer of 1965, getting ready for my third season in the league,
I reported to training camp with the 49ers in Northern California. But
on August 11, I was horrified when tragedy struck the streets of Watts.
What started out as a seemingly routine traffic stop of a twenty-year-
old black man named Marquette Frye exploded into urban warfare.

Knowing the neighborhood, I feared something like this could
happen. There was much grief in Watts. Jobs shrank, housing declined, police brutality rose. But tragically, what began as community
protest flared into out-of-control vandalism. Gang members and
criminals trashed stores and burned buildings, acts of self-destruction
that simply ruined things for everyone left behind.

Most alarming to me, my family lived in the heart of the combat
zone, across the street from Will Rogers Park. Frantically, I tried to
get through on the phone, over and over, but with no luck. There was
no service in the neighborhood.

Back in training camp, I watched the disaster unfold on TV. I saw
national guardsmen trade gunfire with snipers on surrounding roofs.
I saw familiar buildings go up in flames. I wanted to fly down, rush
in, and drag my family out. But no one was allowed in. The neighborhood was barricaded, sealed off. Smoke and flames filled the screen.
Unable to do anything but sit and watch made me want to scream, or
put my fist through the set.

More calls. Still no word. I slammed down the receiver.

———

As night falls and the flames gut Watts, a scene plays out that will
impact my family years later.

A seventeen-year-old black female, named Sondra Lee Holt, sits on her bed in her mother's home. Her back is against the wall and her legs are bent at the knees.

She has not slept for two days. The riots, the noise, the thrill, the fear, the drugs, have all kept her awake.

Now, as she often does, she stares before her at a crack in the wall opposite her bed. It looks like a spider, and sometimes she thinks she sees it move. Other times she is sure of it. Sometimes it gets inside her head, pushing up against her eyes, causing her great pain.

Outside, glass breaks, voices are raised; someone yells, "Burn, baby, burn!"

Inside, through her closed door, she hears a man's voice. "Come here," he says. Her mother laughs in response: too loud, drunken, exaggerated.

Sondra hears a crash, and bodies falling to the floor. Hysterical laughter, then giggling and pawing.

It will all be fun until it isn't, until he starts to hit her. It doesn't matter who he is. It always ends up the same.

Sondra darts her eyes to her door, to make sure it is locked. It is always bad when he comes in. That's what makes her hate.

Focusing on the door makes the spider go away, but not the pain. Every sound is amplified: fire engines, voices, footsteps, slamming doors, and breaking glass. All too damned loud.

She wants to scream, to hit people, to hurt herself.

She reaches for the bottle on the floor, takes two long swigs of whiskey, then returns to her position against the wall. She cradles the bottle under her right arm.

As she leans back she feels her belly move. There has been more of that lately. For a minute it breaks the bad thoughts, hints at something nice.

She takes another long drink.

Her mind stops raging and she rubs her swollen belly from top to bottom, up then down.

She is six months pregnant. Six months ago she met the father-to-be at a party. Now he's in jail, but he will be out soon. She quit school after learning she was soon to be a mother.

Calm thoughts, she now tells herself, she must have calm thoughts. Everything will change with the baby's birth. All will be new and better. Finally, something to call her own, something over which she will have control.

One more drink, and a little more control over her thoughts.

She had heard people say you should talk to your baby, even before it is born. Say nice things and then the baby will be born with nice thoughts.

"It's okay, baby, it's okay," she says, soothing her restless unborn.

She hopes the baby hears her voice, and not the noise.

Inside the house, her mother's man bangs on the door. Her mother is screaming.

Outside: sirens, bullhorns, rage.

She squeezes a pillow over her head to quell the pain.

"It's okay, baby," she chants, as she rocks back and forth.

———

Finally, the following day, I heard from my mother. The family was safe; distraught and shaken up, but safe. But everyone knew the neighborhood would never be the same. The riots caused more than $40 million in damages. Thirty-four people died. More than a thousand were injured, another four thousand arrested. Our street had a new nickname, "Charcoal Alley."

For weeks following, the papers were filled with ominous warnings. The McCone Commission, established by Governor Pat Brown to assess the causes of the disturbance, decried a deep sickness infecting the community, spoke of dashed expectations, frustration, and disillusionment, of illiterate, unemployable youth who quit school to take to the streets. Working as a probation officer in San Francisco in the off-season, I was all too familiar with such problems. I knew the dire predictions to be true. I vowed to move my family out of Watts.

At the time, my career was peaking. I led the team in interceptions. I would soon make All-Pro. I could afford to move them. It was my duty. And when Madee told me that she and my father were separating, the need to move turned urgent. The thought of her living as a single mother in the tinderbox of Watts made me shudder. But Madee, set in her ways and stubborn, resisted the idea. She was attached to her neighbors, church, community, and routine. It would take a near-perfect scenario to convince her to leave these behind.

In 1967, two years after the Watts Riots, I finally succeeded. I rented a house belonging to the wife of a former UCLA teammate. It had been her family home growing up. It was a clean one-floor bungalow on a quiet palm-lined street. The neighborhood was residential, largely white, and with an address of 126 West Fifty-Ninth Street, it was a few houses west of Main, the dividing line between East and West L.A.

This carried great symbolic weight.

This meant that the Alexander family had arrived.

They could now say they lived on the "West Side."

When my brother Gordon first set foot in the house, he was overcome.

He got down on his hands and knees and kissed the floor.

5

MAMA, GO GET 'EM

Seventeen years after my brother Gordon kissed the floor and blessed our good fate, Madee stood in the kitchen and reached for her coffee.

It was a little before eight.

Why was I so late, she wondered. And why didn't I answer as she called my name. And come to think of it, why had I acted so strangely when she last saw me, the day before yesterday. After my visit she had walked me to my car and kissed me goodbye. She then took a seat on her front porch. And for some reason I just kept driving around the block and returning to say goodbye, again and again.

"What's wrong with you?" she had yelled to me as I peered at her out of my car window.

"I don't know," I had answered, smiling uneasily, then repeated, "I don't know."

She just shook her head and smiled.

And I did it again and again, just kept driving around the block. It was like the car was on autopilot, stuck on a track. Something would not allow me to leave.

After my sixth or seventh pass, I broke free and drove away.

She blew me a kiss goodbye.

Finally, I headed home.

Now the footsteps that had fallen through the house came to a stop, just a few feet from where Madee stood in her small kitchen. She replaced her half-finished cup of coffee on the counter. She turned to her left and stared into the hallway.

———

In the back bedroom of the house, my brother Neal and nephew Ivan slept soundly through the early morning hours.

Neal, age thirty-three, was on disability and working through some psychologically tough times. He had returned to the family home in an effort to restore some order and stability to his life. He enrolled in a local community college, where he became obsessed with learning, no matter the subject, with the pursuit itself giving his life a new purpose. At one point he said, "Algebra saved my life."

Due to his intensive studies, we began calling him "Dr. Neal."

Madee was so inspired she decided to realize one of her dreams. Finally free after thirty years of childrearing, she earned her high school GED.

Ivan, fourteen years old, was, like his eight-year-old little brother, Damon, visiting his grandmother for the last weekend of summer. Ivan loved playing football with the family, and like his relatives had been caught up in the Olympics.

For Ivan, a sports-obsessed youngster in a sports-obsessed family, it didn't get much better than this. Finish out the last week of summer hanging out with his All-Pro uncle, take in the Olympic afterglow, and talk sports in L.A.'s golden age: the Rams went to the Super Bowl in 1980, the Dodgers won the World Series in 1981, the "Showtime" Lakers won the NBA championship in 1980 and 1982, and Uncle Kermit's UCLA Bruins had just crushed their opponents in two straight Rose Bowls.

———

Just after eight o'clock on the morning of August 31, Ivan is torn from sleep by the sound of gunshots and breaking glass.

He hears bullets crashing through walls and a woman's screams.

Ivan sees his uncle Neal jump out of bed and run from the room.

In the hallway stands a black man with a long gun. Someone screams Neal's name. Then more gunshots.

Ivan rushes into the bedroom closet and shuts the door.

His mind cannot grapple with what takes place. He keeps asking himself if this is real or just a dream. If it is a dream, he cannot break free.

From the darkness he hears wrestling and thumping, the sounds of a struggle. He fears they will find him.

He then hears footsteps running through the house. Again he cringes, pictures the closet door suddenly thrown open.

He hears the sound of the back door opening and shutting. More hurried footsteps. Again, the back door opens and shuts. Footsteps recede outside the house.

Then silence.

Ivan waits. And waits.

Continued silence.

Slowly he cracks the door.

A sliver of light jabs into the pitch of the closet.

His eyes adjust as he peers through the opening.

————

The telephone rang for the third time before I came to. I was asleep in my Hollywood home, about ten miles from Madee's.

I looked at the clock. It was almost 8:30 a.m. I had overslept.

I had little doubt who was calling. It would be Madee trying to figure out what happened. Why was I so late? What was I doing?

Oh boy, I thought as I shook the sleep from my eyes. She was really going to let me hear it now. Partly in jest, but with an underlying note of gravity, she would let me know that I had dropped the ball, let her down.

It was ironic, because I was especially excited about meeting with her that day. I had some good news I had been looking forward to telling her. But the anticipation of sharing a triumph with the one person who would most appreciate it left me unable to sleep. I often found that Madee's reaction to my good news was better than the good news itself. It was always so inspiring to talk with her. I couldn't wait. And due to my excitement I had gone to bed late and then overslept.

On Thursday, the day before, I had been hired to be the play-by-play color analyst for UCLA football. I was back in the game. It felt like a kind of homecoming. I withheld the news from Madee so that I could tell her in person. She had supported my football career from the start, and had been so excited when I went to UCLA and then when I returned from San Francisco in 1970 to play for the home-town Rams. Now she would be thrilled that I was back with my old alma mater.

For me it was another dream, another moment of arrival, as a long-term gnawing fear could be put to rest. It started as just a glint, but was turning into the full glow of a plan. I wasn't going to be just another retired athlete who faded away. For as soon as one even considered retiring, all of the limitless possibilities of the field were replaced by the realities of life after football. You were great in the arena, now what can you do? Hope dims as retirement looms. The fear of the athlete, where the peak comes so young: All-American by twenty, All-Pro by thirty, forgotten by forty. But now I felt I might find a direction, post-NFL.

As I reached for the phone, I readied myself to go on offense. I would preempt her questions with a quick apology, and the an-nouncement that I had some news for her, that I was dressing as we spoke, that I was on my way out the door, and I would be there in minutes.

"Hello. Madee, I'm so sorry," I prepared to say, as I picked up the phone mid-ring.

But before I could finish "Hello," I was interrupted.

"Kermit," my brother Neal struggled to say, sounding like he was panting. It was hard to hear him. He sounded like a child unable to catch his breath through the tears.

My first thought was that poor Neal was having another episode. What a shame, I thought. Lately he seemed to be doing so much better.

"Kermit," Neal's voice cracked, "why did they do that?"

Now fully awakened by a family member's trauma, I went into problem-solving mode. First goal, help Neal settle down, subdue his demons.

"What did they do?" I asked in my calmest, it-will-be-all-right voice.

More panting, shallow breaths.

"Why would they mess up Mom like that?"

———

As I drive the ten miles to my mother's house every ounce of my steeled self-control is on trial. I'm aggravated by the plodding rush-hour traffic. The time approaches 9 a.m. This will take forever.

My mind screams: Why hadn't I been there? How could I have let this happen? I fear I'm going to lose it.

From the Hollywood Freeway I merge onto the Harbor Freeway. Stop-and-go, then bumper-to-bumper. Moments of acceleration, and I punch the car forward. False hope, false starts, the maddening ebb and flow of the Southern California freeway. The traffic again stalls out, grinding to a halt.

But it couldn't be real. None of this is real. Not real, I keep telling myself. Who would hurt Madee? Why would anyone hurt her? She is beloved. She is known as the nicest lady in the neighborhood. She is a community treasure. No, this is not really happening, I reassure myself, and once I arrive at the house I will learn what a cruel hoax has been played. Please, God, clear up this mess and let things be right.

I turn off the Harbor Freeway at the Slauson Avenue exit. I drive through the old neighborhood. The mirage has already faded. The streets so recently resurrected by Olympic gold now revert to form: a landscape bleak and indifferent, where brother wastes brother with no second thoughts.

Searching for anything upon which to anchor hope, I replay the night of the Watts Riots. I sat there, watching the smoke and flames, the chaos in the streets. My family was at its epicenter. The neighborhood burned, I couldn't get through. But they did. They made it, and they would again. They must.

I brace myself for the turn onto West Fifty-Ninth Street, ready to see the house known for nearly twenty years as the "Alexander House."

Please, I pray, just give me the normal and familiar: children playing, bicycles spinning, neighbors gossiping.

The heart pounds.

I turn onto West Fifty-Ninth.

The heart breaks.

A mass of emergency vehicles blocks the street. Yellow police tape cordons off the front yard. Hundreds of strangers gawk. I instantly feel that the family home no longer belongs to us, already overtaken by tragedy and spectacle.

On the sidewalk in front of me several neighbors are crying. I hear one talking to a police officer. I catch the tail end of her sentence: "They were very nice people."

Another neighbor: "She never did anything to anybody."

A third: "I don't know who her enemy would be. She is a lovely person and has lived here for about fifteen years. I don't understand it. I just can't believe they'd do it to Mrs. Alexander."

From the back of an ambulance a gurney is removed and rolled toward the house.

A neighbor across the street collapses onto her lawn screaming.

I see my family huddled in anguish.

My sister Joan is hysterical, trying to rush into the house as two officers restrain her.

The sun continues to arc over the horizon. Tall, still palms cast long distorted shadows.

Convulsing, Joan shrieks at the officers:

"My mother's in there. Tell me what happened!"

Nearby, a girl hangs on her mother to keep from collapsing. She wails, "They're not dead, Mama, they're *not* dead. Mama, go get 'em. They're *not* dead."

6

OUR FAMILY ISN'T
LIKE THAT

THE ROBBERY AND Homicide Division of the Los Angeles Police Department is responsible, on a citywide basis, for investigating homicides involving serial killers, "arson as a manner of death," "intense media coverage or high profile," and "multiple victims (generally three or more) in one incident."

Located in the Parker Center, or Police Administration Building, in downtown Los Angeles, the RHD, which was established in 1969, had taken part in numerous high-profile investigations since its inception. These included the Manson family murders of 1969, the shootout with the radical Symbionese Liberation Army in 1974, the Bob's Big Boy massacre of 1980, as well as several serial killer cases of the late 1970s and early 1980s: the Skid Row Stabber, Hillside Strangler, Sunset Strip Killer, and Freeway Killer.

By the end of summer in 1984, two new serial killers occupied much of RHD's time.

With two kills in the first half of 1984, an assailant described as having "long curly hair, bulging eyes and wide-spaced rotting teeth" would be dubbed by the media "the Walk-in Killer," or "the Valley Intruder." Eventually linked to at least fourteen killings in Los Angeles and the San Francisco Bay Area, the perpetrator, Richard Ramirez, would come to be known as the "Night Stalker."

Also active by the summer of 1984 was a killer of prostitutes in South Central L.A. Eventually ten were killed, all but two African-American. The suspect was described as "black, with a dark complexion, 30 to 35 years old and 5 feet 10 inches to 6 feet tall. He is said to have black hair, brown eyes, smooth skin, a medium build and muscular arms." As the body toll mounted and the case went unsolved, neighborhood fear and frustration grew. Eventually a group of twelve women picketed in front of police headquarters claiming that because the victims were black prostitutes the police were not pursuing the case with proper vigor.

This was part of a larger pattern during the early eighties, in which several different serial killers preyed upon young black women in South Central. Collectively the murders were considered the doings of the "South Side Slayer."

In addition to serial killings, drug and gang killings were also on the rise, particularly in South Central.

Thus my family's case was the latest in a spate of tragic violence to hit the region. But its extreme nature shocked even the calloused inhabitants of South Central. It quickly grabbed the attention of the press, the police, and the mayor's office.

As my family's case was considered high profile, and involved multiple victims, Robbery Homicide immediately took over the investigation from the division detectives.

————

Inside my family's home, officers from LAPD's Newton and 77th Street Divisions had already responded to the scene. These units were the West Coast equivalents of "Fort Apache, the Bronx," outposts of law and order surrounded by an urban war zone. If the Bronx was made infamous by arson fires and a postapocalyptic landscape, South Central was plagued by the memory of Watts, and the twin scourges of street gangs and crack cocaine.

Located in the heart of South Central and patrolling some of L.A.'s roughest neighborhoods, officers of these divisions affected a certain bravado. They saw in their units that thin blue line protecting society from the forces of disorder and chaos. The 77th Division's motto captures the mentality: "Violent men for a violent society." Newton's nickname: "Shootin' Newton."

But like the battle-scarred residents of South Central, these hardened street fighters found themselves taken aback by what they saw inside. When they left the house, there were tears in their eyes.

———

Upon their arrival at the scene, members of my family were quickly whisked away, taken to nearby Newton Station for questioning. When a family member is murdered, the killer is often one of their own.

In the squad room at the station, my sisters Joan and Crystal were placed in chairs facing different directions and told not to speak to each other. Neither knew any details, nor the extent of what occurred.

Another sister, Daphine, sat separately at the station. Earlier in the morning she had received a call from her son Ivan, who said "something real bad happened in the house." After Ivan's call, Daphine had spent the morning walking around in circles and babbling. Once she composed herself enough to make a call, she phoned her older sister Mary, at work in San Diego.

"Start praying," Daphine told Mary: "Something awful happened."

Daphine then begged the Lord: "Just let them be alive. Let them be on life support. Just let me see them once before they die."

But when I arrived at the station, and my sisters saw my expression through a glass partition, they knew it was all over. The oldest son, and the rock of the family, had no answers. I just stood there numb, with a look of empty shock, my arms hanging helplessly at my sides.

Seeing my face, Joan, an officer in the military Judge Advocate General's Corps, lost control and fell to the floor.

And the questioning by the police continued.

And my family countered with questions of our own.

"Why are we being treated like this?"

"Our family isn't like that," Joan implored. "We don't do things like that."

Crystal, an intensive care nurse who treated terminally ill cancer patients, could not stand the tension.

For Crystal, the suffering that took place within the hospital walls was at least understandable, but this was surreal. An hour before, she walked the halls at work. Now she was interrogated, surrounded by photos of LAPD's most wanted, stared at by killers.

She screamed at the officers, "What's going on in my mother's house?!"

When the police finally explained, Joan hyperventilated and pounded the walls.

"Why would anybody want to do that? Shoot up some kids?"

————

When the police first responded to 126 West Fifty-Ninth Street, they noticed nothing amiss. There was no sign of forced entry. The front door was open, the screen door unlocked. The living room looked neat and undisturbed.

As they made their way through the house, the next room, the dining room, was likewise without any signs of disruption or disorder.

Only when they turned left from the hallway did the spell break.

In the kitchen the body of an older woman, wearing a bathrobe and slippers, lay dead on the floor. An upside-down frying pan covered her chest. She suffered three cranial gunshot wounds. A large pool of blood radiated from her head. All wounds were through-and-through. Evidence of the close-range shots stained the kitchen's east wall and curtains. A wad of scalp rested atop the bananas on the kitchen table.

During the medical examiner's on-scene inspection, a copper-jacketed expended bullet fell from the bathrobe's folds.

A half-finished cup of coffee sat on the kitchen counter. Beans simmered on the stove. Bullet holes dotted the east wall.

As the officers made their way through the house, three more bodies were found in the northwest bedroom.

A woman in her twenties lay slumped in her bed, also shot three times. One bullet went through her chin, another penetrated her right cheek, the third to the right side of her chest near the armpit. Two bullets exited the body, one lodged in the rib cage. Bullet holes pierced the bedroom's west wall. Blood spatter stained it.

A young teenage boy was found lying on the floor covered in his bedclothes. He suffered one gunshot wound to the right side of his forehead. The bullet exited through the back of his skull and lodged into the floor beneath his head.

A little boy lay in bed under the covers. Shot once in the back of the head, the bullet exited his left temple before coming to rest in the mattress.

————

The initial examination of the bodies concluded, the emergency response team prepared gurneys to take them to the morgue, where they would be identified and formal autopsies performed.

Following the removal of the deceased, a latent fingerprint examiner attempted to lift prints from within the house. In the northwest bedroom, where Dietra, Damani, and Damon had slept, the technician took powder, dusted with a fingerprint brush, and where prints developed, placed tape over the print and then transferred it to a card. A total of seventeen prints were taken from the room, including a nearly full palm print recovered from a red storage trunk.

The fingerprint examiner also dusted the southwest bedroom, where Neal and Ivan had slept, and from which she recovered three prints. One was taken from my mother's bedroom, which stood between the other two on the west side of the house.

Ninhydrin, a chemical that reacts and turns purple when it detects the chemicals found in fingerprints, was sprayed on the rough wood of the back door. No prints were revealed.

In addition to the prints, crime scene technicians recovered several expended bullets and bullet fragments from inside and outside the house. Besides the rounds found under the sleeping children's heads, bullet fragments were also recovered from the driveway and house to the west, at 132 West Fifty-Ninth Street. These went through the wall of the northwest bedroom, behind the bed where

Dietra had slept. Other expended rounds came from the area outside the kitchen, embedded in 122 West Fifty-Ninth Street, the blue house to the east. These projectiles had ripped through the kitchen walls and window.

A total of seven expended shell casings were recovered from the kitchen and northwest bedroom. Some of the shell casings bore the head stamp "RP-30 Carbine," while others were stamped "WCC 83." The manufacturers of the casings were Winchester and Remington Peters. The expended casings were ejected from a semiautomatic rifle, indicating a minimum of seven shots fired from such a weapon.

On the front porch a light blue jacket lay crumpled up, just to the left of the front door. The jacket was photographed and taken into evidence.

7

THE HUNDRED-YEAR DRIVE

FOLLOWING THE QUESTIONING, we were all released from Newton Station.

As we walked in silence, I had the queasy feeling that the police believed I was somehow involved, doubted that I had provided them with all that I knew. Whether it was my street instinct, or my experience as a probation officer, from the way they questioned me, looked at me, I could just tell. I was both interviewed as a victim, and interrogated as a suspect. I would be watched. I was a "person of interest," or "POI."

I kept replaying how my sisters looked at me in the police station, then collapsed when they saw I was clueless. Now I prayed that they too didn't distrust me.

Since the crime occurred we had been separated and not allowed to speak with one another. I had to talk to everyone, try to reassure them, figure out what happened. Most important, we needed a plan to protect ourselves against further harm. But before we could meet up, the police told me that someone would need to identify the bodies.

So I drove to the Los Angeles County Coroner's Office on North Mission Road, east of downtown.

Although it was just midmorning, the day already felt endless. As I drove north on the Harbor Freeway, I kept telling myself that none of this could possibly be real, that somehow a great mistake had grown out of control. I knew it wasn't a dream, but I kept holding out hope that somehow everyone was wrong.

But there were my family's screams, the hundreds of onlookers, the yellow crime scene tape, and those gurneys.

As I drove, I saw nothing other than cars, concrete, and the sun. I drove inside a tunnel, unaware of anything around me. Only when I exited the freeway did I realize I'd been driving for the last half hour.

As I pulled up to the coroner's office, as much as I dreaded the task ahead, it still offered a fleeting hope, a last chance to reverse fate. I didn't really believe it, but the slightest flicker remained: somehow the bodies would not actually be there. "There's been a big mistake, Mr. Alexander. You won't be needed here anymore. There are no bodies for you to identify."

But then the bags appeared. And the coverings were pulled back. Numb. For the record I identified the remains.

And as I did, I felt not only sorrow, but rage, self-hatred. The family protector failed to protect. I overslept. I was late. I could have saved them.

But no time for that. From the morgue I had another task.

I called UCLA and spoke with head football coach Terry Donahue. My youngest brother, Kirk, and my son, Kelton, both played as defensive backs for the Bruins. I told Coach Donahue to get them into his office, that I had some sad news to deliver.

He offered me his condolences and said he had already heard. He said neither Kelton nor Kirk knew.

He asked me if I wanted him to tell them.

"No," I said, this was news only I could personally deliver.

He said he would pull them out of the team meeting.

The drive from the morgue to UCLA took forever, more brutal traffic. I needed to get back and talk to Ivan and Neal, find out what really happened inside that house. I needed to help my sisters.

Hoping for answers while stuck on the freeway, I searched the radio. Over and again, "no motive," "the police are remaining tight-lipped," "no indication that it was gang-related," "all we know is that two gunmen burst into the home and opened fire." A man who lived on the block stated, "I heard the shots, then I heard things falling. I saw one male leave, then another one." A woman who lived next door said she saw a pair flee on foot, "one carrying what appeared to be a machine gun." Both neighbors spoke only upon guarantee of anonymity, unwilling to give their names for fear of retaliation. Retaliation from whom? I wanted to scream. Who the hell shoots sleeping children?

And my mother's neighbors kept asking the same question, as they mourned their fallen friend. "They were the nicest people you would ever want to know, they've been there for years, she was a beautiful woman," said one. "Very holy family, she was a very Christian lady," said another.

Then word that the Reverend Jules Mayer of Madee's church, St. Columbkille, had administered the last rites. Mayer described our family as "very kind, gentle, quiet people."

I couldn't believe the cruel irony. My first waking thought, I couldn't wait to drive over and tell Madee the good news about my job with UCLA football. Now I drove to meet the UCLA football coach to tell his players, my son and brother, of the crisis.

The day already felt like one unending drive.

From my home in Hollywood to West Fifty-Ninth, from West Fifty-Ninth to Newton Station, from Newton Station to the Coroner's Office, and from the Coroner's Office to UCLA.

And it continued.

From UCLA in Westwood, I learned that I had to drive to the airport to pick up my brother Gordon. So I headed south on the 405 to Los Angeles International Airport. Gordon was an Army airplane mechanic, stationed up north in Monterey. He had just received the news and was flying home.

As I continued south, I listened to more coverage on the radio.

"Right now we cannot eliminate any possible motives, from disgruntled friends to anything as outlandish as you might think," a police spokesman said. "We are hindered," he continued, "by the absence of evidence left by the suspects."

The words of one of the detectives at the station kept haunting me. He said the crime just didn't seem like the typical gangland drug killings that had plagued the area recently. Something was different about this one. "It just seemed personal."

At times I almost lulled myself into thinking I was simply listening to the news, another violent day in the neighborhood. Like any other motorist that day I was just taking in the horrors of modern urban life. Surely they must be talking about somebody else. These things happened to other people.

Then it would pierce, and reality would scream: this is *my* mother, inside *her* home. A horror movie had become my life.

And then I heard the deep, reassuring voice of my friend Tom Bradley coming over the radio, issuing a statement. I turned up the volume. Maybe the mayor knew something.

"I was sorry to learn of the personal tragedy in Kermit Alexander's family today," he began. "The LAPD is investigating and we hope to make some determination regarding the motive and suspects. I express my heartfelt condolences to Kermit Alexander."

Reassuring voice. Nothing reassuring.

The newscast continued, the reporter's voice returning: "The Alexander massacre is just the latest tragedy to shake South Central Los Angeles in a two-week wave of rising violence."

Cut back to the mayor: "The latest series of shootings have caused us great concern. We want everybody to know that the police department is responding, that they do have a plan, that they have gone into action. And we believe that their actions are going to result in control of these series of shootings."

Bradley concluded by expressing his alarm "at the increasing mayhem," announcing there would be a police crackdown, with additional officers from the department's Metropolitan Division stationed in the area to combat the problem.

Again. Nothing.

As the drive continued, the repeated newscasts were too surreal to grasp, but too real to deny.

As with Kirk and Kelton, I dreaded meeting Gordon. I knew that he too would blame himself for his absence. The curse of the Alexanders: a code of honor without mercy. If a family member is wronged, someone in the family is at fault, someone failed, let them down. Four were dead. Someone must pay.

I also feared Gordon might lose it. He had a volatile temper. He was just another person that I would have to watch.

As I pulled into the airport, I was met by the press. What did I know? Was there anything I could say to shed some light on the mystery?

Not a thing.

I told the reporters, "I don't have anything that would explain it. I'm the oldest in the family and when anything happens that might be a problem, I'm the one my mother would get in touch with. She didn't express any worries to me."

As I spoke with the press, Gordon arrived. We hugged and the tears fell.

We composed ourselves and finished with the reporters.

"As a mother, she was terrific," I said. "She believed in her religion, her family, and everything else was secondary."

Gordon got the last word: "She was the strongest woman I ever met."

———

As we drove from the airport back to my sister Daphine's house in South Central, Gordon and I listened to more news coverage. Mixed with continued statements of shock over the murders were stories on the sudden rash of deadly violence that had hit the neighborhood since the Olympics. Many expressed the opinion that our case—a daylight home-invasion quadruple homicide—sounded a call for action, a desperate plea.

Citizens bemoaned the loss of their neighborhood, their security, and their freedom to walk the streets. "It used to be just a beautiful neighborhood," one woman said, "in which you could walk around any time of the night." Now people went to the market only on the "buddy system," so as not to leave themselves alone and vulnerable. Complaints included the fact that "senior citizens literally run to get off the street before dark," and that "many of the businesses of the South Central Los Angeles area operate during normal business hours with locked doors."

Black Los Angeles was a mix of folks who came west to be free of Jim Crow. But these inner-city residents, enslaved by the fear of violent crime, experienced a sad déjà vu as old threats were reborn. "Don't be out after dark." "Don't get caught on the wrong side of tracks." "Don't look 'em in the eye." "Just cross the street if you see 'em coming."

Now, beaten down and terrorized by their own youth, the people of South Central feared black boys with baggy pants as they once had white men in pointed hoods.

Jesse Jackson would even admit that when he hears footsteps he's relieved when he sees a white face, then followed it up with "After all we have been through. Just to think we can't walk down our own streets, how humiliating."

Yes, how pathetic, for generations we fight for freedom, and when we get it, we imprison ourselves. And my family, my mother, who had endured so much, paid the price.

My mind thrashed. A wave of fury crested.

More driving. Calm, I told myself, as I drove. I must remain calm for my family. I cannot let them down again. I cannot go down in a blaze of road rage.

Gordon was silent, brooding. I tried to refocus on the radio, as if the reports were just the same old accounts of violence in South Central, the same old reports to which we'd all become desensitized.

I could no longer fake detachment. No distance existed. The stories were all personal, immediate. They were mine. Now anything touching upon crime and violence in the city of Los Angeles was ours. Unbelievably, all of this was about us, my family, me. Those same old accounts were no longer about unknown statistical others.

As we drove from the airport east toward South Central, the raw emotion consumed us.

Our past lives no longer existed.

My brother and I broke down.

This cycle of disbelief, quick flashes of detachment, followed by stark grief, became its own reality, claustrophobic, relentless.

I drove in a sort of fugue, unaware of traffic, stoplights, street signs.

Over a hundred degrees, the sun simply washed everything out, leaving behind a scorched gray.

What willpower it took just to function as a zombie.

The city was harsh, indifferent. It did not care.

I kept going, right at the speed limit. I was driving like a kind of automaton, fulfilling a duty, completing chores, one after the other, death chores, the tasks of identifying the dead, burying the dead, winding down lives.

Back to the furnace, back to the roads. I never really noticed I was driving, nor paid attention. It just kind of happened.

At this point I felt like I had been driving for a hundred years.

Back to the radio.

Next report: earlier that day, Eighth District Councilman Robert Farrell submitted a motion to the Los Angeles City Council demanding that Police Chief Daryl F. Gates report on the steps being taken to curb the violence plaguing South Central.

Farrell was a longtime family friend with whom I had spoken shortly after the murders. Prior to our conversation he had been angry about the decline of South Central. Now he was livid.

Farrell, like Mayor Bradley and me, was a black graduate of UCLA with southern roots, born in Natchez, Mississippi, in the thirties. Farrell's council district included many areas of South Central, and he seized on the issue of crime as the most pressing for his constituents. He was at once a harsh critic of the police—blasting the use of the infamous "choke hold" that had resulted in the deaths of several black arrestees—and a fervent advocate of the need for more police presence in his troubled district.

Farrell, waging what he termed a "personal war on crime and violence," proposed a special property tax on South Central residents to pay for additional police, a municipal lottery to finance an anticrime unit, and the closing of Nickerson Gardens and other crime-ridden public housing projects.

Comprising fifty-eight square miles and more than six hundred thousand residents, South Central was a huge part of Los Angeles. However, Farrell said, because the neighborhood was 80 percent black and home to what he called "the working poor," it was being underserved by the police. Had the twenty shootings of the past two weeks "occurred in a more affluent area of our city," Farrell said, "the police response to community concerns would have been immediate. We simply ask for the city standard of service: a police presence sufficient to deal with the nature and the magnitude of the current crime problem."

Farrell's conclusion was then read over the air. "I therefore move that the chief of police be directed to report within fifteen days on the police effort taken with the South Bureau area to combat the recent upsurge in gangland-style shootings." Finally, Farrell called for "the identification of recent parolees who may be involved in these activities, so that appropriate efforts may be made to immediately revoke their paroles."

As my brother and I listened, we realized that our case had struck a nerve, jarring both citizen and politician from their mundane acceptance of street violence, the turning of a blind eye toward black-on-black crime.

The case was coming to stand for something bigger than just one family's plight.

Our tragedy was a symbol of all that had gone wrong in the inner city. The hopes, the promises of the Great Migration, the dreams of finding opportunity out west all felt like a joke.

Like thousands of other black families, we had fled the horrors of the South for the bloodshed of South Central.

8

I NEED TO GO TO
THE HOSPITAL

FOLLOWING THE DRIVE, Gordon and I finally reunited with the rest of the family. It was the first time since the shooting that the surviving family members could speak together in private. We met at my sister Daphine's, not far from where my mother lived.

With the killers at large, and me being watched by the police as a "person of interest," the family would have to band together. Like so many times before—in Louisiana, in Watts—we would have only each other. By huddling together, unbreakable, with their large numbers and fierce reputations, my ancestors had withstood Klan attacks in the South, and my family, gang assaults in the projects. Once again our family was forced to form a tight circle and fight.

The family had been blown apart. Lives filled with routine commutes, bills, and work schedules ceased to exist. With the passage of one early morning everything changed. Just hours ago all was intact. Madee was drinking coffee and watering plants. Dietra would soon have risen to go to work at the department store. Daphine's son Damon and my sister Geraldine's son Damani soundly slept in their grandmother's house. Now all four were gone, simply no longer existed, and that was something none of us could comprehend, nor accept.

Our past lives were over, a new identity branded upon us: from now on, we were all victims of violent crime. For me, who craved strength and control, the title "victim" was sickening.

As the family reconnected, we began reconstructing the events of those early morning hours.

Upon hearing the gunshots and screams, my brother Neal ran into the front bedroom where Dietra, Damani, and Damon slept. As he entered he heard a shot and ducked. He then realized that the killer was not shooting at him, but facing toward and firing at my sister Dietra.

Neal saw the man only from behind. He held a rifle. Neal jumped on the man's back and took him down to the floor, where they wrestled and fought and rolled around.

As Neal knocked the man to the floor the rifle was jarred loose. The man then got to his knees, retrieved the rifle, stood up, and used the weapon to hit Neal in the face. After struggling with the intruder, Neal heard no more shots.

Neal described the shooter as a well-built black man. He said he was sweating and clammy.

Following the struggle, Neal ran out the back door of the house. The man followed him out. Neal hid behind some apartments located directly behind my mother's home. From his hiding place he could not see the back door, and did not know if any other individuals ever fled the house.

At some later point Neal returned to the house and found my nephew Ivan still alive. Neal then called me and the police. Shortly after his call the police arrived. Neal was taken to the station and questioned.

After Neal gave his account, Ivan told us how he was awakened by gunshots. He saw Neal run toward the hallway. Ivan then took cover in the closet. As Ivan hid he glimpsed a black man holding a gun with a long barrel in the hallway.

Ivan said he heard a lot of wrestling. Once the shooting stopped he peeked through the crack of the closet door, saw Neal, and slowly emerged from his hiding place. He described cautiously walking about the house as he and Neal witnessed the aftermath.

Ivan came out of the house screaming, "They killed my grand-mother! They killed my grandmother! My grandmother doesn't hurt anyone!"

Neal then took Ivan to the police station, where a couple of offi-cers questioned him.

Neal and Ivan both reported that the gunman never said a word, just came in shooting.

As we listened, I tried to console Neal. He cursed himself for hav-ing slept too long. He kept stressing that he could have saved them, had he just acted sooner.

I winced, suffering the same guilt. But I kept quiet. I didn't want to make things worse. I just tried to comfort him.

I told him he was a hero. He did all he could to save Dietra's life. He saved Ivan's life. He forced the gunman to flee.

No use. Neal remained despondent.

Later in the day, fearing a nervous breakdown, Neal told the fam-ily: "I need to go to the hospital."

To this day, he cannot talk about that morning.

Everyone expressed their relief that Ivan was alive. But I caught the first signs of his guilt, too. Four died in the house. He survived by hiding. This would haunt him.

Hearing Neal's and Ivan's confessions of guilt, I felt it like never before—that insidious and poisonous regret that jerks one awake in the middle of the night. The endless cycles of what could have been, obsessing over how the smallest counteractions could have changed everyone's lives. Why hadn't I been there? How could I have let them all down?

But aside from the questions of what happened, and why, some-thing more immediate confronted us: our protection and survival.

Someone tried to wipe out everyone within the house, and no one had a clue who did it, or what they wanted. The killers were free and on the streets. Did they intend to finish the job?

For protection and support the family stayed together at Daph-ine's. My sister Joan and I bought guns.

We all wondered, did the killers know where we were? Did

they know where Daphine lived? Were we being watched or followed?

That night, the men stayed in a den downstairs, with the women and children upstairs. Joan insisted on standing sentry by the front door. No one was going to kill any more children, she vowed.

No one was to stand in front of the windows. It made you a target for a drive-by shooting.

No one slept.

Dark thoughts and wailings haunted the night.

Some half expected the departed to return, to walk through the door and explain that the whole thing was just a tragic mistake. Over and over the bereaved swore that this in fact happened. They saw Madee, she just kept walking around the corner, standing there, but then disappearing when they spoke or tried to engage her. Same with Dietra, Damani, and Damon, they were there, they could feel it.

Late into the night sleep teased us, but was always broken by horror, visions, shrieks of disbelief.

"It's not fair! It's not fair!" a female voice screamed into the night. After all Madee had done for us. After all she endured. It could not be. She was not gone.

And the boys, and Dietra. Parents shouldn't outlive children, nothing more unjust than death out of order.

Nothing ripped at me like the sound of my sisters crying out in despair.

Again, "It's not fair!" echoed through the house, followed by shrieks. "Why, Lord? Why?"

The sounds of traffic, footsteps, voices from the street, all sent waves of alarm through the house.

Everyone replayed Ivan's description: the sound of screams, gunshots, and shattered glass.

The family was catatonic.

No one went to work in the morning. No one wanted to leave the house. No one wished to be left alone.

———

One day after the shooting, the police had no suspects and were at a loss as to motive. But they caught their first break.

Two eyewitnesses came forward.

Lashawn Driver, seventeen, told the police that she lived across the street from the Alexander house, and knew Damon and Damani. Prior to 8 a.m. on August 31, she was outside, in front of her house, when she saw two black men, a "clear-skinned guy [with a light complexion] and dark guy," walking from the direction of Main Street toward the Alexander house. The dark guy's hair was "in a little natural," while the clear guy's hair was "braided." The dark guy was about five foot seven to five foot nine and muscular, wearing a dark blue shirt and dark blue pants. The clear guy had a light complexion and a medium build, and wore a red and tan horizontal shirt and light tan pants.

Driver then went inside her house.

Within five minutes after entering the house, she heard shooting. She then went to her front porch to look out. She said several shots were fired, then there was a pause, followed by more shooting. During the time of the pause she saw the dark guy appear from the rear of the Alexander house and then walk down the driveway along the west side of the home. He did not appear to be carrying anything in his hands. Then after the second series of shots she saw the clear guy come running down the same driveway carrying a rifle. Both men headed east toward Main Street.

Venus Webb, who also lived across the street from the Alexanders, heard "many shots," and then looked out her living room window. After the shots stopped she saw a black male with "clear, bright skin" and tan or beige clothing walking "a little fast" toward Main Street. She saw him get into a van, which then pulled away very fast before turning right onto Main.

————

Dr. William Sherry, a deputy medical examiner for Los Angeles County, conducted the autopsies on the bodies of Ebora Alexander, Dietra Alexander, Damani Garner, and Damon Bonner. For all four of the deceased, the cause of death was "gunshot wound to the head."

Peggy Fiderio, a latent fingerprint expert for the Los Angeles Police Department's scientific identification division, compared the fingerprints collected from the Alexander house with those of its residents.

She found that many of the twenty-one prints collected from the scene matched the prints taken of Neal, Ivan, and the four deceased. However, several prints, categorized as "identifiable"—containing sufficient detail of loops, whorls, and ridges to make a match—did not come from any of the family members whose prints were rolled.

In a house trafficked by many people, this did not suggest the remaining prints belonged to the killers. But if the prints matched to anyone without legitimate access to the house, this would provide strong circumstantial evidence of guilt.

The full palm print lifted from the storage trunk in the front bedroom did not match to any family member.

————

From the evidence before them, the crime scene investigation, the autopsy, the victim interviews, and the eyewitnesses, RHD detectives reconstruct the crime:

In the early morning, the killers approach the Alexander house. One is carrying a rifle, which he conceals in a light blue jacket. As they reach the front porch and prepare to enter the house—with his back to the street and no longer concerned with detection—the man removes the weapon and drops the jacket to the ground, to the left of the front door.

The windows are not barred, the front door is open, and the screen door is unlocked. Mrs. Alexander is not living in fear. She expects no intruders.

The killers enter. They hear motion in the rear of the house. The shooter walks through the living room, between the couch and coffee table. Then into the dining room, he walks past the table, through the doorway, into the kitchen.

Now he turns to his left. Ebora Alexander stares in shock. He aims, fires, fires, and fires again. Two shots hit her in the head, blow-ing away the top and side of her skull. The third shot goes through the neck. After leaving her body, the bullets continue their flight, ripping the curtains, boring through windows and walls.

The killer is a good shot, with good hand-eye coordination. This is not his first time. He will have a criminal record, perhaps some kind of specialized weapons training. The three shots hit in rapid succession. The position of her injuries and the bullet trajectories prove that all three wounds are struck before the body hits the floor.

Leaving the kitchen, the killer returns to the front of the house. The time it takes him to walk the hallway explains the break in the shooting described by the witness.

The darker-skinned individual likely leaves the home at this point through the rear door, as he was seen by the eyewitness walking down the driveway from the back of the house prior to the second volley of shots.

The shooter now enters the front bedroom. Dietra Alexander, awakened by the shots, sits up in her bed. She screams. Three more direct hits: two to the head, one to the chest. One shot each to the heads of the two sleeping children, Damon and Damani. Again, the killer is coldly efficient, the bullet-trajectory evidence proving that a standing shooter pointed the weapon downward, firing at the prone victims.

At this point Neal Alexander rushed the gunman from behind and jumped on his back. Neal is strong and athletic. The killer does not go down easily, suggesting he too is powerful, well built, perhaps an athlete himself. Neal wrestles him to the floor, knocking the rifle from his hands. The killer recovers the gun, gets to his feet, and smashes Neal in the face with the weapon. Neal runs out the back door and the killer follows, then, fearing detection, gives up his chase. He retreats to the idling van, where the other man, the darker-skinned individual, already awaits. The door closes and the getaway vehicle disappears to the east, speeding right onto Main.

No words were ever said; they just came in shooting.

The crime showed preplanning and conspiracy. At least three individuals were involved: the light-skinned shooter, the darker-skinned man seen walking down the driveway to the west of the Alexander house, and a getaway driver. The van was poised down the block, ready to tear out as soon as the killers returned.

But the crime was interrupted and altered. Neal's fight with the killer changed the course of events.

The disruption likely produced more evidence. The struggle left the intruder no time to cover up, alter the scene, collect projectiles, or wipe down prints.

A basic rule of investigation, known as Locard's exchange principle, named after forensic pioneer Edmond Locard, "France's Sherlock Holmes," holds that anyone who enters a scene will leave something behind, and take something with them. The perpetrator could leave behind anything from hair and fibers to fingerprints, or clothing. They could take with them anything from stolen goods to the victim's blood.

By cutting the crime short and forcing greater contact with the scene—as the two wrestled around on the floor—Neal's battle eliminated the chance for cover-up while increasing the opportunity for exchange. Neal's acts may also have caused the killer to abandon caution, as he fled from the house with the rifle unconcealed, for all on the street to see.

More important, had Neal not fought the shooter, all six inhabitants would likely be dead. The intruders entered with intent to kill all within.

But what was the motive?

The detectives were perplexed. There was no sign that the killers conducted any search for valuables. In fact the living room and dining room appeared untouched, left in the same order that family members reported their mother ensured: everything neat, starched linens, a set table. No drawers were opened, nothing overturned. With no sign of ransacking, financial gain did not appear a motivating factor.

Further, the known facts did not suggest a crime implicating the victims in their demise: a grandmother, a young fiancée, sleeping children. It simply looked like a preplanned execution.

9

THE LOST LITTER

As the police struggled to find a motive, we did, too.

Days had now passed since the murders. Cooped up in Daphine's house, scared, and without answers, tensions began turning inward. We were passionate, emotional people, and every one of us struggled with our tempers. With each passing hour this grew ever harder.

Desperate for answers, and any sense of control over our lives, family members entered into a kind of crazed speculation. With everyone anxious, angry, and underslept, the ability to focus and think straight broke down. Rumors, no matter how wild, were jumped on as possible explanations. When no explanations existed, we invented them.

The killing was the work of organized crime. Someone in the family had run into trouble and this was revenge. A red Cadillac had been seen repeatedly cruising the neighborhood. An ancient grudge from the bayou had followed us cross-country—something dredged from deep within the swamps.

Family members began mumbling about other family members. Anything even remotely shady from the past resurfaced as the potential cause.

While the family had generally been close, and its members functional, we weren't angels. We had our pasts.

One of my sisters got involved with drugs and dated a series of less than upstanding citizens. Some suspected that one of these past relationships might have resurfaced. A bitter suitor, resentful, high, and out of his mind, would be just the type to commit such a senseless slaughter. Likewise, one of my brothers got into LSD while visiting the Bay Area during the Haight-Ashbury Summer of Love, 1967. Perhaps this explained it. Again, unsavory, unstable elements entering the Alexander family orbit had returned to derail it.

Some also wondered if Madee had ever confronted any one of these bad influences. Never one to back down or hold her thoughts, maybe she tried to set straight someone who didn't want straightening, put them off, induced some kind of drug rage.

Or had Madee at some point called out a neighborhood wrongdoer, maybe scolding some young hoodlum or street vandal, who then returned to send a powerful message, make their name, prove how *bad* they were?

Or it could have been any one of us—who unknowingly set someone off on the streets. With the prevalence of drugs, guns, and the hair-trigger touchiness of everyone these days about being "dissed," or disrespected, any perceived slight would be grounds for violent reprisal.

An incident involving Madee led to yet another theory. About a year prior to the murders, she had been near the Coliseum when a man grabbed her purse. She fought with him and held on tight. When she told us about it, we were horrified, telling her she was out of her mind risking her life like that. She said she could not bear to let go of all the family pictures she kept in her purse. Finally the robber overpowered her. He knocked her to the ground, badly bruised. He fled with the purse. It contained all of her personal information. Some now wondered could the thug who had access to that information have returned to rob her again.

Or could it have anything to do with her relationship with Mayor Bradley, some questioned? We often talked policy with him. Was this politically motivated?

All of these theories had holes. None added up.

And as the family struggled to make sense of the tragedy, one theme returned repeatedly: Madee's absence. Through all the large family's struggles, she had always been there, the stabilizing force, holding things together, battling chaos with faith and grit. Without Madee, the family's ability to navigate the crisis, to come to terms with the loss, was all the more impossible. She was the sun. For all of our lives, the eleven children revolved around her. With Madee gone, we began to break apart, spin out of control. My sister Daphine said that without Madee, we were lost, "like a litter of puppies that had just watched the mother dog get hit by a car."

Deepening the loss was the guilt. For years various members of the family had talked about the need to move her out of the neighborhood. Some had begged her. Some now claimed that others had not done enough. Still others countered that it was pointless—that she would not move until forced. As my sister Crystal said, "I knew she had no intention of moving when she told me, 'I'll only move when God tells me it's time.'"

As the agonizing stretched deeper into the night, and fatigue took its toll, another line of thought intruded. What about that unlocked door?

Surely, some said, this was an inside job, someone whom she knew, who routinely visited. The anger grew at the trusted guest and betrayer. This in turn would circle back to further recriminations about allowing her to stay, allowing her to keep her doors unlocked, and allowing her to let the neighborhood into her home. And this was the worst thought of all, that the killer was known.

No one could match the eyewitness descriptions with anyone we knew. But the descriptions were generic, and the number of people who came and went so great, that "a light-skinned guy and a dark-skinned guy" did little to narrow the hunt.

Still others could not shake the premonitions. Daphine endlessly repeated her son Damon's weird behavior leading up to the killing. Additionally, my sister Barbara said that Madee had made her uneasy when she said she hoped the kids would have a good time at an upcoming concert, and that if she did not see them again she hoped they'd remember her fondly. Given her religious convictions, biblical analogies flourished; it was like Christ prophesying his impending betrayal. Others recalled her saying that just prior to her death, I had acted strangely, circling the block in my car, forever waving goodbye.

Had she suspected someone would do her in? Did she sense it coming? Did she know something she didn't let on?

All of these forebodings again made the crime seem intimate, pointed to the presence of someone near to our lives.

When these thoughts became too unbearable and exhausted themselves, the family, unwilling to go to bed without answers, ventured into the bizarre. It was not internal, they argued, it was distant, ancient, something long thought dead.

It could be Klan related, some said. Like most blacks living in the South, our family had been harassed. But unlike most, we fought back. Coming from a small rural community, we knew who hid beneath the white sheets. And when the time was right, my relatives would find them, drag them deep into the swamps, and "disappear" them. And never another word was spoken. But maybe somehow, with years gone by, something had leaked. Or there were those problems with Kermit Sr., the issue that made him join the Marines and flee town, when local Kluxers found him too "uppity" and said they were going to "teach him his place." But that made no sense, others answered; eyewitnesses said the killers were black. "Didn't matter," was the irrational response; somehow some Klan grudge lay behind this, and they had simply got blacks to kill blacks as revenge, perfect Klan justice.

Murmurs also rippled beneath the surface about some form of voodoo hex. Though we were raised Catholic, from Louisiana to California hidden fears of spells and curses never died. I remembered how during storms, the mirrors were wrapped to avoid cracks and years of bad luck. When we got our hair cut, the clippings were carefully swept to avoid bewitchment. Even the Catholic priests weren't immune to the hidden world of voodoo, and, when outside of formal church services, they indulged family members, invoking secret charms. Saints' images, blood rituals, animal rites, all had meshed together, and from Haiti to Louisiana to California formed a part of our collective memory.

Superstitions, ideas of karmic justice, the way of spirits, and ideas going back to African witches could still enter the family's thoughts. Things didn't just happen, people kept objecting; things happened only to people who had done something wrong. Somebody must have done something to somebody, and that's why somebody did this to us. Coincidence and chance had no power to explain. Omens held answers.

And while all of this conjecture may seem far-fetched, when a people have been the victims of centuries of very real conspiracies, sinister plots ring all too true. Our ancestors really were captured in slave fortresses and shipped across the Middle Passage. The Klan really did terrorize my relatives. Fire hoses, nightsticks, and police dogs really were unleashed, churches bombed, bodies buried. We'd witnessed it. Remote, far-flung, unlikely. Sure. But that didn't make them any less believable, nor terrifying. Our folklore and mythology, based upon our all-too-real experience, are filled with tales of tricksters, hustlers and hijinks, collusions, cons, corruptions, plots and counterplots. When black folk hear about a conspiracy that involves oppression and violence, they're at the very least going to give it a listen. And particularly at that moment, none of us cared about rational explanations. We simply craved answers, and the more emotional the better.

After exhausting theories of bayou revenge—with origins before we were even born—the search for culprits returned to the immediate family. And as this uninformed speculation spun ever further out of control, I sensed an unpleasant trend developing. The feeling among some was that the tragedy must somehow trace back to me.

After all, I was the public face of the family. I was the celebrity and public figure. I must therefore have something to do with it. As this train gained speed, my sisters began to question me.

"Kermit, what have you done to us?" they asked.

A theory centering on a murky "syndicate" began to circulate. According to this explanation, I had gotten myself involved in some shady business down in Texas.

Like my father, I too had a great love for horses. After I retired,

I got involved in several business ventures. One included buying Thoroughbred horses and breeding them in Oklahoma. When the business failed to meet my expectations, I withdrew.

Now certain family members saw in this failed venture the missing link between me and the crime. Horse racing and its mafia connections held the clue. Besides, one of the breeders from Texas had been bragging that he "would kick Kermit's ass." I had burned the wrong people, and now they burned me back, sending me a message, mafia-style.

No matter my protests, some in my family felt no other explanation made sense. Whether through horse breeding or some other means, I had attracted the wrong kind of attention, and now my family paid for it.

The fact that I, as the leader of the family, had nothing to offer only made it more likely that I was to blame. Leaders are looked to for answers. When they fail to provide, confidence and trust decay, anger and resentment rise.

At the time that the family most needed each other, the pressure, and the failure to find solace, began breaking us apart as we splintered into cannibalizing factions.

I couldn't believe what I was hearing. Who were these people? In less than a week they'd become savage, a group I felt like I no longer knew. And then I started to do the same, wondering what secrets they held, what there was about them that I didn't know.

A common enemy unifies. But the enemy must exist, a face to hate, a dragon to slay. Here, whoever they were remained vague and unknown. And since we couldn't lay low a phantom, we sabotaged ourselves.

As we came apart I just wanted to scream. What would Madee think? As she looked down from Heaven she must have been ashamed. Her tragic death didn't bring out the best in her brood, it didn't rally them around her memory. It ate them up, brought out their worst.

And when everyone was worn-out, the voices would die, and a taut stillness fill the room. Every detail was on punctuated alert. Each tick of the clock whacked, echoing off the walls. Outside, a passing car rattled the windows. Footsteps rebounded in the front entryway. The cars, the footsteps, the hot summer wind.

The house was a cage. I had to get away.

And then the voices would pick up again. The same questions hammered upon, the ongoing lack of answers. But no one could let it go, interrupting, yelling, sobbing, interrupting, fingers pointing, interrupting, blaming, voices, voices, voices. How I hated everyone's voice. Silence to screams, more voices, that constant interrupting. There was nothing I hated more. And I did it, too.

Though it was pointless and maddening, everyone somehow felt that if we pounded long enough, somehow we would find something. Something wasn't as it seemed, something lay hidden beneath the surface, undiscovered. If we just yelled and screamed long enough, just maybe we'd uncover it. It was a desperate reach. We all knew it. But we were desperate. And somehow anything seemed better than surrendering to silence.

10

BLACK TOMMY,
SWEET DADDY

O<small>N</small> THURSDAY, SEPTEMBER 6, 1984, *Los Angeles Sentinel* staff writer
Chico C. Norwood wrote an article titled "Mystery Shrouds Alexander Murders":

> Lieutenant Ron Lewis, of Los Angeles Police Department said,
> "The people at the residence, from what we know right now, can be
> ruled out as being into drug trafficking. We don't have anything to
> indicate that there is any drug involvement at that residence at all."
>
> However, he added at this point "we cannot eliminate anything
> as far as a possible motive."
>
> With the aid of witnesses, LAPD artist Fernando Ponce was
> able to come up with a composite drawing of the two suspects.
>
> The first suspect is described as a male Black between 20 and 25
> years of age, 5-10, weighing 190 pounds, dark complexion with a
> muscular build and short hair. He was last seen wearing a dark blue
> t-shirt and dark blue pants.
>
> The second suspect is described as a male Black, with a light
> brown complexion, between the ages of 20 and 25, 5-9, weighing
> approximately 150 pounds. When last seen the suspect's hair was
> braided and laid back in corn rows and he was wearing a red and
> tan horizontal striped shirt and beige pants.

The suspects fled the scene in a very clean 1975 or 1976 brown or light maroon van with a sliding door on the passenger side, two doors and two windows in the back, with brown or tan curtains and a chrome luggage rack on the roof.

Police detectives say copies of the composite drawings will be circulated throughout California, posted in stores, etc.

Lt. Lewis says the department is hoping to generate some information from the dissemination of the composite. . . .

The grisly murders occurred at approximately 8:15 a.m. on Friday, Aug. 31 at the Alexander home on W. 59th St. The suspects reportedly entered the home through a rear door.

Killed in the incident were 58-year-old Ebora Alexander, whose body was found in the kitchen; 24-year-old Dietra Alexander, whose body was found in an outside bedroom; Damani Garner, 12, and eight-year-old Damon Bonner. All four victims were shot in the head.

"I don't have anything that would explain it," said Kermit Alexander, an All-American halfback at UCLA and a 10 year veteran of the NFL.

Police are seeking the public's assistance in locating the killers. If you have any information concerning the slayings call detectives Bob Grogan, John Rockwood, David Crews or Lt. Ron Lewis.

———

The appeals to the public predictably summoned the usual outpouring of cranks, false confessions, and false accusations, as well as the cheats and dead ends of the well-intentioned. In high-profile cases, the problem police most often encounter is not a lack of leads, but an overload of worthless information.

In an effort to sift through the noise, several detectives worked the case. They listened to all kinds of reports that didn't add up. Hearsay upon hearsay, as friends reported what friends of friends had heard on the streets. "Someone I knew from school ten years ago told me that . . ." "A person from Southwest L.A. who used to work at a grocery store said that . . ." "A girl who used to deal dope told me someone who went by the name of Keith knew the shooter."

Information suggested the murders were retaliation for the shooting of a Jamaican drug dealer. Other sources labeled the crimes "cocaine killings" in the "*Miami Vice* school" of senseless violence, perpetrated by organized Cuban, Colombian, or domestic criminals based in Florida. A new drug gang known as "Third World" was also fingered for their involvement. Still others said both killers were black men with long braids. Additional reports noted that the killers still lived in the neighborhood, but had shaved their heads and now wore hats.

Names from the streets poured in as well, amorphous leads pointing to people known as Diamond, Black Tommy, Sweet Daddy, Tweedy-Bird, Eagle, Big Ant, and Scoopy. Alerts were also phoned in warning the police that a ring of individuals who had committed the murders were holed up at the Coliseum Apartment Motel. Other calls suggested the murders were a drug hit gone wrong. The killers had meant to hit a crack house on East Fifty-Ninth Street, not West Fifty-Ninth Street. The killers had meant to hit someone named "Chucky Mac" on Fifty-Ninth Place. Still others claimed the hit was retaliation for a killing that had taken place the night before. The van was not tan, it was black, the weapon used was not a rifle, but a shotgun, not a shotgun, but a machine gun.

Theories regarding me circulated as well. I was a cocaine dealer, it was claimed, and this hit might have been retaliation against me, either because I owed thousands of dollars or because I was selling bad dope. Repeatedly I had been seen at a house in Watts known for drug dealing. It was further claimed that I actually knew the killers and that was why I had remained so calm after the murders.

This information regarding me was followed up, but no evidence was ever uncovered. I explained that as an assistant coach for John Locke High School I was counseling a troubled player involved with drugs, hence my visits to the house in Watts. As to a supposed relationship between me and the unknown killers, nothing materialized. Publicly, my former teammates supported me, refusing to believe I had any involvement. "I was just talking to John Hadl [quarterback on the Los Angeles Rams]," one said, "and the thing we remembered most about Kermit was how much he loved that family." He continued: "God, he was dedicated to his family. He seemed to be always concerned for his sisters and his mother."

While many within the LAPD continued to question whether I held any clues to the murders, a separate investigation of me was never opened.

What about the ex-husband, others wondered. But my father, Kermit Sr., proved a dead end as well. He was driving home from the Pomona racetrack when he first heard about the killings on the radio. His alibi was strong, no evidence linked him, the relationship between my mother and father remained respectful after their separation, and Madee often babysat my father's children through his second wife.

What about some of those active serial killers, others asked. But they too were eliminated. The evidence was dissimilar. The MO, modus operandi, did not match.

As most street crime is local—with the incidents often taking place within blocks of where the perpetrators live and hang out—detectives went door-to-door through the Florence neighborhood, interviewing my mother's friends and neighbors.

Detectives remained troubled by the open door. When the killers' faces were finally revealed, would they be familiar?

Again focusing the investigation locally, in the week following the killing, detectives drove the streets of South Central looking for a brown, tan, or red van.

As expended .30-caliber shell casings were found at the scene, detectives began looking into any .30-caliber weapons that had been used in a crime. The usual neighborhood channels, informants, and snitches were questioned, and came up dry.

With nearly a week passed since the killings, the trail was growing cold. The longer a case remains unsolved, the less the chance that anyone is ever caught: evidence is destroyed, witnesses disappear, memories fade.

In America, less than 65 percent of all murder cases are solved.

And in Los Angeles, this case marked the latest in a spate of open homicide investigations, in what had been a particularly bloody late August. As a prominent case, in which both Mayor Tom Bradley and Chief of Police Daryl Gates held press conferences, the pressure to break it was mounting. But for the detectives working the case, it wasn't just a matter of solving the crime to quiet the brass. The case genuinely haunted them.

Homicide detectives must become desensitized, feel detachment from their victims. They must learn to view dead bodies as evidence and bloodied homes as crime scenes, steel themselves to the point that they can literally laugh in the face of death.

But the sleeping children shot in their beds made this case different.

Over and over again detectives reworked the crime scene, hoping that multiple sets of eyes would seize upon something others had missed. Maybe that magical piece of previously undetected physical evidence would spring forth. Or maybe another viewpoint would see something in the assailant's behavior that would reveal the motive.

Detectives stared at the autopsy photos, passed them around, went bleary-eyed meditating upon the wounds. They retraced the bullet trajectories, focused upon the houses to the east and west, re-examined the holes in the adjacent homes.

They canvassed and recanvassed: door-to-door, block by block. Hadn't anybody seen anything? Did anybody know anything, anybody who might somehow, someway have had it in for that family?

But nothing shed new light. Nothing suggested anything other than what they already knew, that a seemingly innocent and beloved family, an anchor of the neighborhood, had been senselessly killed. Nothing they learned could make the physical evidence tell a complicated tale. It screamed only a maddeningly simple one: four innocent victims were executed inside their home.

11

ETERNAL REST GRANT UNTO THEM

O<small>N</small> FRIDAY, SEPTEMBER 7, exactly one week after the killings, the funeral was held for my four slain family members.

The ceremonies took place at St. Eugene's Catholic Church at 9505 Haas Avenue. The crowd was too large to fit into Madee's regular church at St. Columbkille. Over one thousand people attended, packing the building beyond capacity.

The ceremonies began midmorning. The sun already blazed over the congregation. The temperature would again hit triple digits.

As the police feared the family was still in danger, snipers dotted the surrounding roofs while mourners entered the church. Undercover officers with surveillance cameras were also spread throughout the immediate area, seeing if they could film anyone suspicious, catch any out-of-place behavior, or spot someone who did not belong. Undercovers also circulated throughout the church itself.

Strangers and those who did not belong were one thing. But it was the thought of those we knew that caused me the most grief. As I greeted fellow mourners I felt a queasy guilt as I could not help wondering, was I shaking the hand of a killer? Was I hugging the man who stuck the knife in my back? Were they here among us, posing as bereaved?

This tension hung over the entire funeral. The killers had simply disappeared, and yet they remained a constant presence. And this only added to both the fear and the frustration. What did they look like? At this point they were only shades, something invisible and empty. How to give them flesh and blood? Were they watching me at this moment?

For all assembled, the service did not represent closure, nor an end, but an early step into the unknown. We were in a state of disbelief. It was all unreal and unexpected: a funeral service for loved ones lost in the prime of life, surrounded by snipers and surveillance. And most devastating, the family faced the void as a house divided.

Inside the church it was standing room only, with mourners lining the walls, the balcony overflowing with friends, relatives, and dignitaries attending the funeral mass.

As the congregation entered, my sisters Geraldine, the mother of Damani, and Crystal both collapsed and had to be carried inside. Joan followed them into the church, dressed in her full military uniform to honor our mother, who always expressed her pride in Joan's service.

Upon entry, each mourner was provided with a memorial brochure: "In Loving Memory of the Alexander Family."

Eighteen pallbearers were needed to carry the coffins.

Over fifty relatives filled the front ten pews in the sweltering church.

As the organ played, my father and I wept quietly, staring at the four brown caskets. None were ever opened. Having witnessed the state of the bodies, I insisted they remain closed.

As I watched the sea of mourners dressed in black, I felt I was in a kind of blue haze, unable to focus. It was like trying to think through a fever. I knew I could not stand this any longer, and that once the services were over and the bodies laid to rest, I would begin a new phase.

Right now the heat and the crowd were claustrophobic. The suit and tie were suffocating. I couldn't wait to rip them off.

The eulogy was delivered by Father Joe Shea, a priest at St. John Vianney Catholic in Hacienda Heights, and a longtime family friend.

Father Shea described Madee as "a compassionate, loving woman devoted to her family and church," and "one of the kindest people any of us had ever met." He sermonized about the tragic irony that a woman who loved her neighborhood and community, and remained despite its dangers for its betterment, was senselessly killed because of her residence. Father Shea continued that it was only through people like my mother that such neighborhoods stood any chance of survival.

Father Jules Mayer, the pastor of St. Columbkille Roman Catholic Church, where Madee was a parishioner, said she was a "kind, gentle, hard-working steady churchgoer who was very active in raising funds for the church's elementary school."

It was further lamented that recently she had been in such good spirits. Her youngest daughter, Dietra, was readying to marry and move out, and Madee after thirty-five years of childrearing could finally exhale, reflect on a job well done, and maybe carve out a little time for herself.

Following my mother, the other victims were eulogized as well.

Dietra was described by Father Shea as a shy woman who "loved everyone." She had just celebrated her twenty-fourth birthday and was excited about her upcoming wedding. Coworkers from Zody's department store, on Vermont Avenue, described her as "religious" and "family oriented," and said "that she worked very hard and everyone liked her."

I spoke of Dietra as "the baby" and "the princess," and recalled the time that I served as her chauffeur on her prom night, renting a burnt-orange Cadillac limousine and wearing a suit to match.

Damani was considered to be "a miracle," as his mother, Geraldine, had been told that she would never be able to have children. He was described as a mature boy, "an old man when he was born," and as "old before his time." He made an impression with his "huge hazel eyes," which were accentuated by big Coke-bottle glasses that friends teased him "needed windshield wipers to clean." The family remembered him above all as a trusting boy, "who loved his mom, and worried about her all the time."

The memories of Damon could still make the mourners smile through the tears. They recalled the way he loved to wear a shirt and tie, making him look like "a little midget," or "a little butler." His mother remembered how he liked to watch the Christian station and had said he "wasn't afraid to be with God." Father Shea termed him "a friend of the young and old," while a family friend eulogized him as "loved by everyone in the entire neighborhood [who] would visit the older people every day and report back to Ebora how everyone was doing." Once when he had seemed afraid, his mother asked him if the movie they had recently watched had scared him. "No," Damon said, "that movie wasn't scary. Jaws only eats white people."

As I listened to the kind words over the departed, I agonized not only over the deceased, but over the fact that much of the surviving family had begun to question me, holding me in some way responsible for their pain. It made it impossible to feel any sense of healing or closeness at the service. At a time when we most needed to come together, the suspicions and ill feelings made the tragic day unbearable.

As the service concluded, Ivan walked out of the church and began sobbing, "Damani's dead, Damani's dead, Damani's dead."

Though relatives tried to console him as he exited, his distress ignited additional cries from the crowded church anteroom.

Father Shea, who had earlier tried to soothe the congregants, now slipped into a voice of despair.

"We're not going to be able to see their smiles or touch their hands anymore," he lamented.

"In the face of evil, human wisdom is bankrupt."

———

Following the two-hour service, the mourners drive west on Slauson Avenue to the Holy Cross Cemetery in nearby Culver City. I know the cemetery well, having served at hundreds of funerals as an altar boy in the 1950s. We enter through a wrought-iron gate, drive beside a large ornate cross.

In California's Mexican period the land had been used for cattle grazing and belonged to the Rancho La Ballona, before being sold to the Archdiocese of Los Angeles, which chose the land because of its "rolling hills, peaks and valleys."

Opened in 1939, the Roman Catholic cemetery covers more than two hundred acres and has become a tourist attraction, famous as a resting spot of celebrities. Bing Crosby, Jimmy Durante, Rita Hayworth, Bela Lugosi, and other heroes of Hollywood lie in "the Grotto," up the hill and in the cemetery's southwest corner.

Today, our family procession travels the low hills of Holy Cross, and then buries our four relatives on a gentle slope on the cemetery's northwest side.

Through the proceedings the mourners do what they can to stay cool, fanning themselves, or seeking shade under the scattered trees. By midafternoon the temperature hits one hundred.

The priest makes a final prayer for mercy, then the sign of the cross over each of the bodies.

He speaks for the final time:

Eternal rest grant unto them, O Lord.
And let perpetual light shine upon them.
May they rest in peace.
Amen.
May their souls, and the souls of all the faithful departed,
through the mercy of God rest in peace.
Amen.

After the burial, three metal grave markers are placed in a row in the grass. Damon and Damani each have their own plate, while my sister and mother rest together beneath one. The graves are set in the same plot with the nuns with whom Madee spent her working hours.

Behind the cemetery walls, single-family bungalows stretch for miles. Palm trees intermittently spike the foreground. In the distance downtown Los Angeles and the Hollywood Hills disappear into the late summer smog.

As the ceremony concludes, I stare at the graves.

Ebora Bonds Alexander: April 5, 1925–August 31, 1984

Dietra Louis Alexander: August 15, 1960–August 31, 1984

Damon Andre (Butler) Bonner: January 19, 1976–August 31, 1984

Damani Osei Garner-Alexander: July 11, 1971–August 31, 1984

12

ALONE

FOLLOWING THE SERVICES, I went home to Hollywood and changed my clothes.

Finally, the day was over. It was a kind of torture, a drawn-out moan. Mourning the dead, and always looking over my shoulder, paranoid, fearing the unknown. At least things would change now. I would force them to.

I took off the dark suit I had worn for the funeral services and put on an oversized T-shirt and jeans, tennis shoes, and a baseball hat. I wanted to look like the people in the old neighborhood. I wanted to fit in with South Central, as by night I planned to disappear into its streets and back alleys for as long as it took. I would descend into the urban wilderness to pierce its shadow world, decode its rumors, gossip, and chatter. The secret had to be broken. And no one else was on the trail.

I also packed into my car some other things I thought I might need: a carbine, an M-16, and a .380 automatic with an extended clip.

I would also cease to be Kermit Alexander, instead taking on a doppelganger, or second self. Going forward I would live a double existence, Kermit Alexander, working as an advertising representative by day, and Kermit's friend, the family avenger, prowling by night. This nonreality was my new reality, and instead of trying to resist it, I simply embraced it. I would assume the mantle of the old swamp-hunting great-grandfather of lore.

And it really wasn't a stretch, for that morning of August 31, 1984, was a cleaving point in my life. That morning the killers did not just take my family, they killed me. Any Kermit who lived before that day died that morning. All that he carried with him, trust, joy, hope, went with his relatives to their graves.

As I walked the streets, I refused to give my name, identifying myself only as a friend of the football player who recently lost his family. I hid my identity to protect my siblings as well as my wife and two children. I rented cars and slept in cheap motels so that no one would know who I was or follow me home. Not knowing who was after us, or why, I didn't want to ignite more killings. I just wanted to make sure that whoever they were, I got them before they got me. It was also a mission of vengeance.

During these times I lived like a vampire, sleeping or sleepwalking through the day, coming alive at dusk.

My anger was channeled, but not in a good way. Control fell victim to rage. I had invented a double, a kind of split personality to absorb and express my anger. The same way that football let me vent on the field, this primal character allowed for an indulgent release on the streets. I sought therapy through violence. It was a sacred rage, born of a cause.

I could not take the torment of not knowing any longer. I could not stand the impotence of being a victim, asked to sit quietly on the sidelines, helpless, waiting for someone else to do something. With the police stymied, my family disintegrating, and my guilt overwhelming, I had to take control. At that point I had little faith in the police. If they were keeping an eye on me, how hard were they really trying to solve the case? Further, in the mid-eighties, LAPD's standing in the black community was not good, with few trusting their commitment to protect and serve.

In the wake of tragedy, I retained my faith, but it was wounded. I still believed in God, but I didn't trust him. To ground myself, I repeated a favorite mantra, from Ignatius of Loyola: "Pray as if everything depended upon God, and work as if everything depended on man." For me, faith rested upon action, and only those prayers that were acted upon came true. So I went to work. Armed and disguised with an alter ego, I began to personally scour the streets of South Central in search of the killers.

The South Central neighborhoods I patrolled varied from one to the other: Inglewood, Florence, Hyde Park, Chesterfield Square, Vermont Square, Vermont-Slauson, Central-Alameda. Some spots looked nice, others run-down. Tall palms lined residential streets. Weed-filled lots bordered well-tended lawns. There were homes with barred windows and doors, some simple, like a cell, others decorative and ornate. Many homes remained bar-free. But that would soon change. The main thoroughfares—Slauson, Western, Crenshaw—were filled with small businesses. The skyline stayed low, no large-scale projects, tenements, or high-rises in the neighborhoods.

But as I trawled the streets, I felt one thing for certain: this was a region in decline. The dirt, the litter, the graffiti, the peeling paint and shuttered doors, all spoke of a place whose best days had passed. Despite the Olympic interlude, time was leaving South Central behind.

South Central, which got its name from the southern portion of Central Avenue, was once the heart of black social and cultural life in Los Angeles. However, since the 1960s the neighborhood had suffered a slew of troubles. While problems connected with housing and employment existed for decades, the descent took off after the Watts Riots. Whites and well-off blacks began fleeing the area, moving to the north and west.

In the late 1960s and 1970s the problems were exacerbated by a mass exodus of industry from South Central. Firms manufacturing goods for aircraft, aerospace, and electronics had already begun to relocate to the suburbs as early as 1963, two years prior to Watts. Then between 1970 and 1982 a wave of plant closures devastated industry and changed the face of the region. The corporations leaving South Central included Chrysler, B. F. Goodrich, Uniroyal, U.S. Steel, Ford, Firestone, Goodyear, Bethlehem Steel, and General Motors. And even after the job crisis deepened, blacks continued migrating to Southern California in record numbers. In the 1960s alone the black population of Los Angeles increased by over 50 percent.

This industrial abandonment of South Central changed the relationship between blacks and work. With the disappearance of the industrial union jobs went the prospect of a steady, well-paying position, with benefits and a comfortable retirement. It also marked the start of a trend where blacks without higher education were forced into low-paying service-sector jobs. For many black men this scenario caused a crisis, a sense that they were less able to support their families than in the past, and therefore less of a man. I knew the scenario well. My father worked at the Uniroyal plant prior to its closing.

For disillusioned young men, a sense developed that playing by the rules was a pointless waste of time, leading to a "what's the point" mentality. Crime rates rose sharply in the 1960s and 1970s, causing more businesses and middle-class citizens to flee, leaving behind only the most disadvantaged.

The crime and gang warfare that plagued the area would eventually stigmatize it to the point that the mere words "South Central" conjured images of an urban war zone overrun by street terrorists. To counter this negative view, later in 2003 the Los Angeles City Council would vote to officially change the name of the region from "South Central Los Angeles" to "South Los Angeles."

Now, as I entered the area by night, for the first time under my new guise, I sought to get behind the wall of silence, to get some answers.

Despite being a decade removed from my NFL playing days, at about six feet tall and two hundred pounds of muscle I still cut an imposing figure. Further, for anyone in the neighborhood it would have been obvious by my look, and the way I carried myself, that I was strapped, or armed.

The longer the case went unsolved, the more certain members of my family seized on me as the cause. That during my worst hour, my loved ones felt that I brought this upon them summoned up a murderous rage. That I was blamed for mafia ties or cocaine dealing, while the real killers roamed the streets, made me vow to find them and kill them if needed.

Like a modern-day Philip Marlowe, Raymond Chandler's fictional private eye, I delved into the underside of Los Angeles. Lost in a kind of black noir, I found myself in the city's underworld, questioning liquor store owners, bookies, streetwalkers, pimps, drunks, vagrants, and gangsters. Some I begged, others I bribed, while still others I straight-up threatened. I even leaked information through the grapevine that there was a $25,000 reward.

Due to my time as a probation officer in San Francisco I had learned how to interrogate criminals, developing a keen ability to tell truth from lie. Additionally, during off-seasons, I spent more than five years as an Army reservist, and was well trained in the use of firearms.

As I questioned people, some were sure I was a cop and offered me leads on other cases, if I would just call off the heat on them. I assured them I sought information only on this one case. Others thought I looked familiar, and swore they had seen me before. I assured them they hadn't. Some, watching my temper flare, thought me only crazed, another casualty of the streets, and gave me space. Out of fear and anger I had become hypervigilant, hypersensitive to sounds, noises, sudden movements, any sense of danger. Quickly I turned on people, yelled at them, drew my weapon, accused them of lying to me.

Many thought of me as a kind of vigilante, seeking to hunt down the killers of an innocent family, and thanked me for my work. The year 1984 marked a kind of high point of the "fed-up citizen," as seen by New York City's embrace of its subway vigilante, Bernhard Goetz, who shot four unarmed black teenagers on a downtown train before disappearing into the darkened tunnel. A jury acquitted him of all shooting charges. Thus, for frightened citizens of South Central, fed up with living in fear of gangsters and hoodlums, a strong, angry, heavily armed black man was just what they were looking for, a kind of guardian angel, avenger of community victims.

When a possible lead developed I would follow it, only to be disappointed. Just like the police, I received endless bad tips and false leads, based upon vague and fleeting rumors. Everyone knew of the case, but no one seemed to quite get it. No one could make sense of it.

Sometimes, out of sheer frustration I would draw a gun and demand information, or grab someone and roughly pin them against a wall or over a parked car. This produced only cowering and more useless speculation. I repeatedly heard muddled accounts that the murders were said to be some type of retaliation. I also heard rumors that the killers had meant to hit Fifty-Ninth Place, a street well known for drug sales. But I could never turn the street gossip into a promising lead.

I felt that my life was over. I was at that dangerous nihilistic stage where I simply didn't care about anything other than revenge. I really didn't care if anyone killed me. I swore that I would never be captured and sent to prison. As I plied my way deep into gang territories I almost dared them to shoot me. I was prepared to die a "suicide by gang," forcing them to kill me, rather than be taken and imprisoned, sent to another hell, devoid of control.

In the weeks following the murders, I continued to check the papers daily for anything new on the case. On September 13, the *Los Angeles Sentinel* reported the detectives working the case stated: "Nothing new has developed yet." "We're getting telephone calls but nothing has panned out."

———

When exhaustion and depression overtook me, I usually crashed in cheap local motels. On other occasions, late at night, I climbed the walls of the Holy Cross Cemetery and slept among the graves.

I would sit down in the surrounding grass and relive the past weeks. The parts of my personality I liked least now dominated; the out-of-control, angry and vengeful Kermit could not stop raging until some kind of closure was reached. As I stared at the four graves the throbbing in my brain was unbearable.

Half awake, conversations, accusations, images, voices looped through my mind, obsessive and circular.

Conversations with Madee at that kitchen table, on that front porch flashed before me. We talked about the neighborhood. The neighborhood—the same one over which my brother Gordon had fallen to his knees in joy—had changed. It got worse every year. Another Watts could happen at any time, we both agreed. The same tensions were building, over the same set of problems: lack of jobs, opportunities, resources, a racist and brutal LAPD. Only this time, armies of angry young men roamed the streets heavily armed. It would be worse this time, much worse, more violence, more destruction.

We reminded her, all of us did, we talked about it, how the sound of gunshots was more common, and how she had to force the children and grandchildren to "get down." They would all remain crouched below the windows. Then the police helicopter, the "ghetto bird," would circle above, the blades pounding the night sky, the spotlight irradiating the neighborhood, bringing a kind of militant reassurance to the streets below.

But as in Watts years before, Madee was in no hurry. She was about to turn sixty and was set in her ways. Her routine was fixed and revolved around her neighborhood. And while I understood she was her own person and made her own decisions, in light of what happened it was clear I had failed.

Voices on the street echoed my doubts: Why couldn't the All-Pro get his old mom out of the old hood? And family members mumbled under their breath, why hadn't I shown up on that particular morning, like I always did? This added to the suspicions that I knew something I wasn't letting on.

And as answers failed to materialize and doubts multiplied, I sometimes wondered if it was possible that somehow, something I had done had in fact brought this down. I was the only public figure. Could a past act have so antagonized someone to commit quadruple murder? Always be responsible, prepared, I had preached. If you want to ensure that you can be dominant for four quarters, be ready to play eight, I liked to say. Keep as much under your own control as possible, I told people. So what had I failed to control? What had I done, or failed to do, that brought this on? What was there hidden in the past that I was missing? A word, an object, a memory, something I wasn't seeing?

As I sat in the cemetery on a warm California night, I relived my life frame by frame—from Mount Carmel, to UCLA, to the 49ers, Rams, and Eagles, to my post-NFL life as a broadcaster, businessman, and volunteer—searching for any incidents, any clues that could possibly trace the motive for the murders back to me. I dredged up past romantic disillusions, family disputes, business disagreements, trying to imagine any sequence that could have led to this outcome.

It certainly was unpleasant, digging up all my failings and wrongdoings, but it didn't get me anywhere. I found no clues. Nothing fit together. Nothing added up to four counts of home invasion homicide. Nothing equaled children shot in their sleep.

Surely I had made enemies over the years, I had pissed a lot of people off, no doubt; but such incidents centered on football and my aggressive play on the field, and my relentless support of the NFL rank and file as president of the NFL Players Association.

I had exchanged words with many an owner, coach, and player, notably George "Papa Bear" Halas of the Chicago Bears and Green Bay Packers head coach Vince Lombardi. And most famously, in 1968, I had blown out Gale Sayers's knee, ending his season. Actual footage of the play was used in the TV movie *Brian's Song*, the story of Brian Piccolo's fight with cancer and his friendship with Gale Sayers. The footage graphically shows me, number 39, diving through a hole in the line and injuring Sayers. For months I received hate mail and death threats, and was decried as dirty by Bears fans. But I had carried Sayers off the field, visited him in the locker room after the game, and apologized, and Sayers himself later said the hit was clean. And besides, these were incidents on the field almost twenty years ago. It was ridiculous, as worthless as my family's late-night speculations. Surely the ghosts of Halas and Lombardi hadn't somehow returned to take out my family in revenge for some distant football infraction.

But I just kept digging for anyone I had wronged, upset, antagonized. Nothing. But it did serve to drive my depression deeper, load up more guilt. Keep thinking, keep on thinking about everyone you have wronged, hurt, let down, displeased.

Outside the cemetery's walls Los Angeles continued on as always.

It was the weekend. Before me in the distance, the lights poured from downtown. People ate, drank, clinked glasses, and went on dates.

When I looked at myself I wondered if I had lost it, cracked up. The sociable athlete from the big family, always surrounded by brothers, sisters, friends, and fans, now sat alone in a graveyard in the middle of the night, cradling guns and pretending to be someone else. Was it really me, after all, who needed to go to the hospital?

As sleep began to muddle my thoughts I just couldn't put it out of my mind that I must somehow be to blame. I did not feel the crime had distant origins—in Jamaican drug lords, or Colombian cartels. I felt it was local and personal.

But what was I missing? I feared the source of it all would somehow lead back to me, like a riddle from a Greek tragedy. I knew not what I did and that would end up being my sin, and my undoing. I imagined myself out on the streets hopelessly looking for the real killer, and somehow ultimately discovering that in some way I was looking for myself. The fake Kermit with no name and a disguise was actually tracking the real Kermit. My God, I should check myself into the hospital.

The twisted sequences became all-too-confusing and unpleasant and I jerked from my sleep, my heavy head falling toward my lap as I remained seated upright in the grass. I knew I had no hope of banishing the thoughts; the more exhausted I became, the more truth they took on. It was somehow my doing. It must be. I did it. My own family and the police sure seemed to think so.

Another cycle of guilt and beatings: What if I hadn't overslept? I would have been there. I would have killed them, or at least died trying. What if?

As I again stared at the graves, more dark thoughts pounced. It wasn't just the four deceased victims, but the two survivors. Neal, who had shown such potential, as an athlete, as a student, but who always battled inner demons, on disability, trying to recover at our mom's house, was put over the edge by the tragedy. Even years after the event he would say, "Every time I have to talk about it I see it all again."

And what plagued me devastated Ivan. If I felt derelict in upholding the family creed, Ivan couldn't face himself. "I wasn't responsible, Uncle Kermit," he said repeatedly. "I wasn't responsible." No matter how we stressed that hiding in the closet saved his life, that had he not, there would have been five victims, not four, Ivan beat himself up. Like survivors of any tragedy, he couldn't understand why he lived and others died. "Why did they kill them?" he asked. "They didn't do anything."

Near dawn, my head became heavy then fell to the side. Finally I gave in, stretched out on the grass, and fell asleep.

13

THE MAYOR WANTS
TO SEE YOU

As summer turned to fall, and the Santa Ana winds blew the hot desert air off the Mojave and into the Los Angeles basin, the cause of the murders remained a mystery. Weeks had now passed, and a sense of dread infected South Central.

Despite all the conflicting rumors, most residents continued to believe that the killers were local and therefore still within.

No longer were doors left unlocked. Bars began appearing on more doors and windows. Neighbor peered at neighbor with suspicion. Community time was curtailed.

In an effort to understand the tragedy, longtime Angelenos began dredging up the city's most notorious crimes for purposes of comparison. Most commonly they invoked the Manson family murders. Los Angeles County District Attorney Ira Reiner would do so explicitly, emphasizing "the degree of monstrosity" found in both cases.

In the August 1969 killings, armed invaders slaughtered innocents within their Benedict Canyon home. Celebrity was also an issue in the Manson murders, as the actress and wife of director Roman Polanski, Sharon Tate, was one of the five killed. The night following the Tate killings, another couple, the LaBiancas, were tied up and murdered in their Los Angeles home. The motive was elusive and for months the crimes remained unsolved. Finally, the case was broken and the bizarre motive unwound as the prosecution showed that the seven murders were part of cult leader Charles Manson's plans to ignite a race war and eventually rule the world.

In our case, like the Manson murders, the crime was highly atypical, with detectives stymied: a home invasion homicide in which blameless victims were killed at close range. As detectives in the Manson investigation suspected that the controversial director Polanski was the source of the hit, here they continued to question whether the known personality lay at the heart of this case.

Likewise, others referenced another notorious murder case that had just recently made its way back into the news. On August 24, 1984, Louisiana-born author Truman Capote died in Los Angeles of an overdose of pills, in the home of his friend Joanne Carson, ex-wife of Johnny Carson. Capote's death, occurring the same week as the Alexander family murders, raised discussions of the similarities to the crime portrayed in his 1965 "nonfiction novel," *In Cold Blood*.

The subject of Capote's book was a quadruple homicide that took place in Holcomb, in western Kansas, in 1959. Two intruders entered the large farmhouse of Herbert Clutter in the early morning hours of November 15 and with a shotgun executed Clutter, his wife, and their son and daughter. Three of the victims were shot while tied up in their beds. Mr. Clutter had his throat slit before being shot. For months no motive could be found. The Clutters seemed to have no enemies and all that was taken from the house was a small radio, some binoculars, and forty dollars in cash. The case was finally solved through a jailhouse informant who revealed that one of the assailants, Dick Hickock, believed that there was a safe within the house containing $10,000. The house contained no safe and the family was senselessly slaughtered.

————

In late September 1984, I was dressed in a dark three-piece suit as I drove my Jaguar sedan to a business meeting. It was nine in the morning. I was in Marina del Rey, an affluent seaside community in Los Angeles County.

Since the murders I had given up the UCLA broadcasting job, put on hold my volunteer work, stopped speaking at local schools about the dangers of gangs and the virtues of education. I just didn't have it in me. At the time, I was ill-equipped to inspire and motivate. Instead I worked a mindless advertising job. My heart wasn't in it, nor my head, but it gave me a paycheck and something to do.

It was another blistering morning. I stopped and bought a cup of coffee and a morning paper. I wanted to see if there was anything new in the case. Otherwise, I hoped that reading the paper might help take my mind off things.

Back in the car I began drinking the large coffee and opened up the paper. I knew I had to quit the caffeine habit. My doctor said it was bad for my blood pressure. But those days, hardly sleeping, without a pot of coffee I couldn't function. I also wasn't very concerned with my health at that time. My blood pressure was probably through the roof anyway.

As I read the paper, I began with the world news. A Soviet diplomat, S. Tsarpkin, a key architect of the 1963 Comprehensive Nuclear Test Ban Treaty, had died. In another Cold War story, an Afghan rebel leader claimed that the Soviets planned a major new offensive, intending to "finish Afghanistan" in a campaign of "genocide and oppression." In the Middle East, the six-nation Gulf Cooperation Council said military security measures were the top priority in ensuring no disruption of oil flow through the Persian Gulf during the Iran-Iraq War.

Nationally, Reagan was confident in his reelection bid and was stumping for Republican congressional candidates, holding out the promise of even lower taxes in a second term. Reagan reacted with "anger and sorrow" at the latest suicide bombing against Americans in Beirut, Lebanon, declaring, "we can't just withdraw in the face of this kind of terrorism." Vice President George H. W. Bush was heckled by nuclear freeze advocates, who chanted "Vote for Peace." Bush responded that Reagan had secured peace without backing down, and the protestors were "out of step with the country." As Democratic candidate Walter Mondale spoke on the campaign trail, he was heckled at USC by the Trojan College Republicans, who chanted "four more years" and "peace through strength." The Sierra Club announced it was endorsing Mondale.

In Florida, the murderer of an elderly civil rights worker "enjoyed" a last meal of a dozen oysters, with hot sauce and crackers, as well as half a cantaloupe and grapefruit, before dying in the electric chair. In Chicago, a symposium shed new light on a condition known as anhedonia, "the inability to experience pleasure," in which sufferers are socially isolated, operating on automatic pilot and simply going through the motions with no joy.

In California, San Diego's mayor, Roger Hedgecock, along with three political backers, was indicted on fourteen counts of perjury and one count of conspiracy regarding illegal campaign contributions. Joselito Cinco, a man charged with killing two San Diego police officers, faced the death penalty. Cinco pled not guilty and broke into tears when the judge refused to grant bail.

In sports, ex-Dodger Steve Garvey was leading the San Diego Padres as they closed in on their first National League West title with just a week to go in the season. In the American League the Angels were a game and a half out of first after defeating Kansas City bullpen ace Dan Quisenberry on a Bobby Grich eleventh-inning single. In college football, UCLA starting quarterback Steve Bono, suffering from a sprained ankle, was unlikely for the upcoming game against number-one-ranked Nebraska at the Rose Bowl, said head coach Terry Donahue. In the NFL, former Raider QB Dan Pastorini, along with the NFL Players Association, was suing the Raiders for payment of a $1 million arbitration award.

Locally, the weather was finally supposed to cool, after a month of sticky sweltering heat, as a "low-pressure trough from Alaska was expected to take the edge off."

Coverage of our case was fading fast. Weeks ago front-page news, then buried deep within other local stories, now it was either nothing, or more of the same: "No concrete motives," "Nothing's new," "Little progress made." The other news felt distant and meaningless. Political or sports-related stories that would have captured me weeks ago now seemed irrelevant, boring, or maddening. I couldn't focus or care about sports, even UCLA. The Cold War and Middle East had no effect on my life, and murderers eating oysters and crying over bail seemed absurd and insulting. The only thing that made any sense was that story about the mental condition.

But where was news of our case? They had better not forget about us, I seethed. I threw the paper down onto the passenger seat in disgust. Everyone else was moving on. That's how these things went. I knew it. I got it. Four more murders, black people, South Central, statistics. And back to our regular programming: elections, wars, politicians, corruption and convictions, pennant races and injured QBs, and now for the weather.

As I dwelled on the stalled investigation, I felt my anger rise. No options, no hope. When I began my search for the killers it had a certain sick thrill of the new. Now it foundered as well. Nothing I could do. Nothing the police could do. Impotence, gnawing. I barely resisted an impulse to fling the half-filled coffee cup against the windshield. Instead I squeezed the steering wheel and jammed the accelerator.

As I sped through an intersection I noticed another car turn the corner and speed up behind me. It was a patrol car. Next came the flashing lights.

I had just blown through a stop sign.

I pulled to a sudden stop. Red and blue lights lit up my rearview mirror.

As the officer approached the driver's side of the car, I reached for my wallet and pulled out my license.

As the officer took the license, he barely glanced at it, instead staring past me and onto the passenger's seat.

"Exit the vehicle," he said. "Keep your hands visible."

Underslept, overcaffeinated, and with a hair-trigger temper, I had no patience for this. As I got out of the car and he started to search me in a disrespectful manner, I let him know I wouldn't take it.

"Look," he said, pointing at the pile of discarded newspapers on the front passenger seat. "I have to take you in."

From beneath the stack of papers, the butt of a handgun protruded.

As the officer removed the gun and searched the rest of the car, I explained to him who I was and that I needed the weapon for protection.

The officer then took me to the Pacific Station, where I was questioned. Following the interview, the desk sergeant made some calls, hung up the phone, and said, "The mayor wants to see you."

14

I'M AFRAID HE'LL
TURN INTO ONE

Built in 1928 in the style of an ancient ziggurat, City Hall intentionally conjured the image of Los Angeles as a modern Babylon—a fantasy city where anything was possible. Echoing this theme, Mayor Bradley had declared that City Hall "must be a beacon to people's aspirations." When no structure in downtown topped twelve floors, the thirty-two-story City Hall towered over the cityscape and remained L.A.'s tallest building for decades. A symbol of the city's draw and mystique, as well as its newly won status as the state's epicenter, City Hall's construction utilized raw materials from all fifty-eight of California's counties and water from all twenty-one of its historic missions. An image of the iconic tower has been on the LAPD badges since 1940. The mayor's office is located in room 300.

Mayor Bradley, now halfway through his third term, and still riding the Olympic high, greeted me in his outer office, then led me inside to his private chambers and offered me a seat. I had known Bradley since his days walking a beat in South Central when I was a young man living in the Jordan Downs housing projects. We had remained friends over the years and worked together on various projects involving sports and the community.

During and after my NFL playing days I was involved in charitable events, including golf tournaments, fund-raisers, and motivational speaking tours of middle and high schools.

In 1970, after seven seasons with the San Francisco 49ers, I came home, when I was traded to the Rams. For my family it was a dream come true. For me, it was the greatest moment in my career. From then on, every time I took the field for a home game I knew that Madee and company were cheering in the stands.

But coming home was also depressing. The old neighborhood was in bad shape, run-down, with kids cutting school, hitting the streets, joining gangs. Trying to provide an alternative, I sponsored a Pop Warner youth football team, hoping that football, like it did for me, could help steer kids away from trouble.

Pop Warner leagues went back to the thirties, named after coach and innovator Glenn Scobey "Pop" Warner. While the leagues are designed to teach kids how to play football, the goals are greater. By playing in Pop Warner, kids are taught the values of teamwork, how to overcome challenges and work together. Warner saw this firsthand at the Carlisle School in Pennsylvania at the beginning of the twentieth century, where displaced Plains Indians, including the legendary Jim Thorpe, thrived under his leadership.

For me, having grown up in South Central, I wanted to give the kids a meaningful way to spend their time, an opportunity to make positive attachments, and a chance to be a star on the field, not the streets.

One of my sisters and her husband ran the team. I provided the funding. My friends from the Rams, Rosey Grier and Deacon Jones, also helped me raise money. We even took the Wildcats to a Rams game to inspire them as to what they could be.

Likewise, Mayor Bradley, as a young police officer, organized youth baseball and football leagues to provide positive options for at-risk kids. The mayor and I were convinced that sports provided a way to channel both rage and talent, that sports stressed discipline and focus, that playing the games was satisfying and built a sense of pride and self-worth. Currently, Bradley saw to it that portions of the Olympic surplus went to fund youth athletic programs.

Additionally, the mayor and I had discussed my off-season work as a San Francisco probation officer during the 1960s. We both felt that I could use my influence to help turn lives around. Just get them to listen, just get them to think about their lives. The hardest thing to do was to get the criminals to take any responsibility. It was never their fault, it was the drugs, it was the police, it was the radical movement—in the late 1960s every gangster was revolutionary. They all called me "brother," and went on about "power to the people." "Man," I'd say, "you aren't in my family, and you sure as hell don't have any power." They didn't listen. No matter what, it was always something other than them that caused the crime. With these guys it was always "SOD," we would laugh around the probation office: "Some Other Dude." I always believed that once someone could actually take time out, look at their life, and own it, then great change could occur.

Any little moment has within it life-changing potential. This view was born of a personal interaction between Bradley and me when I was just a boy. When Bradley was a beat cop and I was about twelve, he had called me out regarding my recent theft from a corner store, asking me whether I wanted to amount to something or start down the path to ruin. As a young man, Bradley himself was caught for the same offense and received a whooping from his mother that he never forgot. Bradley never told my mother what I did, for which I was forever thankful. I always remembered Bradley's words. The event marked another turning point in my life, like my father dressing me down and asking if I wanted to be a star athlete, or just another killer.

Since the murders, Mayor Bradley had personally offered my family his condolences and held press conferences outlining the police response to the tragedy. But with little progress after nearly a month, he shared my frustrations. He knew I could blow at any moment.

As a police officer, a city councilman, and now as mayor, Tom Bradley had developed a reputation for knowing what happened within his city. And word of my midnight rambles had reached him.

Well aware of my personality and my current sense of desperation, he feared I could kill someone, or get myself killed. Either result would be a public relations disaster for the city, highlighting the failure to solve the case and control violent crime.

Now, reclining in his high-backed chair, the mayor spoke in a calm baritone as he attempted to put me at ease. At six feet, four inches tall and dressed in a dark suit, Bradley had a commanding presence. He pushed his fingertips into a pyramid, exhaled, and slowly leaned forward. He empathized with me and my family, he assured me. Bradley too had been very close with his mother, who had just recently passed away. The mayor also lived by the creed that you needed to take control of your own life, and understood my refusal to simply sit passive. But, he stressed, leaning back into his chair, my vigilante act could only bring further tragedy. He concluded his plea by telling me that LAPD chief Daryl Gates was on his way up to the mayor's office. Gates, Bradley said, would detail for me all of the LAPD's current efforts and convince me that the police could handle this matter.

———

Daryl Gates was appointed chief of police in 1978. Gates was a protégé and onetime driver of the iconic chief William Parker. Modeling himself after Parker, who headed the department from 1950 to 1966, Gates believed in a modern, efficient, and professional police force, organized upon a military model and reliant on the most up-to-date technologies. Gates shared Parker's intolerance for police corruption and brutality, as both thwarted the will to effectively fight crime. But Gates, like Parker, took criticism poorly, was slow to acknowledge errors, and failed to perceive the racial divide splitting the police from the city's minority citizens.

Since becoming chief, a central issue facing Gates was the growth of street gangs, particularly in South Central. Believing that U.S. Supreme Court Chief Justice Earl Warren's "due process revolution" emboldened criminals at the expense of the law-abiding, Gates spearheaded numerous "get tough" programs designed to "take back the streets." Gates's philosophy was that if you caused others to fear leaving their homes, then you did not deserve to be on the streets, and would thus have a problem with the LAPD. Faced with the new murderous gangs, Gates forged a police force that even the most hardened gangster would fear. This made Gates highly controversial, embraced by law-and-order advocates as a last best hope, condemned by civil libertarians for running an L.A. Gestapo.

LAPD's CRASH Unit (Community Resources Against Street Hoodlums) exemplified the Gates way of fighting gangs. CRASH, originally TRASH (Total Resources Against Street Hoodlums), was born out of South Bureau's 77th Street Division. Relying upon aggressive proactive policing, favored tactics included gang sweeps, heavily armed raids of crack houses, and widespread use of stop-and-frisks. CRASH's motto, "We intimidate those who intimidate others," as well as the logo, a skull wearing a cowboy hat, sent the message that L.A.'s streets were the new Wild West. Like Gates himself, CRASH was divisive. Critics questioned its constitutionality, seeing it as just another excuse for the head-cracking LAPD to harass minorities while ignoring underlying social problems. Gates defended it as the only way to protect terrorized citizens stuck in gang war zones.

As the 1984 Olympics neared, Gates had made a name for himself with his full-force assault on gangs. Leading fifty separate law enforcement agencies, LAPD saw that the summer Games went off without incident. Fearing that gangs would intimidate patrons, as well as potentially ally with foreign terrorists, Gates and his security team relied upon gang sweeps and mass arrests and secured fences and barricades to prevent suspected gang members from nearing the Olympic Village. While generally applauded in the spirit of Olympic euphoria, Gates had his critics. Some criticized his tactics as an "Olympic siege," turning the streets of Los Angeles "into occupied Belfast."

While Bradley and Gates had cooperated in the name of Olympic unity, the preceding years had seen their relationship grow ever colder. They could grit their teeth and exchange wooden handshakes at press conferences, but the bad blood left the two barely speaking. Gates felt the mayor punitively starved LAPD of resources due to a long-held grudge that the department had discriminated against him as an officer in the 1940s. Bradley saw Gates as a loose-tongued cowboy, out of touch with the realities of modern-day Los Angeles and hostile to the concerns of the city's growing nonwhite population.

For Gates the situation was complicated. African-American leaders, such as City Councilman Robert Farrell, demanded more active policing for the terrified residents of poor minority districts. Farrell and others also argued that had white people been frequent murder victims, a very different police response would have been seen. This pressured Gates to solve black-on-black crimes and prevent them going forward. Gates said this could be done only through persistent and aggressive strategies. On the other hand, Gates and LAPD were under constant assault by civil rights groups complaining that such tactics in minority neighborhoods constituted racial profiling and put disproportionate numbers of young black men behind bars.

Now, in a rare moment of harmony, Bradley and Gates agreed that getting me off the streets served their collective interests. Gates did not want the message sent to the community that a black family's murder was not prioritized, that the police could not handle their business, and that vigilantism was acceptable. This would erode respect for law and order. And Bradley, a seasoned campaigner, understood all too well the importance of crime as a political issue. In 1982 he lost a heartbreakingly close gubernatorial campaign to George Deukmejian in which law and order, victims' rights, and the death penalty were the lead issues. Deukmejian had cloaked himself in the mantle of crime fighter and surrounded himself with victims and their families. Bradley was hurt by the defeat, and angered at being branded soft on crime. Thus as he geared up for future campaigns, Bradley felt the emotional impact of violent crime and knew its effects on his political fortunes.

Bradley and Gates therefore assured me that my case was a top priority, and that going forward, a "drastic change" in police protection would be seen. More officers would be assigned to divisions policing South Central and even more active CRASH units would be put into action.

Gates explained that LAPD had linked a lot of the recent gang violence to a concert held at the Coliseum on August 18, which had been attended by hundreds of gang members wearing their colors. Since that concert, numerous gang-related killings had occurred. While Gates could not say whether the murder of my family was related to this spate of killings, he commented that the police did not feel that the majority of the attacks were random, as they once had, but represented "targeted" attacks against certain individuals.

"But why would anyone target my family?" I asked.

Gates wasn't sure, but said it may have been a drug-related retaliatory hit gone awry. And he conceded that the initial police reaction was that the crime had no apparent gang connection.

I remained unconvinced, still seeing the police as clueless. It sounded to me like Gates was spinning his wheels, simply trying to mollify me and avoid a violent confrontation. It was gang related, it wasn't gang related, it was random, it wasn't . . . on and on. I felt he meant well and that his heart was in the right place, but nearly a month after the killings the police just weren't getting anywhere.

But out of respect, I continued to listen patiently.

As their next approach, Bradley and Gates guaranteed me that they would personally explain to my family that I had no role in the killings and was not considered a suspect. Finally, they agreed that they would keep me abreast of developments in the case going forward, and that the investigating detectives would be instructed to give me regular briefings.

Bradley then reiterated his heartfelt feelings for my family and his commitment to bringing the killers to justice. Gates concurred and ended with some small talk, noting that he, like me, was involved with Pop Warner football, where he coached nine-year-olds. Gates reminisced over his days playing football at Franklin High, where he too lined up on both sides of the ball, at fullback and outside linebacker.

As the meeting concluded and I worked my way toward the door, the two adversaries once again spoke as one, stressing that for the good of all, my parallel hunt must end.

Having a long-term relationship and great respect for Bradley, and an impression that Gates was sincere in his promise of stepped-up police efforts, I nodded in agreement. However, my need to be personally involved remained. I would do my best to stay out of the way, but I could not just sit idle. I would have to be more careful, and covert.

"Find his killers," the mayor said to the chief as we parted, "or I'm afraid he'll turn into one."

15

AN EPIDEMIC OF VIOLENCE

It kept me from being a killer. It was my savior.

The game is colorful and fast, complex and creative, electric. But it's brutal and fleeting. The road to the pros is one long struggle. And every player knows that every play may be his last. The average NFL career is about three years. NFL means "not for long."

Thousands of hours of practice, conditioning, two-a-day practices at training camps beneath the blazing summer sun, repetition, reps, reps, reps, sacrifice, knockouts, see stars, reps, reps, reps, more stars, more reps, grind it out in youth leagues, high school, practice, commitment, then more reps.

It's been called a "murderous sport." That's why people love it. The violence is seductive. A psychology professor at UCLA would come and watch practice, then marvel. "I don't get it," he'd say, "but I'm just fascinated by the violence." The game is raw, played in blizzards, "Ice Bowls," "Fog Bowls," and subzero temperatures described as "inhumane." It is a model for manly living: vigorous, strenuous, punishing. It's the ultimate subculture, tribes in uniforms and helmets, with a secret language and a coded plan of attack. Vince Lombardi called it "a game for madmen," and General Douglas MacArthur thought it ideal battlefield training. It is a war. It is fought in the trenches. Gladiators face off in the Coliseum, warriors at Soldier Field, troops at Veterans Stadium. Guys nicknamed "Tank," battle for yards against "the Assassin" and "the Hit Man," offenses wage an aerial assault, led by the "Mad Bomber." Defenses blitz.

And my day was a different world from today's NFL. Many players in the 1960s and early 1970s made little more than the average worker. Baseball was still the "national pastime." Our salaries didn't come close. We all had off-season jobs. We were blue-collar, lunch pail tough, that's why they loved us in hardscrabble towns like Pittsburgh, Cleveland, Detroit, and Oakland. We drank at local pubs with steelworkers and machinists, plumbers and cops. We hitched a ride to practice and carpooled to games to save money on gas. Practice fields were muddy, sometimes gravel strewn. Until the mid-1970s the Super Bowl didn't sell out.

We didn't call them concussions. You got knocked out. You got your bell rung. And as long as you could stand up and "answer the phone," you got back in the huddle and ran the next play. The fear was constant: you miss time for injury, you lose your job, the world hypercompetitive, everyone behind you on the depth chart just begging you to go down, give them a shot. The pressure was intense: play hurt for your teammates. We were a unit, a battalion. Be there for them, don't let them down. The guy next to you depends on you, trusts you. Have his back. He has yours. Play through pain. He does. Why not you? Not tough enough? Do it. Don't worry, the adrenaline and injections will numb it just fine. It's in the job description, it's just part of the game, perform or go home. Life lessons on the gridiron.

In the scrum, or battle for the loose ball, unspeakable things occur, grabbing and grappling, biting and scratching, hands to the face, eyes, mouth, and worse. Until just the last few years, TV highlights glorified hits that are now illegal, bringing suspensions and fines. In my day we played for those hits. But now the toll is there for all to see: Oiler running back Earl Campbell sits in a wheelchair at age fifty, Raider center Jim Otto has undergone forty knee surgeries and has no cartilage left, Patriot wide receiver Darryl Stingley, with broken vertebrae, became a quadriplegic at age twenty-six. On the date he was injured Stingley was to become the highest-paid player in the league. The game was in Oakland. The Patriots flew back to New England, leaving him behind, alone in the hospital with a breathing tube in his mouth. The contract was never signed.

But that was the game. The object was to knock the best player off the field. Everyone knew that was the goal, always had been, as long as the game had been played. When I played in the 1960s and '70s it went without saying. With the Saints of 2012, it was labeled "Bounty-Gate," put a bounty on other teams' best players, collect cash for injuries.

The other major struggle in my early years was racial. When I began to play football, in the 1950s, race was still a major barrier in the sports world.

In 1951, the University of San Francisco Dons went undefeated, but were denied a bowl bid. Two of their star players were black, Ollie Matson, a future NFL Hall of Famer, and Burl Toler, who would become the NFL's first black referee. The Dons actually *were* invited to play in the Orange Bowl in Miami, to decide the national champion. But the bid came with a condition: the team had to leave the black players behind. Refusing to be Jim Crowed, the team unanimously declined. Without the Orange Bowl revenues, USF could not afford to continue to field a team, and like Pepperdine and other Catholic universities I had once dreamed of attending, it shut down its program.

When I played at UCLA, our nonconference games were scheduled only in northern cities. It was too explosive to put black players into the South, where sports and race did not mix. And when black athletes from California and the North would go down south, they were shocked. They couldn't eat meals with their team, could not stay in the same hotels, could not use the same facilities. Guidebooks existed especially for black travelers, leading them to safe places that would serve them. Often black players, unable to find accommodations, relied upon local blacks in the area to put them up for the night. When I began with the 49ers and we played in southern cities, armed guards lined the stadiums for our protection. Just a year before

I entered the NFL, 1962, the Washington Redskins, playing in D.C., finally integrated, and only under stiff federal pressure.

In my day, only certain positions were open to black players: typically running back and defensive end, but never quarterback, center, or linebacker, the positions that called the plays and directed the action.

To play a role in challenging these conditions, I became the 49er player representative, and then in 1976, after my retirement, the president of the NFL Players Association. At the time, I was only the third president in the association's history, and the second black, after Colts legend John Mackey, who himself was a sad reminder of what we were fighting for, as he suffered severe bouts of dementia later in life.

And it was a fight. Our union was new and weak. We were nothing like the Major League Baseball Players Association. But we all believed in the game. We knew what we were getting into. We just demanded that we be fairly treated, compensated for the wild risks we took. We all knew that our survival as individuals, and the game's future, depended on making the game as safe as possible, while still keeping it football. On several occasions in its early history, the game came close to extinction. In the early twentieth century, after several deaths on the field, avid football fan President Theodore Roosevelt called for reforms to keep the game alive.

Today the racial conflicts belong to the game's historical past. But the tension over safety remains. We condemn injuries. We crave violence.

––––––

High rates of violent crime were nothing new to California or Los Angeles. In the height of the Gold Rush in the early 1850s, towns in the Sierras hit murder rates fifty times higher than late-twentieth-century America. Los Angeles, in the mid-1850s, while still a sleepy and undeveloped frontier pueblo, set the all-time homicide record.

One of the reasons for Los Angeles's outsized murder rate was its small population, ensuring that just a handful of killings could spike the per capita rate. However, Los Angeles during the transition from Mexican outpost to major metropolis was, like the Wild West in general, a dangerous place. From 1830 to 1860 the revolver became the favorite weapon, adding to the potential for lethal violence.

By the end of the nineteenth century Los Angeles's homicide rate was one and a half times that of the United States and more than three times the rate of New York City. With increasing railroad access, the city's population exploded, from 100,000 in 1900 to 600,000 by 1920. This growth, however, was not accompanied by an increase in the homicide rate. Murder in America and Los Angeles hit a low point between the Great Depression and the post–World War II years. These low rates have been attributed to the end of Prohibition, high employment, more stay-at-home parents, an increase in law enforcement, and an antiviolence attitude of returning soldiers.

Like most American cities, Los Angeles experienced a sharp homicide increase in the tumultuous 1960s, fueled by racial tensions, civil unrest, and New Left protest movements over the Vietnam War. Over the next decade, homicides continued to rise, hitting a modern high in 1980.

By 1984, L.A.'s overall homicide rate had declined, but a clear trend was developing: an increase in black-on-black homicide, specifically, drug- and gang-related murders, an intraracial explosion that would be termed an "epidemic" and "a black genocide." Homicide became the leading cause of death for young inner-city black males.

This was the issue addressed by Eighth District councilman Robert Farrell on the day of the murders. Likewise, Tenth District councilman David S. Cunningham Jr., also black, urged the chief to "do whatever you can" to clamp down on crack cocaine markets, stating that the drug was "going to destroy the black community."

16

HYDE PARK

On SEPTEMBER 27, 1984, as part of an increased effort by the LAPD to crack down on drug-related violence, Detective Manlove, of the L.A. Narcotics Division South Bureau CRASH, supervised a fifteen-person task force assigned to the area of Sixty-Third Street and Tenth Avenue in the Hyde Park neighborhood of South Central.

One of the oldest neighborhoods in Los Angeles, Hyde Park was established in the late nineteenth century as a stop on the Atchison, Topeka and Santa Fe Railway. In 1887 the Atchison, Topeka and Santa Fe broke the Southern Pacific's monopoly on transcontinental travel, cutting the cost of a railroad ticket by more than 80 percent, opening up the West to mass settlement and spurring Southern California's boom of the 1880s.

Originally a small independent city of a little under three square miles, Hyde Park was incorporated into Los Angeles in 1923. Like nearby districts of Westchester, Gramercy Park, and Chesterfield Square, Hyde Park was given a charming classic name to entice settlers. By the end of the twentieth century the neighborhood would become largely black, with census data showing its residents to have one of the lowest percentages of four-year degrees and highest rates of single-parent households within Los Angeles County.

Within Hyde Park, Tenth Avenue, a residential street, ran north to south with no center divide. A strip of grass separated the street from the sidewalk, setting the homes back several yards from the curb. American cars, mostly from the 1960s and 1970s, parked along the street: Valiants, Darts, Dusters, Mustangs, an occasional van or truck. Palm trees, bushes, and chain-link fences fronted many of the buildings; a mix of single-story bungalows, duplexes, and low two-story apartment complexes. Gang graffiti streaked walls and buildings.

As officers approached Tenth Avenue, a crowd of black teens stood in front of an apartment complex. They dressed in black and blue, in baseball hats and sneakers.

The police task force was engaged in an undercover narcotics operation. This portion of Tenth Avenue was known for drug sales, most recently a new form of cocaine, called "crack." The police were focused on a "rock house," a fortified residence where crack was sold. As time went on, the rock houses had ever-thicker steel doors, reinforced with multiple locks, and only a narrow slit through which the drugs and money were exchanged. The reinforced doors were to thwart desperate addicts as well as robbers. They also served to slow police entry, allowing sellers time to escape, and stash or destroy the evidence. LAPD first employed small explosives referred to as shape charges to shatter the locks, and eventually turned to armored vehicles, used as battering rams to, in the words of Chief Gates, "hit with precision the exact spot on the house they wanted to punch a hole through."

First hitting the streets of Los Angeles in early 1980s, crack was a form of cocaine that had been heated or cooked with bicarbonate of soda. This distilled the cocaine into a kind of rock or nugget that could then be smoked, typically in a glass pipe. As the rocks were smoked they made a crackling sound, giving the drug its name. The crack cocaine craze was the latest fad or rush to hit California, this time the nuggets white not gold.

The small rocks were cheap, making the drug instantly popular among the poor. Additionally, the high from smoking the rock cocaine is extremely intense, creating feelings of euphoria and omnipotence, as dopamine, a neurotransmitter providing a sense of pleasure, is temporarily spiked. However, the high is also very short-lived, lasting between five and fifteen minutes. Once the effect dissipates, the euphoria quickly fades as dopamine levels plummet, leaving the user feeling irritable, angry, and disoriented. The user now craves the high, making crack instantly addictive. As dopamine levels take time to recover, the next hit will not bring the same result as the first, causing the addict to smoke ever more in an effort to regain the initial high. This cycle of craving became known as "chasing the ghost."

The effects of crack cocaine devastated inner cities across the country, as millions became addicted. Dealers quickly realized the power of the drug, with some offering free samples, as one go-around was often enough to create an addict. Desperate to recapture the magic, addicts would literally sell themselves to get another high. Females who sold their bodies for a crack hit were referred to as "crack hos" or "strawberries," while males were called "raspberries." Crack houses sprang up like mushrooms. Outside the houses, the most desperate groveled in the dirt, on hands and knees, foraging for the tiniest grub that may have slipped to the ground. Locals called this "kibbles 'n' bitsing."

Once hooked, the addict's life revolved around getting the dose and maniacally attempting to sustain a high. Unable to function without the drug, and often staying up for days at a time, crackheads became incapable of handling everyday responsibilities, abandoning work, family, and any semblance of a normal social life. With brains chemically damaged by the drug, they also ceased to think rationally, acting paranoid, hostile, and erratic.

While the supply lines of the powder cocaine originated in Colombia, Peru, and Venezuela, before being smuggled up through Mexico, the cooking of the powder took place in the States. The distilled crack, or rocks, was then sold on the streets by black street gangs, who spread the drug through their own communities. As the crack trade was highly competitive, dangling the promise of high profits, street-level dealers began heavily arming themselves in an effort to protect their stash and drug-dealing turf.

Now, in Hyde Park, the narcotics task force prepared to make a "buy-bust," an operation in which an officer in plain clothes posed as a drug buyer. When the drugs and money were exchanged, the seller was busted and placed under arrest.

As the police engaged in the operation, they saw a black teenager hiding behind a fence. He was holding a gun. He was someone referred to as a "boner," an armed gunman guarding the rock house against robbers.

When the police identified themselves, the teen fled. The police chased him, caught up with him, and eventually captured him. When they did, the weapon was gone.

Officer Duran, who had accompanied Detective Manlove on the raid, searched around the bushes and then found where the teen had stashed the weapon. He returned holding an old rifle with a folding stock.

It was a .30-caliber M-1 carbine, containing live rounds of ammunition in the clip and barrel.

It was tarnished and scuffed. The letters PBG had been scratched onto its wooden base.

Police took the weapon, as well as the live ammunition, and booked it into evidence.

The teen was handcuffed, put into a police car, and booked. He was seventeen years old, and he lived in an apartment complex on Tenth Avenue. His name was James Kennedy. On the streets he was known as Little Cat Man. He belonged to a Hyde Park gang called the Rolling Sixties.

———

"Stop it!" I yelled. "Just stop!"

Someone was pulling at me, shaking me. A loud noise rang in my ears.

"Don't make them go away. Don't let them leave again," I pleaded.

The shaking and ringing continued.

"They're not dead, Mama, they're *not* dead. Mama, go get 'em. They're *not* dead."

That little girl again, in front of Madee's house.

"I know," I said, "I know. They're not, they're right—"

"Kermit, wake up," my wife, Clarice, said as she shook me. "Wake up and get the phone."

"What? What?"

"Phone call, answer it," she said. "It'll be for you, probably the cops again."

She put the ringing phone on my chest.

It was early evening and the autumn sky was just beginning to darken. By night I prowled; by afternoon I slept.

Earlier that day I had cleaned out my mother's house. The landlord needed to rent it.

I had carried a box of photographs into my house and fallen asleep next to them. In my dreams my slain relatives lived. Now the phone had killed them again. One more ring.

"Hello."

"Kermit?"

"Yes. Who's this?"

"This is Tony. Tony Anderson, from Juvenile Hall."

It took me a minute to compute as I came to, still shaking the dream from my mind.

Tony was a friend of mine.

"Yes, yes . . . Tony. What's up?"

"Got a minute?"

"What is it?"

"I'm not supposed to be making this call. I'm going outside of channels, but I felt there was something you needed to know."

"Go ahead. I'm listening."

"I don't know if this is legit or not, but there's a kid down here, sixteen, seventeen. He just got arrested, and I overheard him talking about a murder. Sounds to me like it's your case and he might know something about it. Actually sounds like he might have been involved."

Now fully awake, I sat up and began calculating. I had no idea if this was another false start, but I had to act on it as if it were real.

"Kermit, what do you want me to do?"

"Isolate him. Don't let him go anywhere."

I wanted to give him as little time as possible to concoct stories or excuses.

"Will do, are you coming down here?"

"No way, if I did I'd rip his head off."

17

GLADIATORS, PANTHERS, AND TALES FROM THE CRYPT

Black street gangs in Los Angeles have their roots in collective acts of juvenile delinquency in the 1930s, but became a permanent fixture only following the World War II migration. As the numbers of blacks living in Los Angeles increased dramatically in the 1940s and 1950s, the informal boundary lines separating black and white neighborhoods began to blur. White Angelenos worried about property values, and desiring racial homogeneity, attempted to draw new lines beyond which blacks could not cross.

White youth living in these borderlands began acting as racial regulators, forming street groups, most infamously a gang known as the "Spook Hunters." Such organizations sought to intimidate blacks, curtail their movement, and prevent entry into white enclaves. This street terrorism, in addition to the governmental tactic of restrictive housing covenants, served to concentrate blacks in limited areas. It also prompted some blacks to question whether Los Angeles represented any improvement over the Jim Crow South. It led others, such as the black noir writer Chester Himes, to conclude that it was worse. Moreover, the white regulators spurred some younger black males to form their own defensive groups, which provided their members with a sense of safety, of power in numbers, as well as feelings of acceptance and belonging.

While these black street organizations, or "clubs," as their initiates called them, may have begun as defensive mechanisms, they soon took on a life of their own, and began turning their aggressions inward, competing and fighting among themselves, primarily over local disputes ("beefs"), as well as turf. The Slausons, Gladiators, Businessmen, and other clubs began to mimic the pattern against which they had initially rebelled, as they carved up portions of South Central Los Angeles and claimed them as their own. Neighborhoods, blocks, parks, and other hangouts were declared as belonging to one club or another. The newly constructed housing projects, including Jordan Downs, Nickerson Gardens, and Pico Gardens, where many young people congregated, also became hotbeds of gang membership.

The youth from the clubs typically liked to dress up, show off their cars, hang out, look cool, and try to impress the young ladies. But if members of another club attempted to cross a line or infringe on their turf or action, this was taken as a challenge, often resulting in a physical altercation. The gang fights of the 1940s and 1950s typically involved fists, brass knuckles, tire irons, and bicycle chains, occasionally knives, but seldom guns.

By the 1960s, several trends converged to change the nature of the black street gang. First, the number of blacks migrating to Los Angeles accelerated, placing ever greater strain on the traditionally black areas to absorb and contain the newly arrived migrant population. Second, the early stages of deindustrialization and its erosion of the inner-city economy destabilized black job markets and employment opportunities. Finally, intertwined with the burgeoning numbers and diminishing prospects was disappointment at the civil rights movement's inability to deliver timely and tangible benefits to urban blacks. While the Civil Rights Act of 1964 and the Voting Rights Act of 1965 represented ideological victories and promised to improve conditions in the rural South, the pace of change in northern and western cities, to which so many blacks had migrated in recent decades, remained maddeningly slow.

These collective dynamics dovetailed with a generational shift. The first waves of African-American migrants relocating in Los Angeles applied a relative perspective to their situation, comparing the opportunities of the West favorably to sharecropping and Jim Crow. The earlier migrants also shared a culturally ingrained sense of deference, inculcated since birth. You showed white people respect—or else. You lowered your eyes, and submissively vacated the sidewalk when they walked by. Thus, while it wasn't perfect, in general the way whites treated blacks in Los Angeles was a big improvement from what they and their ancestors had faced, and from which they had fled. The idea that L.A. represented something new and different for blacks is exemplified in the words of the African-American scholar and Harvard sociologist W. E. B. DuBois, who after visiting Los Angeles in 1913 declared the city "a new heaven for black people."

However, for the younger generation that never knew Jim Crow, and who came of age under the rhetoric of civil rights, a different set of expectations prevailed. Impatient for change and frustrated by what they saw as a selling out of the promise of equality, many younger blacks began challenging the established order. They rejected the "yes sir, no sir" obsequiousness of their elders, bucked under the restrictions of movement imposed by racial boundaries, and fought to resist unequal treatment at the hands of the LAPD.

The tensions that had been building then erupted in the wake of a traffic stop on August 11, 1965. The Watts Riots, which involved the active participation of L.A.'s black clubs, would end up changing the nature of black street gangs in Los Angeles. Following the riots, the gangs called for a kind of truce, as members of once-rival clubs became the new disciples of a politically motivated group, called the Black Panthers, as well as a competing organization known as U.S., or United Slaves. For Southern California in particular, the Watts Riots of 1965 marked a political dividing line, separating the Martin Luther King–led civil rights movement of the 1950s and early 1960s from the radical Black Power era of the late 1960s.

Founded by Huey Newton and Bobby Seale in Oakland in 1966, the Panthers became the vanguard of the Black Power Movement.

The Panthers, along with Malcolm X and the Nation of Islam, and Ron Karenga and U.S., sought to distance themselves from the non-violence of Dr. King and to demand change through the doctrine of armed resistance. Initially called the Black Panther Party for Self-Defense, they adopted the symbol of a panther because it was known as an animal that acted peacefully if left alone, but fought to the death if cornered and threatened. Dressing in black leather coats, army boots, dark glasses, and berets, the Panthers projected an image of power and militancy. Following after police cars, armed with guns and penal codes, the Panthers checked the officers' actions against the language of the law in an effort to curtail police abuses of discretion. On May 2, 1967, the Panthers created a national stir when they stormed the California Capitol building in Sacramento wielding shotguns. In addition to such militant acts, the Panthers also exerted a presence in the community, organizing breakfasts and literacy drives, performing charity work on behalf of the inner-city poor.

The legacy of the Panther Party and other radical black political organizations remains contested. For some, the channeling of street energies into a politicized movement marked a positive development for L.A.'s inner-city black community. As one black studies professor states, "In the wake of the 1965 Watts Rebellion young men began to abandon the territorial differences that had become part of the established norm of street organization culture in favor of organized black radical politics. The Black Panther Party would come to reflect these aspirations, serving as the vanguard of the youthful movement. As a result of this process of radicalization, black-on-black violence in Los Angeles would come to a virtual standstill."

Leading national and local law enforcement figures viewed the Panthers differently. FBI director J. Edgar Hoover called them "the greatest threat to the internal security of the United States." Similarly, Chief Gates remembered the Panthers as "a criminal gang," "who sought power for themselves, not the people. They were hoodlums. . . . They were mean. They were violent. And that got them into difficulty with us."

Many of the members of the Black Panther Party of Los Angeles, including its leader, Alprentice "Bunchy" Carter, had come from the early black street organizations, particularly the Slausons from the east side of South Central. Conversely, many of the members of the more culturally directed U.S. organization, including prominent member George Stiner, had been Gladiators, from the west side. The question of whether the newly politicized members of these organizations had embarked upon a community-enhancing mission, or whether they were simply street thugs in a new guise, looking to prey upon their own, is not easily answered. The best that can be said is that they were probably both, politically motivated gangsters who sought to profit through their community deeds.

For while the Panther Party championed a far-left, Maoist ideology and engaged in social work, its members' behavior often devolved into criminal acts of street violence and drug abuse. Huey Newton was arrested for several shootings, including the killing of an Oakland police officer. George Jackson was sentenced to prison for murder, where he in turn killed correctional officers. Eldridge Cleaver fled to Angola to escape a rape charge, and drew further ire for stating that raping white women constituted political action.

The blurring of political acts with street crimes played a major role in the Panthers' demise, as many of its leaders self-destructed, consumed by drugs and violence. In addition, indigenous disputes and power struggles crippled the advancement of the party. Finally, added to the internal disintegration, the Panthers were relentlessly targeted by law enforcement, in particular by FBI director Hoover's COINTELPRO (Counter Intelligence Program), as internal enemies of the state. Through COINTELPRO, the FBI wiretapped, harassed, antagonized, and infiltrated the Black Panthers in an effort to ravage its organizational viability.

Thus, through a combination of debilitating drug use, illegal activities, internal feuds, and external governmental surveillance and interference, by the end of the 1960s the Black Panther Party had effectively been destroyed, most of its leadership intoxicated, imprisoned, forced underground, or killed.

The demise of the Black Panther Party, and street-level orga-

nized black political resistance, is viewed by those sympathetic to
the Panthers as a failed turning point, a lost moment when street
gangs stopped feuding and came together for the betterment of the
community and the race. On the other hand, most law enforcement
agencies viewed the Panthers as nothing more than thugs and gangsters who opportunistically hijacked the language of politics to ad-
vance their own criminal agendas and in the process bred fear among
the law-abiding, who according to Chief Gates "called us repeatedly,
saying 'Why don't you do something about them?'"

Whatever the truth regarding the Panthers, many African Americans in South Central felt a void following their downfall. And
regardless of the underlying nature of the Panthers, with the party's
demise the individuals subsumed under its umbrella began to again
factionalize according to neighborhood, giving birth to the next generation of black street gangs in L.A.

———

In 1969, a seventeen-year-old named Raymond Washington attended Fremont High School, on the east side of Los Angeles. Having grown up at the feet of some of L.A.'s now-legendary Panthers,
including Alprentice "Bunchy" Carter, Washington sought to create
a new street-level organization that would fill the void. Attracted
by the idea of local control over the streets, Washington and his
confederates emulated the "cool" style of the Panthers, dressing in
black leather, with berets and fedoras. As Carter had been a member
of a group called the Avenues, Washington began calling his group
the Baby Avenues, or the Cribs, which due to mispronunciation over
time would transform into "Crips."

While other explanations for the name abound, these are dismissed
by founding members. The term did not come from the fact that they
crippled people, nor did it originate from the comic book and movie
Tales from the Crypt. The idea that it represented an acronym for a
community-based organization—Community Resource Inner City
Project, or Community Revolutionary Inner City Project—has also
been rejected.

Ultimately, pieced together from rumor, myth, and informal street histories, no two sources tell the same story regarding Crip origins. But one thing is generally agreed upon: Washington's Cribs were not to be a political organization, nor did they possess a revolutionary mind-set. Raymond Washington was a talented street brawler, whose techniques rested upon rat-packing victims. Targets of their attacks were those who had desirable items upon them, particularly leather jackets and Stacy Adams dress shoes. Another of Washington's techniques was to identify the toughest individual in a rival group, beat him up, and then convince him to operate under Washington's authority.

In 1971, a west side teenager attending Washington High School named Stanley "Tookie" Williams would unite his gang with Washington's. As Williams writes, "Words such as 'revolutionary agenda' were alien to our thuggish, uninformed teenage consciousness. We did not unite to protect the community; our motive was to protect ourselves and our families."

In the early 1970s, in an effort to defend themselves against the aggressions of the Crips, other neighborhood youth gangs, such as the Pirus and Brims, formed a loose counterorganization, initially called the Anti-Crips, before taking on the name Bloods, derived from a greeting used by black soldiers serving in Vietnam.

For members of the gangs, style, a mentality, and a way of life emerged. "Crippin'" and "Bloodin'," which meant to be or to act like a Crip or Blood, allowed these inner-city youth to form a subculture with its own rules, norms, and codes. It also enabled them to find meaning and purpose, to justify violent and antisocial acts as part of a greater mission or cause. While the Panthers sought to subsume their every activity under the aegis of political action on behalf of the racially oppressed, for the Crips and Bloods everything was done in the name of the dignity and reputation of the neighborhood or block, the "hood." Crippin' or Bloodin' was an escape from the strictures of society, an internal world, before which real-life concerns faded. Parents, family, school, and work all became secondary to the needs of the gang.

And it is the needs of the individual that lead them into the gang in the first place. For while much is made of the "push" or pressure to join a gang, the threats that an "unaligned" individual receives, and the youngster's ultimate decision to join the gang based upon fear and for his own protection, the more persuasive explanation centers on the "pulls" or attractors that entice the individual. As Eight Tray Gangster Crips member "Monster" Kody Scott states, the gangs exert a "gravitational pull" before which all else pales. The gang allows inductees to feel they belong to something. It provides quick and easy praise. It bolsters self-esteem. Typically joining the gang anywhere between the ages of ten and seventeen, the insecure young person might be mistreated at home, humiliated in school, but on the streets, as long as they stand up for their hood, they are rewarded.

And the rewards are substantial to the teenage mind: the seductions of money, girls, cars, drugs, and above all status, power, and feelings of acceptance. They are now a part of something respected and feared. By creating an alternative universe, based upon youthful fantasies and instant gratifications, the gang functions as a world unto itself, in which the individual role-plays and takes on a new identity. It is liberating, leaving behind the boring world of childish insecurities, failures, rules, and restraints, for the excitement of the streets. Even in particularly gang-infiltrated neighborhoods, on average only one in ten youth join gangs, suggesting that it is youngsters who feel most intensely that the gang will satisfy their needs, and provide them with what they are longing for, who choose to join.

For young men growing up without fathers, raised by mothers and grandmothers, the gang offers the corrective of a tough, macho world. No longer a weak "mama's boy," the teen enters a hypermasculine arena in which violence is used to settle scores and exorcise fears and insecurities. They will fight their way into momentary feelings of superiority and dominance. And in the process, the induction myth promises, they will make enough money in the "alternative economies" of drug sales and robberies that they can avoid the mainstream labor markets that have no place for them and return to financially support those mothers and grandmothers who once took care of them.

Once a kid joins a gang, he enters a special teen world. Ironically, this gang world is just as dominated by rules and regulations as the mainstream society it rejects. The key difference is that the gang rules are their own. The youth are in control, imposing the rules on themselves, not taking orders from anyone on the outside.

Upon entry the inductee assumes a new identity, taking on a street name, or gang moniker. The name may be due to a physical attribute, a smile, "Smiley," size, "Monster," or a name, Noel "No No." The name may also come from a street mentor, with the original gangster called "Big," and then succeeding generations "Little," "Tiny," "Baby," and "Infant." They learn a particular way to walk; in the Crips this is called the "Crip walk," shoulders back, knees bent—cool, defiant, uncaring. Members also "dress down," wearing a uniform, for Crips blue, and Bloods red, including bandanas (originally to cover the face during robberies), baseball hats, sneakers, oversized T-shirts, and baggy pants. They also learn a foreign language. Crips would not use the letter *b* to start words as this might be seen as legitimizing their enemy, the Bloods. Instead the letter *c* is substituted to demonstrate their dominance over their rivals; so for example, *because*, *been*, and *baseball* become *cecause*, *ceen*, and *caseball*. Likewise, for the Bloods, *Compton*, *car*, *Coke*, and *cigarette* are transformed into *Bompton*, *bar*, *Boke*, and *bigarette*. Each gang denigrates the other's name in a similar fashion. Crips refer to Bloods as Slobs, while Bloods call Crips Crabs, or more properly Brabs. Each gang also has a special greeting, "what's up, blood," to fellow Bloods, and "what's up, cuz," for the Crips. Members of the gang are referred to as "homies," standing for those from the home turf. Each gang has its unique hand signals, or gang signs, which they "throw up" in a greeting or statement of territoriality, twisting their fingers into various shapes and patterns to denote their street or neighborhood: a *B* for Bloods, a *C* for Crips, a *W* for Watts, and the Roman numeral VI representing Sixties.

An individual gains entry through some combination of being vouched for by someone who is "reputable," an OG, or Original

Gangster; by being jumped in, beaten for a period of time to demonstrate strength and a tolerance for pain; or by shooting your way in, establishing your credentials by killing a rival. While most gang members are male, about 10 to 15 percent are female. Females can gain entry by the three means above, but can also be "sexed in," by having intercourse with male gang members. Once in the gang, members are expected to "put in work," typically through acts of violence against enemies, or by engaging in other activities beneficial to the gang, such as selling drugs or conducting burglaries or robberies.

This set of codes and regulations refers to members only, and anyone who is not "in the game," or "banging," is a "civilian." And while most gang violence targets rival gangsters, civilians are sometimes caught in the crossfire. This is typically dismissed as "collateral damage," or a "cost of doing business." "Civilians" living in gang neighborhoods avoid wearing red or blue, instead dressing in black or other "neutral colors" when walking the streets, and respond, "Nowhere," when asked, "Where are you from?" a challenge designed to reveal the individual's gang affiliation.

The gang member's world is an insular one, beholden to specialized codes within highly circumscribed geographical spaces. Waging wars over tiny bits of inner-city real estate, gangbangers remain largely oblivious to the external world. Like the street youth in *A Clockwork Orange*, or the stranded boys in *The Lord of the Flies*, the social order at large disappears, replaced by a dystopic microsubculture.

While the media has exploited the image of armies of blue-clad Crips warring against red-draped Bloods, the reality is more nuanced. The black gangs of Los Angeles are generally disorganized. Neither gang possesses the kind of pyramidal hierarchy associated with the mafia, with a godfather, consigliere, captains, and soldiers. There is no unified Bloods or Crips, as each gang is broken down into myriad "sets," or subgroups. Each gang has thousands of members distributed throughout the various sets, which exist according to neighborhood. These sets, particularly among the Crips, often war among themselves. Over the years the Crips have killed far more Crips than they have Bloods. Because of their significantly larger numbers, the Crips tend to engage in more internecine killings than do the smaller Bloods, who view intragang feuds as more dangerous to their overall survival.

The nature of the intragang feuds often has little to do, at least initially, with matters specifically gang related. For example, two Crip sets, the Rolling Sixties and the Eight Tray Gangsters, have been "at war" for more than thirty years. The dispute, which began in the late 1970s, was over a stolen girlfriend in junior high. This intergenerational feud has resulted in hundreds killed and injured, as present-day gangsters, most with no clue to the original cause, carry on the bloodshed in the name of the set. In addition to girlfriends, "beefs" have arisen over stolen bicycles and sneakers, as well as dirty looks and other signs of disrespect. These conflicts may stem from individual and personal insults, but in the world of "banging" they ultimately become subsumed under gang business, demanding the loyalties of fellow members, pitting set against set, gang versus gang.

The larger the gang the greater likelihood of breaking down into factionalized sets. These sets, if large enough, will in turn splinter into smaller subgroups, or cliques, which often feud among themselves. As the largest Crip set, with several hundred members and several hundred more associates, the Rolling Sixties break down into several primary cliques. The Sixties have become so big that most members have no idea who their fellow gangsters are.

The gang name derives from the Hyde Park neighborhood where most members live. The streets are numbered in the sixties and take on a rolling quality as one drives south. For the Rolling Sixties, Hyde Park breaks down into three primary sections: the Fronthood to the East, the Avenues in the middle, and the Backhood or Overhill in the West.

James Kennedy was from the Avenues, and as he lived on Tenth, he belonged to the clique referred to as "the Dime."

Kennedy was now in police custody and about to enter an interrogation room.

18

LITTLE CAT MAN

Fᴏʟʟᴏᴡɪɴɢ ᴍʏ ᴄᴀʟʟ to Detective Crews, Robbery Homicide detectives responded to the Los Padrinos Juvenile Hall to talk to James
Kennedy.

The detectives had him in an interrogation room at "the Hall," as
the delinquents called it. The room was a tight cubicle, three chairs
and a small table, no windows. Gang graffiti covered the walls. Interrogation rooms are psychological mind plays, meant to leave the
suspect ill at ease, and stress the power dynamic: the police have you
cornered and there is nowhere to go.

As the detectives began to question him, Kennedy claimed he had
been a member of the Rolling Sixties for only two to three months.
He got in, Kennedy said, when a guy known as Cat Man told him he
could be in the gang. When Kennedy agreed, he became Little Cat
Man.

The Rolling Sixties initially made their reputation in bank robberies, giving rise to the slogan the "rich Rolling Sixties," and "rich
and rolling, mafia-style." Gang detectives described them as "a bunch
of killers" and "the biggest and most active Crip gang in L.A." In addition to robbery, they were heavily involved in narcotics, burglary,
and an array of violent crimes.

When asked what the gang signified, one Rolling Sixties member
responded, "It carries dirt, it carries murder."

The Sixties were also known for having the highest amount of intra-set violence, leading to the saying "You're not a Sixty until you kill a Sixty." Members who kill their own are referred to as "homie killers."

With the gang's reputation for drug sales and violence, finding Kennedy guarding a rock house with a loaded firearm was nothing unusual. But the weapon he held was a .30 caliber, same as the rifle used in the murders. And it sounded like he at least had information regarding the killings.

As the detectives sat with Kennedy in the small room, they wondered if they were looking at one of the killers. Not in the gang very long, they thought, certainly no "OG." And his criminal record at the time was limited to property crimes and minor violence.

But these initiates were always looking for a way to "prove themselves." What a start—only in the gang a couple of months and you "put in work" with a quadruple homicide.

Besides, these young, newly minted gangbangers were often the most violent and reckless: lacking in restraints and self-control, unable to handle the effects of drugs and alcohol, and eager to make a name for themselves, show they were "down for the hood."

The police had come across killers as young as eight years old. Gang culture was indoctrinating kids from the crib. Officers had seen three-year-olds throw up gang signs.

When asked where he got the gun, Kennedy answered, "From some dude on the street."

"Who was the dude?"

"He was just some guy," Kennedy said, "a basehead," a street term for a crack addict.

"You're lying."

"No, man, I was selling dope and got the gun from a basehead."

"Stop lying to us."

"No, this dude said he needed dope and he had the gun. I gave him a fifty of rock for it."

The detectives didn't know if the gun fired the bullets found in the house, but they did know Kennedy was not telling the truth, and that he knew more.

Once again they wondered if they were looking at one of the killers who had eluded authorities for the last month. If so, they knew he acted with others. At least three people were involved. Who put him up to this? the officers wondered. Where would this gun lead?

While gang members swore to codes of silence and a refusal to snitch, like the mafia's *omertà*, the reality was quite different. Generally, the more of them involved, the greater the likelihood someone could be pressured to talk, to "flip," and point the finger at his homies.

Kennedy was young, and did not have a long history in the gang. But for the moment he held to the Rolling Sixties motto, "Never Open Up."

———

Jimmy Trahin, a firearms identification expert for the LAPD, compared the bullets recovered from the crime scene with a bullet test-fired into a cotton recovery tank from the .30-caliber M-1 carbine seized from James Kennedy.

The M-1 carbine was a lightweight semiautomatic rifle that became a standard weapon for the U.S. military in World War II. The name derived from the French word *carabine*, referring to light horsemen and the weapon they carried. Carbines were typically shortened versions of full rifles. The particular model taken from Kennedy was the A-1 model, containing a collapsible wire stock extension and a forearm grip. Made for paratroopers, it was compact and easy to use in close-quarter assault situations such as urban warfare. The rifle could hold up to thirty rounds, with each one fired as fast as the shooter could squeeze the trigger.

In analyzing the fired rounds, Trahin used a stereomicroscope containing two adjacent positions. He placed a bullet in each position, end to end, aligning the marks on the test bullet and the bullets recovered from the house, to see if the stria, or tool mark lines, matched.

Each manufacturer has a certain set of rifling specifications, with the lands and grooves in the barrel of the rifle individual to the particular company. The rifle barrel is bored with tools, which leave their own unique marks in the rifle bore. The bore's particular tool marks are then transferred to the bullet when the gun is fired. If the lines in the recovered bullets match those of the test-fired bullet, then both were definitely fired from the same gun. The tool marks left on the bullet are like a fingerprint. No two are identical.

As Trahin stared through the comparison microscope he concluded that four of the bullets from the house definitely came from the tested rifle. While the other recovered bullets could have been fired from that gun, they were so damaged—from hitting bone, wood, glass, and concrete—that no comparison was possible.

Trahin also used the comparison microscope to test whether the expended shell casings from the semiautomatic rifle matched those left behind at the crime scene.

The casing is the portion of the cartridge or projectile that contains the powder, primer, and bullet. When the firing pin, which is like a nail, strikes the rear portion of the cartridge, it too transfers individual tool marks to the soft metal of the casing. When the firing pin strikes this cartridge the bullet exits. As the bullet goes forward, under Newton's law—of equal but opposite reactions—the casing is thrown backward, striking the bolt face, which contains the firing pin. At this point the bolt face leaves unique tool marks on the back side of the casing. Finally, in semiautomatic weapons when the round is fired the casing is ejected from the gun by an extractor, a little claw that grabs the casing and pulls it from the chamber. The extractor also contains one-of-a-kind markings that are left on the side of the casing during the cycling of the weapon.

As Trahin studied the ejected shell casings recovered from the house, he determined—based upon the firing pin, bolt face, and extractor marking—that all seven casings positively came from the .30-caliber M-1 rifle.

The gun seized from James Kennedy was the weapon used by the shooter on the morning of August 31.

———

If the LAPD and my family were both at a loss as to what occurred on August 31, the residents of Hyde Park were equally confused.

In the weeks following the crime, the quadruple homicide was a constant topic on the streets. But the gossip regarding the shooting was often conducted in hushed tones. The mood on the streets was described as eerie, with all types of rival rumors circulating.

Some said the crime was in retaliation for a hit that had been carried out weeks before. That hit in turn was rumored to have been payback. If that was the case, the hit on my family was revenge for a retaliatory hit, revenge for revenge. But no one seemed to know who the first two hits were waged against, nor any of the underlying circumstances. Another line of thought circled back to the familiar idea that the football player somehow brought this upon his family, either through drug use, drug dealing, or some other shady venture.

Another theory snaked its way along the neighborhood grapevine that the killer was on PCP at the time of the crime, and had lost it. Developed as a synthetic drug, PCP (phencyclidine) has been a street drug since the 1960s. It is referred to with a variety of names, including *wet, sherm, bobbies, amp*. It is associated with extreme violence, and was highly publicized in the media as an "evil drug" throughout the 1960s and 1970s. Among its many physiological symptoms are a rising heart rate, blood pressure, and body temperature, along with flushing and sweating. Psychologically, its users often feel an immense sense of power and the ability to take on anything. Those who have taken PCP have said, "I would fight anyone who touched me," "When high, I would attack people. I was extremely violent," and "I was on the racetrack all the time because the PCP told me we could conquer the world." The behavior of people on PCP is manic and chaotic. While heroin was popular with inner-city blacks in New York and on the East Coast, PCP remained a drug of choice with blacks in L.A.

Regardless of the theory regarding the crime, and the source of the gossip, a few common threads stitched together in the rumor mill. No one was ever able to link detailed motives to specific names. Something always remained murky and elusive about the facts, with no one quite sure why whoever it was they were secretly discussing had picked that particular house and killed its inhabitants. Additionally, the eerie sense pervading the streets of Hyde Park came from the gruesome nature of the crime, which was ever changed and exaggerated with each retelling: The inhabitants had been dragged down the stairs and into the basement before being executed. Everyone in the house had been killed. The killers were lying in wait as they tracked down other family members.

Finally, there was the sense that the killings were part of something bigger, that the shooters were not acting alone but rather had operated at someone else's behest. Only no one knew who that someone else was. This made folks leery about saying too much. Who knew what might set off the killers or their overseer again?

On the streets, gossip is a kind of currency, providing valuable information that can be used for personal gain. But particularly in tense and unknown situations, it also poses risks. Passing on rumors is one thing, while snitching, the cardinal sin of the underworld, is another. The dividing line is often thin, and tends to be flexible, held in the eye of the beholder. People who talk too much play a dangerous game.

For while no one seemed to understand precisely what took place, this was clear: the case was high profile, and the pressure on LAPD intense. Everyone noticed an increased police presence on the streets since the crime occurred. Whomever they caught, whomever they could pin the crime on, that homie was going to get the gas.

———

Later, armed with the firearm examiner's findings, the RHD detectives continue to interrogate James Kennedy.

Who knew if he had any role in the actual crime, but he was talking at the Hall, and was caught in possession of the murder weapon, which represented the first major break in a case that had otherwise ground to a halt.

"Where'd the gun come from, James?" they repeat.

"I already told you, man, from some basehead."

"And you gave him fifty dollars' worth of dope for the gun."

"That's right."

"Name, give us a name."

"Can't. Don't know it."

"You seen him around before?"

"I don't know, maybe. Just another doper."

They know he's lying, but they want to keep him talking, sweating.

"If we took you around the hood could you ID him for us, point him out?"

"I don't know."

The detectives are going in for the kill.

"When did you get this gun from the basehead?"

Kennedy pauses, trying to figure out what the officers are driving at. What did they want him to say, he wonders. "I don't know," he says, pauses again, then, "Like a couple of months ago."

"When, like before Fourth of July?"

"No, later. Like early August."

"First part of August?"

"Yeah, about, I guess."

"Then you had it when the murders occurred."

"Murders?"

"Yeah, you know those kids and that old lady that were killed over on Fifty-Ninth?"

"No, I don't know nothing about that."

"Nothing? Word is you were boasting about having done it. Never said anything like that?"

"Nope."

"So if we brought someone in and they said they heard you boasting—"

"They be lying."

"I don't think so."

"I do. Just trying to hang me out to help their own—"

"Look," a detective interrupts him. "We tested the fuckin' gun."

The detectives realize that the tit-for-tat over whether Kennedy spoke about the crime is going nowhere. For the moment they will abandon that tack and focus on the physical evidence.

"See I didn't say—"

"Let's forget what you said. I don't care about that right now."

"But you said—"

"Just listen, James," one of the detectives says, leaning forward, now less than a foot away from Kennedy. "You can tell us whatever you want, but the fuckin' physical evidence, it never lies—"

"He's right, James," the other interjects, "never."

"And right now," the other continues, "it's pointing a real big finger right at you."

"I already told you—"

"Yeah," the other detective continues. "That gun that you had, tested positive." He pauses.

Again, the other detective jumps in. "That gun killed those four people." He pauses. With raised voice, "While they slept in their house."

"I don't know—"

"Well, you better start fuckin' knowing, because we got you cold with the murder weapon. So either you name names or—"

"Look, man, I don't know nothing about no murders."

"Who are you afraid of, James?"

"Ain't afraid of nobody."

"Well, you better start being afraid. Because right now you're going down for four counts of first-degree murder, and you know what that'll get you?"

Kennedy says nothing, looking down at the floor.

"Well, I'll tell you—the gas chamber."

"That's right," the other detective adds, nodding. "They're going to drop the pellets. New governor means fuckin' business."

Kennedy remains silent, staring down, making no eye contact with the officers.

"This is your last chance, James. Where'd you get the gun?"

Still nothing.

The detectives begin to get up to leave the room. One is already at the door. He stands with his right hand on the knob.

"Hey, wait a minute," Kennedy says in a low, weak voice.

The detective standing by the door stares down. The other pauses in his act of standing. "Yes?" he says.

Kennedy balks, then while continuing to look into his lap, mumbles something inaudible.

He is in the process of crossing a line. He is just about to go over, his last act of half resistance. He gives up the name, but says it so that it cannot be heard. He knows he is gone, but just cannot quite commit.

"Who?"

"Fee," he again mumbles downward. This time it is audible.

Now he has crossed over and knows it. But two months into a gang he isn't going to eat four murder convictions and go to death row. In the hierarchy of fear, the dread of the gas chamber has trumped the threat of the streets. He has broken the code. He is a snitch: selling out a homie to save his own skin.

"Who's Fee?"

"Li'l Fee."

"What?"

"Little Fee," Kennedy now enunciates.

"Who's that? Never heard of him. Give us his real name."

Kennedy pauses, does not look up. He mumbles a name, again, inaudible.

"Who?"

"Tiequon Cox."

19

HE TOOK A WRONG TURN

In early october 1984, Peggy Fiderio, of the scientific identification division, stared into a comparison microscope.

On the left side she had the palm print recovered from the red trunk in the front bedroom of the house. On the right side was a palm print that had been taken by the Los Angeles Police Department of Tiequon Aundray Cox, following his arrest on September 6, 1984.

As Fiderio studied the characteristics of the prints, the ridges, whorls, loops, and bifurcations, she knew she needed at least ten points of comparison before LAPD would consider the prints to match. When she reached twelve matching points, she stopped her examination and declared that the palm print found on the red storage trunk was the right palm print belonging to Tiequon Cox.

Fiderio described "the smooth, nonporous" metal trunk lid as a "delightful surface" from which to lift latent prints.

Five other latent print examiners would confirm that the palm print on the trunk matched the right palm print of Tiequon Cox.

On Wednesday, October 24, 1984, the *Los Angeles Times* reported:

A South Central Los Angeles man already in custody in County Jail was named by police late Tuesday night as a prime suspect in the August 31 slayings of former UCLA and Los Angeles Rams defensive back Kermit Alexander's family.

Los Angeles homicide detectives identified the suspect in the shooting deaths as Tiequon Cox, 18, a reported member of the Rolling 60s street gang. Cox was being held in jail on a charge of being an ex-convict in possession of a gun. Detectives said there was no immediate indication that street gangs might have been involved in the shootings.

Police Lt. Dan Cooke said announcement of Cox's possible involvement in the quadruple slayings was delayed Tuesday until after a jail lineup was conducted.

A second gunman is being sought by authorities. . . .

. . . Cox was not in custody at the time of the shootings, detectives added.

The Thursday, October 25, 1984, *Los Angeles Sentinel* added:

At this time the detectives refused to release the names of the witnesses who faced Cox in the lineup and refused to say whether they had identified him as one of the pair seen at the Alexander dwelling.

They declined to do it to protect them from harm or threats in view of Cox's gang affiliation and the fact that his alleged partner is still outstanding, also posing a threat to the well-being of those who had knowledge of the crime, officers said.

———

Tiequon Cox would be remembered variously as "a mind-boggling football player who moved like O. J. Simpson," "a gymnast," "a sociopath," "evil," "a Nazi storm-trooper," "a monster," "a ghetto idol," "a stone cold killer," "a monk," a "mythological creature," "someone who had great influence over others," "someone who could have been special ops," "someone who could have been a college professor," "all that," and "a bad motherfucker."

Physically, people described Cox as "having very light skin," and "long corn-rowed hair"; "six feet tall and two hundred and forty pounds without an ounce of fat," "a physical specimen," "one of the first gangbangers to tattoo his neck . . . that was hard core," "the most piercing eyes I've ever seen," "a reptile, with almond-shaped eyes, that were green or hazel—depending on his mood."

————

On August 31, 1984, Tiequon Cox was uncharacteristically out of custody. Since he had turned fourteen, he spent the majority of his life incarcerated, either in juvenile hall or the California Youth Authority (CYA).

On March 18, 1984, after serving two and a half years for carjacking, he was released from CYA, the parole board stating that "he has done a real turnaround in relationship to gang involvement," and that his "success in dealing with this problem will stand him in good stead while on parole."

Cox's release was over the district attorney's objection.

On September 6, 1984, less than six months after his parole date, Cox was pulled over on a traffic violation, and a .32-caliber handgun was found inside his yellow Cadillac. He was arrested as an ex-felon in possession of a firearm.

Following his arrest, Cox was placed in Module 4800, where Crips were housed in Los Angeles County Jail. Described by Cox's attorneys as a "cauldron of pernicious violence," 4800 was famous for its overcrowding and fights, which included stabbings, razor blade slashings, and other vicious assaults. Inmates complained of brutal and racist guards who, they claimed, referred to them as "assholes" and "faggots" and at one point burned a cross in the unit.

In Module 4800, Cox, with his light skin, green eyes, and long braided red hair, was constantly challenged.

In an effort to ward off attacks, Cox affected a persona of toughness and menace. One guard said Cox "created chaos just to entertain himself," while another said he had "murder and chaos in his eyes." Said a third, "violence was like a drug to this killer."

He also developed a maniacal exercise regimen. An inmate housed next to him in Module 4800 said that the workout going on next door sounded so intense he swore there were two people exercising in the cell. Another cellmate stated that Cox was so wound up and agitated, he seldom seemed able to sleep. He described Cox as "the most physically busy prisoner in our housing area. I don't know if he did this because he enjoyed it. I don't know if this was something he literally had to do."

It was further noted by inmates in 4800 that Cox was "hypervigilant," or extraordinarily cautious, sensitive, and suspicious as to what was going on around him. The inmate noted:

> He always stood in front of my cell with his back against the wall and watched the cells on either side of mine. He had a way of talking to me while looking around, watching for who might come up on the tier, and taking everything in that was happening further up the row. He did this moving his eyes around but not his head.

The same inmate would also describe Cox as depressed, keeping a front or guard up, a kind of mask:

> He was quiet, watchful, shy, and kept to himself. He stayed that way with nearly everyone on the [cell] row and did not open up. . . . He was afraid of getting hurt or being let down and protected himself against that hurt by walling himself off. . . . He withdrew . . . instead of asking for help or letting on that he was hurting.

Cox himself would later state: "There was a point in my life when an elder might have stepped in and given me a sense of hope, but I had learned early on that you can't rely on anybody but yourself."

———

Based upon the statement of James Kennedy and the results of the ballistics testing, the palm print comparison, and the live lineup, Detective David Crews went to Module 4800 of Los Angeles County Jail on October 25, 1984, to rearrest Tiequon Cox, this time for four counts of first-degree murder.

Cox said he had killed no one, but said nothing more.

The Los Angeles County District Attorney's Office would charge Cox with four counts of first-degree murder with special circumstances—the killing of multiple victims—which if found true by a jury would send him to the gas chamber.

———

When Detective Crews called and told me of Cox's arrest, I could tell he viewed it as a major victory. I sensed that there was great relief at Robbery Homicide that an arrest had finally been made. He seemed pleased he had cracked the case.

While I said nothing of it to Crews, I took some secret personal satisfaction in knowing that my own attempts at finding the killers had pushed the mayor's office and the chief of police to step up their efforts. These increased patrols and intensified drug searches had flushed out James Kennedy and the gun. Further, it was my friend at juvenile hall who provided the information that Kennedy was boasting. These efforts in turn led to Kennedy's interrogation, which ultimately led to the discovery of Tiequon Cox.

My acts had altered events.

Otherwise, I took little solace. While I was pleased that the case finally showed a break, I knew that Cox's arrest marked only the first phase in what would surely be a long process.

While the ballistics results and palm print were strong evidence that Cox was the shooter, he refused to make any other comment. He clammed up and was then appointed a lawyer. At his arraignment he pled not guilty.

We were still left clueless as to what took place, or what was coming next.

Cox's persistent silence frustrated my family, as well as the authorities. Later it would poison relations with his own attorney.

With the arrest of Cox, the police believed they had my family's killer. But they still lacked a motive, accomplices, and leads as to who orchestrated the crime.

For my family, the arrest, while welcome, provided neither security nor closure. Here was the killer, but why had he targeted us? Who were his confederates? Were they still after us?

Cox wouldn't say. Whatever he knew, he kept to himself.

With no answers and ongoing uncertainty, fear continued to grip us all.

My sister Joan's mental state was typical. She was scared, and unable to lead a normal life. "It took me five minutes just to open my door I had so many locks on it," she said. "And before I even got to the door, I always grabbed my gun."

———

Following the arrest of Tiequon Cox, his great-grandmother's house on West Seventy-Seventh Street was searched. When the search was conducted, Cox's great-grandmother, with whom he lived, was described by police as "greatly upset by the series of events." She showed them the part of the house where Cox stayed, which was a garage that had been converted into a "bachelor pad."

Within the house the police found numerous trophies and awards Cox had received for being an outstanding athlete. The trophies were from Little League baseball, and for his performance as a running back while playing in youth football leagues.

"He had the potential of being a top player in either sport," said Detective David Crews.

"But somewhere along the way he took a wrong turn."

20

IT WENT TO MY HEART

O N   T H E   E V E N I N G   of October 25, 1984, Linda Lewis was in her
apartment on Tenth Avenue, in Hyde Park, across the street from
where James Kennedy was arrested. Lewis and her god-sister, Cassandra Haynes, routinely sold drugs on Tenth Avenue. Haynes ran a
"rock house–type operation," and Lewis served as her "banker."

Shortly before 11 p.m., a member of the Rolling Sixties, Horace
Burns, came over to Lewis's apartment and asked if he could watch
the eleven o'clock news.

The news broadcast the story of an arrest in the Alexander murders and announced that Tiequon Cox had been arraigned earlier
that day.

As he watched the television report, Burns, a skinny nineteen-year-
old with a medium-length Afro, known as "Horse" or "Death Lock"
on the streets, told Lewis that he did not have to worry about his fingerprints being found in the house because he didn't touch anything.

Burns also said he did not have to worry about Cox snitching on
him "because he knew his homeboy wouldn't do him like that."

The following day, Cassandra Haynes, who was outside on Tenth
Avenue selling drugs to customers in cars as they drove up, heard
Burns, who was standing by the gate outside, talking about the crime
to other gang members, including "Shoes" and "Eddie-Boy."

Haynes, who had known Burns for less than a year at the time,
heard him say that Cox had kicked the door in, and was "just like

a time bomb that exploded and when he entered the house he just started shooting everybody everywhere." Burns said he was in the house and "stood there and watched."

For Burns, the explanation of the crime was that the Rolling Sixties had robbed a dope house on Sixth and Broadway. The people from the dope house had then retaliated and shot up the house of a member of the Rolling Sixties. The hit of August 31 was revenge for the retaliation.

Burns would tell others that Cox did it out of revenge for a retaliatory hit on Cox's house.

Burns said he did not know why the Alexander house was hit.

When asked about the killing of children, Burns responded, "That's just something that just happened."

————

On November 3, 1984, members of the Gang Enforcement Unit arrived at 6310 Second Avenue in Hyde Park. Officer Tony Moreno exited the police car and walked to the front door. Moreno, a legendary gang cop, was known on the streets as "Pacman," because for years he drove a bullet-riddled yellow Ford Fury and was said to gobble up gang members like the little yellow video game character. Moreno was the model for the CRASH officer later played by Sean Penn in the 1988 movie *Colors*. Detective Crews, of Robbery Homicide, not wanting a big show of the arrest of Burns, had walked down the hallway of Parker Center to the Gang Enforcement Unit and asked Moreno if he would arrest Burns.

As Moreno approached the front door, he saw Burns make a break for a window to the left. Another gang officer waiting outside grabbed the fleeing Burns and took him into custody, booking him for murder at Central Division.

Following Burns's arrest, Chief Daryl Gates stated: "We believe that these two individuals [Cox and Burns] were involved in the rip-off of a narcotics dealer," and were recognized. In retaliation for the rip-off, there was retaliation against one of the individuals, "so this is a payback for the retaliation."

The chief continued, "We believe we know the reason for the Alexanders' murder. We believe it was about as tragic a situation you'd ever, ever find."

While the press ran with the chief's version, it would take years to uncover what actually took place. The true facts were very different from those broadcast by Gates.

———

Following the arrests and arraignments of Tiequon Cox and Horace Burns, the case entered a second phase. Both defendants were provided with attorneys and the legal proceedings began.

Unlike most high-profile murder trials, this case had a strange, disjointed feel about it. The case was incomplete, as the prosecutor, Sterling Norris, approached it without any clear understanding of motive. While under the law, the prosecutor does not have to prove motive, since it is not an element of the crime, it is unusual to have a murder case where it is not addressed, since juries want to know the reason behind the defendant's act. Figuring out the motive answers that most basic question—why did he do it?

Without knowing that reason, we found no solace, and had little confidence that the trials would end well. Norris kept assuring us that the evidence was sufficient to try Cox and Burns and that technically, all he needed to prove to sustain a conviction for murder was malice, that is, that a human being was intentionally killed without any excuse or justification.

In early December 1984, Norris prepared for the preliminary hearing, the stage in the proceedings when a magistrate determines whether there is enough evidence to bring the defendants to trial.

Not only did the prosecutor not have a clear motive at the time—giving as possible theories gang-related, drug-connected, or a contract killing—but it was also unclear what role Burns played in the crime. For my family the combination of not knowing if all involved had been arrested, as well as the ongoing uncertainty as to motive, left us nervous for our immediate security, and afraid that Cox and Burns would somehow beat the case and be set free.

———

In the weeks leading up to the preliminary hearing, Linda Lewis, who was subpoenaed to testify, repeatedly called the police in a state of panic.

The phone would ring. She answered to dead air, breathing, a hang-up. Every day, every night, dozens of calls, always the same ending, the thud of the hang-up. Several times people attempted to break into her house. Cars stopped outside her home, a rock crashed through her window, people yelled "Rolling Sixties," and tires squealed as cars sped away. On the eve of the hearing a note was left in her mailbox. It said, "You talk, you die."

Despite the repeated threats, Lewis said it was the nature of the case that compelled her to come forward.

Of her decision to testify, she said: "Being on Tenth Avenue, I see a lot of things as far as drug transactions, killings and beatings and everything else; but when it involved kids, that went a little further than any means and that's why I came forth."

Lewis had never informed the authorities on a case before, but, she said, the nature of this killing "went to my heart."

———

Going into the trial our family was an emotional wreck. But from the start we were pleased with the choice of prosecutor, Sterling Norris.

While the deputy district attorney who tries a criminal case is formally a representative of the collective community, he ends up feeling like the attorney for the victims' family. The prosecutor keeps the family updated, explains courtroom procedures, and most important, fights for justice on our behalf. For victims' families suffer not only the horrible loss of loved ones, but an agonizing sense of unfairness. Trust, confidence, feelings of control are obliterated. And the anger that injustice spurs is unbearable, that violence has been unleashed on your family, yet you are forbidden from action, breeds a kind of cancerous impotence.

So in the wake of the crime, unable to go on with their daily lives, victims pour all their emotional energy into restoring justice, into rebalancing the world. And the immediate goal of those efforts is the conviction and punishment of those who caused the suffering. We sought clarity and solace. On at least one thing my fractured family stood as one: justice could be found only if the killers received the maximum possible penalty.

If I had it my way, I would have taken out the gangbangers who killed my family on my own. But it didn't work out that way. And now I, along with the rest of my family, put our trust into Sterling Norris to achieve justice, and at least begin the process of restoring our lives.

Norris was a veteran prosecutor who specialized in highly charged murder cases. He was an emotional man himself and channeled our family's passions. A *Los Angeles Times* reporter described Norris as "a straightforward, no-nonsense lawyer with a red face, white hair and a voice made hoarse by heartfelt conviction." He had run unsuccessfully for district attorney of Los Angeles on more than one occasion. He had anger, passion, an ax to grind. And in him we placed our faith.

He was a firm advocate for capital punishment. A picture of every member of California's death row hung on his office walls. Tacked to his door, a flyer: "Free the Nightstalker. Retain Rose Bird." This referenced the notorious serial killer and California's liberal Supreme Court chief justice, who famously opposed the death penalty and repeatedly voted to overturn capital convictions.

Norris also had high-profile capital case experience. Several years earlier he tried and convicted the "Freeway Killer" William Bonin, for the sex-torture murders of more than twenty young men.

When asked about our case Norris termed it "especially brutal."

He continued: "We know from the facts that there was a bang, bang, bang. The mother and sister were shot. Then there was a pause, and the kids were killed. [The shooter] went back for the kids; the witnesses. To go back and kill kids—that's gross."

Norris assured us he would do everything in his power to send the killers to death row.

———

The preliminary hearing began in the first week of the New Year, 1985.

While my family did not attend this hearing, Norris filled us in on the proceedings.

He said that despite his twenty years of experience, he was unprepared for the insolence and defiance that met him in the courtroom. Even though Cox and Burns were both handcuffed to the chairs, he still felt they posed an ongoing threat to courtroom security.

Los Angeles Times reporter Paul Ciotti described Cox as "smoldering," and said he just got the feeling that at any time he could "bolt from his seat and try to kill everyone in the courtroom."

Los Angeles Municipal Court Judge Candace Cooper ordered the courtroom, in the downtown Criminal Courts Building, cleared, and checked all entrants with handheld metal detectors. Inside, three marshals guarded the two suspects while three other marshals stood by the doorway.

After hearing evidence from James Kennedy regarding the gun, as well as ballistics, fingerprint, and eyewitness testimony, Judge Cooper found probable cause and ordered the two men to stand trial on January 18, 1985, for four counts of first-degree murder with special circumstances.

Since Norris was seeking the death penalty, he would have to prove, on top of the first-degree murder charges, that a special circumstance existed. Special circumstances are something extra that renders the first-degree murder particularly heinous. Examples include killing a police officer, lying in wait, using poison, or torturing the victim prior to death. In our case, the special circumstance was multiple murder victims.

––––––

On January 31, following her testimony at the preliminary hearing, Linda Lewis was "dogged" (stared at intensely) while out at a nightclub. She recognized the individuals as people who hung out on Tenth Avenue. She pulled a gun on one of them and they ran. Lewis reported this to Detective Crews.

———

In February 1985, as Sterling Norris prepared for the upcoming trials, the prosecution caught another break.

Horace Burns, housed in Los Angeles County Jail, kept on talking, naming names of other gang members he said were involved. Due to Burns's loose lips, several threats were made on his life. Burns was then moved into the "snitch tank," or protective custody. For Burns this was the first in a string of humiliations that would erode his standing within the gang.

While Burns sat in protective custody, another inmate, David Mangola, came forward, telling the police that Burns had been talking about the murders. Mangola told the authorities that Burns was housed in the cell next to him for about two months, and stated that the murders at the Alexander house were a botched hit on a drug house, and that the Rolling Sixties were paid $20,000 to $30,000 for the hit.

These statements pointed toward a contract hit as the motive.

Los Angeles County District Attorney Ira Reiner wrote a letter asking for federal leniency on behalf of Mangola in exchange for his testimony, stating: "Mr. Mangola refused to testify without specific assurance on the federal violation of parole. He will do his state time regardless. Because of the monstrous nature of the Alexander killings, I must ask you to provide specific assurance of leniency for Mr. Mangola on the federal violation. Mr. Mangola's prior actions may not be those of an ideal citizen but neither are the acts of these violent defendants in taking the lives of four innocent people."

———

At the very end of February 1985, more than a month after the preliminary hearing of Cox and Burns, LAPD received an anonymous phone call.

The caller provided a description of a van, and said that it was the one that had been used in the murders of August 31. The caller provided specific details as well as a location.

The van was a 1975 Chevy, maroon. It had a passenger-side sliding door. It had no rear side windows.

The license plates were traced to a thirty-seven-year-old black woman named Ida Moore.

———

As the prosecutor prepared for the first trial, my family braced itself for the ordeal ahead. I planned to attend, to do whatever I could to ensure that justice was served. While my role had been turned from active street hunter to passive courtroom observer, I still needed to exert my will. I hoped my presence could bring control.

In an effort to keep myself calm and adjust to this new role, I relied upon my experience as a probation officer. When a defendant walked into our office, we would just sit there, quiet, say little or nothing, and let them hang themselves. I would do the same here. I would provide a steady presence for my family, for Norris, for the jury, but I remained quiet. In the courtroom I would watch the killers sentence themselves through their own words and deeds.

As I readied myself, I thought of my father, and his arduous study of the Bible, his ability to recite from memory.

When issues of justice and atonement arose, Leviticus 24:19–21 was sure to be heard.

"And a man who inflicts an injury upon his fellow man just as he did, so shall be done to him, fracture for fracture, eye for eye, tooth for tooth. Just as he inflicted an injury upon a person, so shall it be inflicted upon him."

21

THE THIRD MAN
FACES DEATH

THE DEATH PENALTY has existed in America since the beginning. So has the challenge of a constitutional execution.

After independence, the United States abandoned most of Europe's methods. Burning at the stake, breaking on the wheel, crucifixion, stoning, and the notorious Roman *culeus*—where the condemned was sewn into a sack with a live serpent, ape, and dog, then heaved over a cliff into the water—along with other slow, torturous deaths were eliminated. And while more than two hundred crimes could lead to the gallows in the Old World, in America capital crimes focused on murder and treason.

The first method used in America was hanging. Viewed as an ignoble way to die, this was the traditional way to kill common or lower-class criminals. The key to a successful hanging was for the executioner to correctly calculate "the drop." If the rope was too short, then the neck would not break, causing the condemned to suffocate, leaving him writhing. But if the drop was too long, this risked yanking off the condemned's head as the plummeting body jerked to a sudden stop. Either way struck observers as both cruel and unusual.

Also used was the more noble and martial death by firing squad. Here a team of marksmen would fire in unison, taking aim at the condemned's heart. The defendant was seated, restrained, blindfolded, or hooded, while beneath the chair a large pan or bowl caught the blood. As with hanging, botched executions alarmed critics. Marksmen sometimes flinched and missed the mark, maiming the condemned. Efforts to get around the effects of nerves included a firing machine and the use of dummy rounds for some of the shooters, allowing them to question whether they fired the lethal round.

Beginning in New York in the late 1880s, the search for more "scientific" executions made the electric chair the dominant mechanism of death. Electrodes were placed on the condemned's leg, chest, and head, then the executioner flipped a lever delivering thousands of volts of electricity. Over time, the chair too came to be seen as gruesome, cruel, and inhumane. Botched executions included the repeated efforts needed to kill Ethel Rosenberg in 1953, and the chronic malfunctions of Florida's chair, nicknamed "Old Sparky," as it produced smoke and the smell of singed flesh.

Seeking to improve upon the technology of the electric chair, in 1937 California switched to gas. In an airtight chamber, modeled on a bathysphere, the condemned was strapped into a large metal chair, sitting above a container of potassium cyanide pellets. When the executioner threw the switch, the pellets dropped into a solution of sulfuric acid, generating hydrogen cyanide gas. When a defendant was sentenced to death by gas, the saying went, "They're going to drop the pellets on him." The chamber, due to its color, was nicknamed the "Mean Green Killing Machine." Some inmates tried to hold their breath as the invisible gas filled the chamber; others sucked in deeply to speed the process. Regardless, within minutes the condemned was pronounced dead.

In 1985, the gas chamber was California's sole means of execution.

———

As Burns and Cox stood accused, Ida Moore admitted to driving the van. Her friend Delisa Brown rode shotgun. Both denied any knowledge of the killers' intent.

In exchange for immunity from prosecution they agreed to testify in the upcoming trials.

They also provided the police with a third suspect who they said rode in the van on that early morning last August.

————

Darren Charles Williams was one of the first generation of Rolling Sixties. He was twenty-four years old at the time of the murders.

Williams had done time for mail fraud, robbery, and assault. He was known as a bully. Throughout his life he was big and muscular. By the time of the crime, however, this began to change. Williams, known on the streets as CW, C-Dub, and C-Dove, was addicted to crack cocaine. He lost weight and became paranoid.

Rumors spread through the streets that Williams had been shot at several times following the murders, but no one knew who called the shots.

On February 27, 1985, six months after the murders, following the lead from Ida Moore and Delisa Brown, RHD detectives traveled north to the San Francisco Bay Area. At the time Williams was staying at his father's house in Richmond.

Initially the police had some difficulty locating Williams, but finally tracked him down, brought him to the Richmond police station, and interrogated him. When the police questioned him, he gave a rambling seventy-page statement. Despite denials, lies, contradictions, and inconsistencies, by the time the detectives finished with Williams they had for the first time a clue to the events of six months prior.

The full motive would not become clear until Williams's trial the following year.

Williams, like Burns and Cox, faced the gas.

————

On March 2, 1985, as preparations for Burns's trial continued, LAPD responded to the home of Burns and his mother on Third Avenue in Hyde Park.

Based upon the statements of David Mangola and Darren Charles Williams, both of which indicated that the Rolling Sixties had been paid for the murders at the Alexander house, the police obtained a warrant to search the Burns residence.

Additionally, based upon the theory that there was a hidden stash, ten officers, armed with shovels, dug up the small backyard behind Mrs. Burns's bungalow.

No money was found.

————

The death penalty the three men faced had not been imposed in California for twenty years.

In the liberal moment of the 1960s, majority opinion saw prison's purpose as rehabilitation. Environment created criminals: victims of social injustice, racial discrimination, poverty, and poor education, the "root causes" of crime. In the 1960s society reformed itself through mass movements. And so too could the criminal be remade, reemerging as a new man, retrained as "a productive member of society."

Such times left the death penalty both out of touch and out of date. In 1972, in *Furman v. Georgia*, the United States Supreme Court held that the death penalty, as then applied, was unconstitutional, finding it to be arbitrary, and thus cruel and unusual. The Court found that too many crimes were death-eligible without sufficient guidelines, leaving it solely to a prosecutor's discretion when to charge the case capitally. This lack of guidelines, the Court held, left the state free to discriminate based upon race. This was most troubling in the South, where prosecutors most often sought death.

In eliminating capital punishment, the Court reversed the death sentences of over six hundred condemned inmates nationwide. This included Charles Manson and his followers, as well as Sirhan Sirhan, the assassin of Robert F. Kennedy.

In the 1970s, as violent crime soared, a backlash surged against the 1960s' rehabilitative vision. The "tough on crime" movement gained political force, and in 1976, in *Gregg v. Georgia*, the U.S. Supreme Court set forth guidelines for states wishing to bring back capital punishment.

While death penalty opponents saw *Furman* as the beginning of the end of capital punishment in America, it marked only a pause. Following *Gregg*, more than thirty states drafted new capital statutes designed to limit the chances of arbitrary enforcement.

When a Utah firing squad executed double murderer Gary Gilmore on January 17, 1977, the new era of the death penalty dawned.

In the wake of Gilmore's execution, California sought to revive capital punishment, passing a new law with provisions designed to reduce arbitrariness. Only certain types of egregious first-degree murder would qualify. Capital trials would be cut into two phases: guilt and penalty. And the defendant, if sentenced to death, gained an automatic appeal to the Supreme Court of California.

Now, in March 1985, the attorneys began picking a jury in the case of *The People of the State of California v. Horace Edwin Burns.*

22

HORACE VS. HORSE

A DEATH PENALTY CASE differs from a noncapital trial in many respects. Because a life is at stake, the process is longer and more complicated, with its own set of rules.

While, as in any criminal case in California, a jury of twelve is chosen and a unanimous verdict required, in capital cases all twelve jurors must be willing to impose death.

Additionally, death penalty cases tend to be high profile, with widespread media coverage. This means a high percentage of potential jurors have already formed an opinion on the case prior to trial.

Therefore, in this case, after determining financial hardships, and establishing which members of the panel were unable to serve due to medical or other reasons, the judge heard challenges based upon publicity.

As the media had extensively covered the murders, the judge dismissed jurors who felt they could not remain fair and impartial in a case with such facts.

The judge then instructed the remaining jurors on their unique role in a capital case:

If the jury finds the defendant guilty beyond a reasonable doubt of first-degree murder and then further finds beyond a reasonable doubt a special circumstance to be true that at that point the jury would be asked to go into what we call a second phase of the trial, known as the penalty phase. And in that second phase you would be asked to determine whether the punishment should be the death penalty or life without the possibility of parole.

Unique to capital cases, the death penalty jury is both the trier of fact—determining whether the evidence is sufficient to convict—and the sentencing authority, deciding whether the defendant will live or die.

The back-and-forth in jury voir dire, the process of picking the jury, is the first taste the jurors get of the gamesmanship marking a capital prosecution.

Sterling Norris warned our family that the trial was a kind of artificial world, with strange rules and procedures that wouldn't make much sense to us. He let us know that the legal hoops would often be time-consuming and likely frustrating to us as the proceedings unfolded. I knew this world well from my time as a probation officer. For the rest of my family it was a new realm.

While we did not attend jury selection, Norris kept us updated throughout the process. He advised us that picking a jury in a capital case was a lengthy affair. He also stressed the importance. It was vital, he said, to excuse anyone biased against capital punishment.

While we didn't know it at the time, this kind of capital case minutiae would end up consuming our family for years.

In a death penalty case the prosecution and defense are each afforded a limited number of what are called peremptory challenges. These allow an attorney to dismiss a juror without stating any reason. With a peremptory challenge the lawyer can rid himself of a juror who for whatever reason they feel will not be sympathetic to their case. The dismissal can be based upon hunch, vibe, intuition, anything other than sex or race.

Peremptories are a precious and limited resource, and therefore the attorneys wish to exclude as many potentially hostile jurors for cause, which means those who express an antagonism toward their side: those who will always or never impose the death penalty regardless of the evidence. Any time the attorney can dismiss a juror for cause, a peremptory is preserved.

THE COURT: Now, let me ask you this. Are your feelings about the
death penalty such that you would always vote for the death
penalty regardless of what evidence?

PROSPECTIVE JUROR: Probably I would vote for.

THE COURT: Is that regardless of the evidence, no matter what the
evidence was?

PROSPECTIVE JUROR: Yes.

THE COURT: You would vote for the death penalty?

PROSPECTIVE JUROR: Yes.

THE COURT: And regardless of what evidence was presented in the
trial? Would you do that automatically, in other words?

PROSPECTIVE JUROR: Yes. Um-hum.

DEFENSE ATTORNEY: Challenge for cause.

THE COURT: The challenge will be granted.

Conversely, some on the panel felt they could never sentence to
death:

THE COURT: Are your feelings about the death penalty such that
you could never vote for a verdict of death regardless of any
evidence that might be developed at the trial?

PROSPECTIVE JUROR: Well, I was always for the death penalty, but
now that I'm here and actually going to get on it, I don't know
whether I can or not.

THE COURT: Do you understand that with regard to the imposition
of the death penalty, the jury would have to agree unanimously
to impose the death penalty?

PROSPECTIVE JUROR: Yes.

THE COURT: So all twelve jurors would have to agree.

PROSPECTIVE JUROR: Yes.

THE COURT: So each individual juror would have to agree to the
death penalty.

PROSPECTIVE JUROR: Yes.

MR. NORRIS: What that really means to you is that it would be your
vote that would sentence another human being to death.

PROSPECTIVE JUROR: I just don't think I can vote for the death
penalty.

DEFENSE ATTORNEY: Under any kind of case? Hitler? That type of
person, could you vote death if you had someone like that? So
you're saying no matter what the evidence is—

PROSPECTIVE JUROR: I'll have to say that. I'll have to say that, yes.

MR. NORRIS: Now, after you've considered all this, is it your opinion
as you sit there now that you could not personally yourself ever
impose the death penalty upon another human being?

PROSPECTIVE JUROR: No.

After impaneling hundreds of prospective jurors, a jury of twelve,
along with four alternates, is finally selected. All swear to apply the
law and impose death if the evidence so merits.

From the prosecution's perspective, this is the only way the death
penalty can function. Were it otherwise, and jurors categorically opposed to capital punishment were allowed to find their way onto capital juries, it would render a death verdict impossible, no matter the
evidence. This would mean a total rejection of the voters' will, as they
overwhelmingly supported the death penalty's reinstatement in 1978.

For the defense, and death penalty opponents, the process en-
sures that capital juries are both predisposed to vote for death—as all
twelve have assured the judge and attorneys that they can do so—and
also more conservative, as citizens who favor capital punishment tend
to be right of center.

———

Due to issues of timing—Cox and Burns were arrested long before
Williams—and to legal prohibitions on using Williams's statement
against the other two defendants, the cases were severed, with each
defendant tried separately.

While this would drag the proceedings out for much longer, I
felt it would provide the prosecution with a psychological advantage.

So much of the persona and the swagger of the gangster is tied to
the group, and the proximity of the homies. They feel safe, insulated,

caught up in the fantasy of the mob. Collective presence emboldens, convincing them to remain tight-lipped and unified, not wishing to be seen as weak or to let down the crew, and perpetuating the fiction of street warriors against the world.

Sitting alone he is stripped of his protective illusion. He is isolated, out of his comfort zone. No eye contact, smirks, hand signals, or gossip, none of the little street reassurances. Severance leaves him vulnerable and insecure, sending the message that the power dynamic has flipped. He will now be judged by society's standards, not those of his subculture. Killing of innocents will now be condemned, not lauded.

Additionally, the three defendants posed less of a threat to courtroom security when separated.

Once the death-qualified jury of eight men and four women was sworn in, testimony in the Horace Burns case began in April 1985, in Department 132 of the Criminal Courts Building in downtown Los Angeles, Honorable Aurelio Munoz presiding.

My family and I sat in the first row of the gallery. We were scared, angry, and confused. We also remained divided. The murders had ripped the family apart. We hoped a guilty verdict could help put it back together.

But we knew it would be taxing, that until all three trials were over our lives would be on hold, dominated by the fits and starts of the legal system. For years we would be forced to relive the crimes, subjected to autopsy photos, defense arguments, and the ongoing presence of the killers.

———

Heading into the Burns trial, the defense was confident, the prosecution uneasy.

Burns's two attorneys were both experienced criminal defense lawyers who had tried death penalty cases since capital punishment returned to California.

Gerald Lenoir was five feet, three inches tall, described by a colleague as "brilliant." He had migrated to California after graduating from a small African-American college in Missouri.

Lenoir's co-counsel, Hal Miller, was a lifetime resident of Los Angeles. He attended UCLA, and in 1956 ran on the same track-and-field team with Olympic gold medalist Rafer Johnson. Miller's family migrated to Los Angeles from Oklahoma and Kansas in 1906.

Hal Miller's uncle, Loren Miller, was one of L.A.'s most famous black attorneys, working with Thurgood Marshall on *Shelley v. Kraemer*, which declared restrictive housing covenants unconstitutional, and *Brown v. Board of Education*, which struck down school segregation.

Lenoir and Miller posed a challenge for me that I would deal with throughout the trials. These defense attorneys seemed like decent men and we shared similar pasts. Logically, I also knew that all of the defense attorneys were just doing their jobs. But none of this overrode my anger when they argued on behalf of my family's killers. This pattern would hold for all three trials. I could feel it in my nearby family members as well. When the defense attorneys spoke, a kind of electric tension pulsed between us.

I knew the justice system well, and dealt with it for years from the inside. What a difference when it's no longer a job, but your life.

In the Burns trial, both Lenoir and Miller felt an acquittal was likely. The prosecution's case, as far as they could tell, would rest largely on the testimony of drug dealers, drug users, accomplices, and informants. Of the three defendants Burns would be hardest to convict.

In the first week of trial, the prosecution relied upon police testimony and forensic evidence to establish the murders. Norris also put Linda Lewis, Cassandra Haynes, and Burns's county jail cellmate, David Mangola, on the stand, to prove Burns's knowledge of the crime.

The star witnesses for the prosecution would be Ida Moore, the driver of the van, and her front-seat passenger, Delisa Brown. Both were granted immunity from prosecution in exchange for their testimony at all three trials.

Unknown to the authorities at the time of the January preliminary hearing of Cox and Burns, Brown and Moore would now reveal what took place inside the van in the early morning hours of August 31, 1984.

————

Before Moore and Brown could take the stand, the Burns case took a strange turn.

Attorney Miller would later say that in a matter of seconds, the case changed from likely acquittal to a mad scramble to beat the gas. The defense was broken. Miller said Norris grinned like the Cheshire Cat.

Despite the advice of his attorneys that there was nothing that Cox or Williams could do to help him, Burns refused to believe them and took action. A week into the trial, Burns attempted to contact Cox.

At 6:45 p.m. on April 8, 1985, as a Los Angeles County deputy sheriff escorted Cox and several others to a visiting area in the county jail, Burns dodged into the line and jammed a bunch of papers into Cox's hand. Cox took the papers and tried to stuff them into the left breast pocket of his jacket. A deputy witnessed Cox's moves and confiscated the papers, which he said were "folded up in a fashion as if a very large item was contained in the envelope."

The papers were a jailhouse "kite," a secret communication between inmates.

The ten handwritten pages, described by some as looking like "chicken scratchings," were examined by an LAPD handwriting expert, who said he was "completely certain" that all ten pages were written by Burns. He added that when Burns was brought into the room with him he exclaimed: "That's my writing. I wrote that."

The intercepted letter was at once a revealing look into the violent world of the Rolling Sixties, a damning piece of evidence against Burns, and a depressing window into the antiliterate world of the streets.

Norris said the kite was "better than a ten-page confession . . . because what this gives is the innermost understandings, the innermost feelings of this defendant in relation to the crime, in relation to his conspirators. . . ."

Norris would use the letter to prove that Burns shared the intent to kill on that early morning. He would also use it to show Burns's efforts to escape justice, citing the language "Let's beat this DA" and "two of us should spring the one." The kite also showed a common cause between the three gang members. Finally, the letter exhibited an arrogant lack of remorse.

Norris summed up the sentiment: "We're going to be able to do whatever we want. We're going to be able to work our will. Not just the crime. But in accomplishing our will wherever we want to."

The symbol RSC, for Rolling Sixties Crips, is at the top of the letter, and Burns tells Cox, "I love you homie." This was strong evidence that the crime was done with an understanding between Cox and Burns and on behalf of the gang.

The margins of the letter contain dozens of names of other gang members. Many have question marks after them, indicating Burns's suspicions regarding the commitment and loyalty of these individuals: "Mumbles? Snoop? J. Bone? Slip Roc?" Others like Catman are crossed out, indicating that they had snitched and should be killed.

The letter, filled with misspellings, street slang, and the purposeful substitution of the letter B, for Bloods, with C, for Crips, provides a window into the thinking of a Rolling Sixties gang member.

The primary theme was how the three could beat their respective cases. Burns writes to Cox, "Let Mumbles and Mup Read this an you get your think cap on and see can we try to get out of this mess."

Throughout the letter Burns weighs the strength of the evidence against each of them, concluding that the case is weakest against him because he did not leave the van, and therefore, every effort should be made to free him so that he could help the others escape.

Key to this theme is the upcoming testimony of Ida Moore and Lisa (Delisa) Brown. The two women would place Burns in the van and show that he had knowledge of the intent to kill.

"The bitch said I knew about it and she didn't. So the things are looking like none of us are going to beat this," Burns writes.

Attempting to demonstrate to Cox that he, Burns, was their only chance, he continues, "Now C. Dove made statements that's going to hang him, and you got to mush against you and Me by those bitches put me in that van and I new everything that was happening."

The testimony of Ida and Lisa angered Burns on two other counts.

The first concerned the advice of his attorneys: "My punk ass lawyer said I am not going to beat this case by saying I was not in that van. He said the only way I will beat this case is by saying I was in that van or if C. Dove or Fee say you was not in the van."

On his displeasure with his lawyers, he continues, "Now my lawyer are triping they are telling me that the jury is going to celieve those bitches So they want me to say I was in the van and did not know Nothing. But I'm not going to do that cecause they are going to ask me who was in their with you and that's like snitching which I never would do."

A second theme regarding Ida and Lisa's testimony is Burns's disbelief that his "homies" on the street had done nothing to prevent "those bitches" from coming to court.

"And rest of are SoCall homies they aint shit cuzz Nobody did Shit for us just let us go to prison nigas with those checks. Five years from now we would see forgotten by most of are so call homies they did not even try to stop those bitches from coming to court on me."

The lack of support by the homies on the street is made clear because "[t]hose bitches did not even move out of the hood."

This passage shows the desperation. The romantic dream of being a modern-day highwayman or bandit has come to an end. The code of the street is breaking down. Homies snitch to save their hides. No one comes to the rescue.

Burns continues: "Now the homies out there on the streets do not give a fuck about us. They just going to watch us hang. Now who is going to take care of us? We are just going to be three homies that fade away in darkness."

Burns laments that he would be all alone in prison, stating, "I might go crazy and kill everybody in sight and probly wine up dead my self I can't see how you are taking this so well cecause I am realy swetting this right now an is real scared." He continues: "I don't know what to do cecause I do not have know female that I could get marrie two," and, "My mother is not going to talk to me no less take care of me, ain't got no bitch."

Now Burns feels the only hope the three have is if one is set free: "When one could see out their making sure the other two is well tookin care of. We can not help each other out by seeing in jail—am serious two of us should set the one free. If you want to cefore all three of us get sent up for the crime."

Burns then says to Cox: "I wish their was a way to Set you free you get the job done. I love you homie and would die for you. I know you love me homie those white folks are trying to kill us. Now think about all this we can Not let this fucking DA. Get all three of us."

After expressing his love for Cox and fear of the DA getting them, he bemoans what this whole affair was doing to the families of Burns and Cox: "Now forget about the homies for a minute and think about are familys and what they are going threw. It is killing them to even think their sons were involve in something like this."

Next, Burns reflects on the bleakness of his situation. "Sometimes I feel like taking my own life but then I don't because I'm scared of hell."

Burns then makes his pitch to Cox to testify that Burns was not in the van: "I'm asking you this cecause I'm the only one that might have a Slim chance." He continues by analyzing the evidence and indicating to Cox how he can help Burns beat his case: "All we have to do is think Now nobody has seen me at all nor my fingerprints in the house nor James is not saying I new nothing about It. Now here were you come in at by saying Lisa and Ida were involve and I was not in the van. That's the only way you could spring me is by testifying I was not in that van at all and they got to Release me."

Burns tells Cox that if he is released the witnesses will be taken care of and unable to testify against Cox: "They got to Release me and I'm going to get out and show you how a real homeboy do it those bitches family going to suffer for all this and that's on mom's. When you come back on appeal I make sure know witness shows up."

Finally, Burns assures Cox he will not receive the death penalty because he was not the mastermind in the crime: "You won't get the gas cecause you did not plan it you was doing what you were order."

Other gang members need to be consulted and a strategy worked out: "Now I'm going to talk to C.Dove. Please Show Pochie and Mumbles and Keith Rat and tell me what they think."

After expressing his hopes that someone will save him from his fate, Burns concludes the kite, exposing his two conflicting sides.

"Love you Homie," he writes to Cox, followed by "don't See that I'm Just Scard." Burns then signs the letter "Horse. RSC [Rolling Sixties Crips]. Notorious W/S [West Side] Rollin Sixties. Rich an Rollin Mafia Style."

The two sides present a different kind of case, one that takes place inside the young man's head: *Horse v. Horace.*

The fantasy life of Horse: a street soldier with a gang moniker, a warrior fighting to protect his turf. He belongs to something meaningful, he is a reputable member of the notorious Rolling Sixties, gangsters who control Hyde Park, brothers bonded in blood, sworn to secrecy till their dying day. He speaks in coded tongue, flashes underworld hand signs, and flies the blue flag. He plots escape and revenge, scheming to bring the world of the streets crashing into the courtroom to win his freedom. He is feared, respected, acknowledged. He is a Rolling Sixties Crip, rich and rolling, mafia-style.

The reality of Horace Edwin Burns: He is a scared nineteen-year-old kid recently arrested within his mother's home, where he still lived. He is unemployed, uneducated, and functionally illiterate. His father left him, and his adoptive family, the black street gang, is disorganized, without any inclination or ability to break him out and secure his freedom. His circumscribed world of a few blocks of Hyde Park has collapsed upon him. Horace is alone and abandoned. According to the street code, he is a snitch, giving up his gang in open court. To society he is simply another cowardly, boasting thug. He is neither rich nor rolling. On the morning of the killing he was unable to conjure two dollars for gas. He now fears that the only one who ever genuinely cared for him, his mother, will finally cut the cord with her murderous spawn. He is caught in the teeth of the law, his future options life without the possibility of parole or the gas. Upon death he fears he will be sent to Hell.

23

NOTHIN' ABOUT NOTHIN'

WHEN THE TWO women came to court to testify in April 1985, Ida Moore was in her late thirties, Delisa Brown her early twenties. Both bore the scars of crack's charms.

Certainly not ideal witnesses: drug addled, uncouth, and with unclean hands.

This was unsurprising, to be expected.

The district attorney's old adage: *When the play is cast in Hell, don't expect the actors to be angels.*

———

It is sometime before 6 a.m. on August 31, 1984. Moore and Brown are awake. They are in Moore's house on Third Avenue and Sixty-Fifth in Hyde Park.

The two have stayed up all night partying, smoking crack, while Moore's husband, Leon, worked the night shift.

It is still dark outside, and Moore's children, ages twelve and fifteen, are asleep. Stanley Cheatam, "Cheater," is crashed out on the couch.

At some point Darren Charles Williams (C-Dub) and Horse enter the front room. C-Dub speaks with Brown and then goes into the kitchen to make a phone call. C-Dub then returns to the front room, hands Horse his car keys, and tells him to go get someone.

Moore knew C-Dub as a dope dealer. She was afraid of him. He was "pretty crazy."

C-Dub then asks Ida to take him in her van to pick up some money from a girl. The van is a maroon 1975 Chevy.

Moore agrees, but says she needs money for gas, because the van is empty. C-Dub says he will pay her once they arrive at the girl's house.

About ten minutes after being sent out, Horse returns with Fee. This is the first time Moore has met Fee. He wears his hair in French braids.

Upon Fee's arrival, C-Dub says, "Let's go."

They leave Moore's house. It is now light outside.

Moore gets in the driver's seat, Brown gets in the front passenger seat, and C-Dub, Horse, and Fee climb in the back. They sit together on the "built-in bedlike seat" about ten feet behind the front seats.

Moore has not seen any of the men carrying anything.

Moore drives north on Third Avenue and stops at Burns's house. He says he will get some gas money from his brother. Burns gets out and returns a couple of minutes later, stating that his brother did not have any money.

Moore does not look at Burns upon his return to the van, and does not notice if he has anything in his hands.

Moore then says she will use her own two dollars to buy gas.

She drives her van to the corner of Slauson and Western, pulls into the Shell station, gets out of the van, and pumps two dollars' worth.

Upon her return she sees a big gun in the back of the van.

As she pulls out of the gas station, C-Dub comes forward from the rear of the van, kneels between the two front seats, and tells Moore to drive east on Slauson. From Slauson he directs her to West Fifty-Ninth Street.

As they slow on West Fifty-Ninth, Brown sees C-Dub looking at some writing on a torn piece of a paper bag. He then reads out an address, peers out the window, and says, "There it is."

C-Dub tells Moore to stop the van about thirty feet down the street from the house, and keep it running.

Other than C-Dub's directions, there is no conversation.

As the van slows to a stop, C-Dub says, "We are going to go in there, kick in the door, and scare them up, and shoot them up." Fee and Horse remain silent.

Moore then hears someone in the back say they are going to kill everyone in the house.

The sliding door on the passenger side opens. C-Dub and Fee get out. C-Dub tells Horse to stay in the van.

The motor is running. Horse sits on a pillow behind the driver's seat. Moore and Brown remain seated in the front. The sliding door is open.

Fee holds a long gun wrapped in a blue coat. C-Dub pulls an automatic pistol from his waistband.

Fee and C-Dub walk down the street toward the house. C-Dub walks first and Fee follows.

Upon seeing the two men with the guns, Moore asks Horse, "What they gonna do?"

Horse replies, "They just going to shoot it up."

Minutes after the two leave the van, shots ring out.

A couple of minutes after the gunshots, C-Dub runs to the van. He still holds the pistol.

"Let's go," he says.

"Aren't you going to wait for your friend?" Brown asks.

C-Dub does not respond.

After another minute or two, Fee returns. He still holds the long gun, but no longer the jacket in which the gun was wrapped.

After Fee gets in the van, he slides the door shut. He and C-Dub tell Moore to drive.

———

Burns's jailhouse kite forced the defense to do something they never intended—to put Burns on the stand. So damning was the letter, it left them no choice. They would do their best to spin Burns's words into something they were not.

On the stand, Burns, dressed in street clothes, came across as angry and aggressive, and according to his own attorneys, with an off-putting attitude of "Why am I here?"

Burns denied any knowledge of plans to kill, and stressed his fear of the older C-Dub, that he simply did what C-Dub said without any understanding of a larger goal, and without giving it any thought. Additionally Burns attempted to explain away the incriminating aspects of his letter, stating that he had not sought a violent breakout, or elimination of witnesses, but had merely wanted his homies to come and visit him in county jail.

Through his testimony, Burns shed more light upon the secret world of the black street gangs, continuing to make statements viewed under the gang code as snitching.

On direct examination, his trial counsel threw him softballs, while on cross-examination, the prosecutor hammered at inconsistencies as well as his past crimes.

Burns testified that in August 1984 he hung out at Tenth Avenue and Sixty-Third Street, about eight blocks from his house.

On Tenth Avenue he was "gangbanging, rolling dice and socializin' . . . and drinking beer." At about three in the morning on August 31, Burns went to bed after a night of drinking. Sometime around 6 a.m., CW woke him up, told him to go to Ida Moore's house around the corner.

Upon arriving, CW told Burns to drive CW's Fiat and pick up Fee. Burns got Fee at his house on Seventy-Seventh and Crenshaw and they returned to Moore's house. According to Burns, CW said he was going to his girlfriend's house to pick up some money and asked Burns, "Why don't you ride with us?"

From this point, Burns's narrative corresponded with that of Moore and Brown, with the addition of Burns's repeated comments as to how frightened he was.

Burns confirmed he could obtain only fifty cents for gas, that CW gave the directions, told Burns to stay in the van, and carried a pistol.

Burns testified that upon arrival at West Fifty-Ninth Street, "I was surprised. I said, 'What you doing?'" CW answered, "We're going to scare the people up." Fee "didn't say nothing."

At this point Fee and CW disappeared. Burns "was scared."

Burns said he thought CW was going to kill his girlfriend.

Shortly thereafter Burns heard eight or nine shots, making him so nervous that he was shaking as he sat inside the van.

CW then returned to the van and sat on the bed in the rear. CW looked scared.

Burns then heard a second round of shots. At this point CW, from the rear of the van, said, "Let's go. Bone out."

Fee then returned, threw the rifle on the bed, and closed the door. Fee did not look scared.

CW again said, "Bone out."

CW directed Moore to Vermont and Gage.

Burns at this point "was so scared and was so in shock, you know, I just didn't say nothin'."

Burns said he then took a bus home, got a forty-ounce beer and "took it to the head," and then went to sleep. He then went to his mother's workplace, a nursery school six blocks from his house. He asked her for twenty dollars, and he went over to Tenth Avenue and gambled with the money she gave him.

Burns said he felt taken advantage of by Fee and C-Dove. Between June and August 1984 Burns said he and Fee were together every day hanging out, "date difference girls . . . go to the beaches . . . go to outings on Friday and Saturday nights like to a skating rink, to the A.M./P.M., to the street races."

Burns did not know CW well. He was older, "was like the leader of the Rolling Sixties; and he really, if you don't do what he say, you're in real trouble." CW "called the gang meetings and the shots out there on the streets." Burns received numerous threats from CW after he learned that Burns had flown the kite.

Burns concluded with a string of denials. He never boasted about the crime. All the witnesses were liars. He and Fee were friends, but did not engage in gangbanging activities. He did not pick up the pistol and rifle from his house. The kite was simply his way of stating he had nothing to do with the crime. He never received any money in connection with the crime. He planned to sue the city of Los Angeles for false arrest and false imprisonment.

———

When asked about the Rolling Sixties on cross-examination, Burns described it as "a group of individuals in one neighborhood fighting. Really, it's like a war. It's like a small country war."

Burns further stated that the gang engaged in robberies, dope dealing, and shootings, but he denied participating in any of these activities. He had been a member for two to three years, but engaged only in gang fights.

As to his membership Burns stated: "It's just like—it's just like I was to socialize with one of them for my protection. I got to get along with the people in my hood. You hear what I'm saying? So I hang out with them."

In trying to defuse the intercepted letter, Burns testified, "The real fact was it was only one person that can go, and that was the person that was completely innocent, and that was me."

He said he wanted the letter shown to others because "Fee he don't think at all, you know. He don't—his mind don't register. He just take the demands and follow through with them. He ain't— he ain't very bright is what I'm sayin' and there were older people, probably bright, and they know how to deal with the situation."

As to the reason for the crime, Burns testified, "As far as I know, I don't know nothin' about no money or nothin' about no real motive." He would continue, "There's nothin' about no hit, nothin' about no pay. Nothin' about nothin'."

The prosecutor concluded his cross-examination:

"In your letter to Fee, Mr. Burns, is there anything in there that you could point out to us in relation to any remorse in relation to the killing of these four people?"

Burns: "I don't understand."

Norris: "Remorse, being sorry?"

Burns: "What did you say? No, sir."

24

KILL THEM ALL

THE PROSECUTOR'S CLOSING argument was filled with emotion, recalling the four victims who would never again awaken.

Norris stated that the intent to kill everyone in the house had already been formed in the "death van" on the ride over. He termed the killing the "Fifty-Ninth Street Massacre," arguing that "Nazi storm troopers have done no worse."

The van was needed, Norris argued, because it was a "hit vehicle," easy to get in and out of, unlike CW's little Fiat. He stressed the horror of the cold-blooded executions and linked them to Burns's role in the case. He quoted Lisa Brown's testimony: one of the men in the back of the van said, "We're going to kill everyone in the house."

Norris pounded on the callousness of the killers, Burns's statement to Cassandra Haynes that the dead children were just "what happens." Further, Burns boasted of the crime, his role, his involvement in the retaliatory hit team.

As he spoke of the killings Norris waved the murder weapon in front of the jury, arguing that either CW and Burns brought the rifle with them, or Burns got it when he went to pick up Cox, or when they stopped at Burns's house to supposedly get gas money. Norris further suggested that the letters "PBG" scratched onto the gun indicated it came from the Playboy Gangsters, a Crip set friendly to the Rolling Sixties at the time, and argued that the gun may have come from Horse's PBG friend known as Insane.

In establishing Burns's liability, Norris stated that "those who directly and actively commit the act constituting the crime, or those who aid and abet the crime are principals. It is the contention of the People in this case that Mr. Burns falls under both categories."

Norris then quoted the law:

A person aids and abets the commission of a crime when he (1) with the knowledge of the unlawful purpose of the perpetrator, and (2) with the intent or purpose of committing or encouraging or facilitating the commission of the offense, either by act or advice, aids, promotes, encourages, or instigates the commission of the crime.

As to motive, the district attorney listed several: a retaliatory hit, a hit for a drug deal, a hit for a businessman, and a Rolling Sixties–ordered hit. But it made no difference. Motive was not an element of murder. As long as the defendants went there with the intent to kill, beyond a reasonable doubt, guilt was proven.

Norris concluded, "You have something just as bad as your Nazi storm trooper upon that street when they come down to the house where the Alexander family is. . . . Convict Mr. Horace Burns of what he righteously deserves, that is, all four murders as well as the special circumstances."

———

The defense pointed the finger at CW, saying that the prosecution witnesses had lied to protect him and instead fingered Burns. The defense focused on Ida Moore's relationship to CW and that she was an accomplice whose testimony had to be viewed with great caution.

The defense continually stressed that a jury should not convict based upon the testimony of lying dope dealers, accomplices, and jailhouse snitches who cut deals in exchange for testimony.

The defense criticized the prosecutor's closing argument for throwing out four possible motives: a drug hit, a retaliatory hit, a murder for hire, and a Rolling Sixties gang–ordered hit. The defense argued that this asked the jury to convict based upon speculation.

For the defense, Burns was "a nonfactor sitting in the van."

The defense concluded:

"Your not guilty verdict will not tell Horace that you endorse his lifestyle. You can rest assured this case will be implanted in his mind the rest of his life." "I'll give you my assurance, that with Mrs. Burns—I'm going to give her my assistance—to turn this boy around. I have not said this in any other case I've had." "He is eighteen, nineteen. He's gone through that period of time which is very difficult for single parents to rear boys."

"I say to you, jurors, from this evidence, this case, I've never seen anything like it. Don't convict this young man on this type of evidence."

Because the prosecution has the burden of proof in a criminal case, they get the opportunity to rebut the defense argument.

Norris concluded by quoting the jury instruction on murder: "Motive is not an element of the crime charged and need not be shown. . . ."

He then stated: "If you can imagine to go back in time, we haven't had the killings; Ebora and Dietra and Damon and Damani are still in there alive, and at the door is Fee and CW. You ask them: Does it make any difference in the world as to what their motivation is? You think they care? The question is the intent to murder, the intent to kill when they go out."

Finally, "They walked to that door. That is the important thing. They had an execution squad to kill human beings when they walked to that door."

On May 23, 1985, the jury found Burns guilty of four counts of first-degree murder.

The defendant sat motionless as the jury rendered its verdict.

The special circumstance of multiple murders was likewise found to be true. The jury would next decide whether Burns would receive the death penalty or life in prison without parole.

Following the verdict Burns was led back to jail.

Our family left the courtroom in tears. In the hallway we embraced as one.

It was my sister Joan's thirty-seventh birthday. She called the verdict a "beautiful birthday present." But she also said, "This was just the beginning."

Norris called the verdict "a message to the gangs of Los Angeles County that not only have the police gone to the fullest to prosecute, but the community itself is tired of gang warfare and of being ruled by the gangs on the streets."

———

In the penalty phase of the trial the defendant's background and character are at issue. The district attorney presented evidence of Burns's nine prior arrests, primarily for gun charges.

Burns testified that he did nothing to merit any of the arrests and that they were all cases of police harassment. Burns was brought to court on only one of the cases, a robbery charge stemming from an incident at Crenshaw High School, which was pled as a misdemeanor charge of brandishing a weapon.

The prosecutor also presented evidence from another jailhouse informant who testified that Burns wanted to have witnesses, jurors, and the district attorney killed.

The defense showed that Burns had attended church every Sunday, sang in the choir, and taught Sunday school. Burns's mother, Edwina, testified on his behalf, stating that he had been close with his father before the latter left the family when Burns was fourteen. According to Burns's mother, his father had been shot and injured by the LAPD and left L.A. because he feared for his life while living in the city. Burns testified that he had missed his father very much.

In the penalty phase the jury considers aggravating and mitigating factors in determining whether to impose death. In reaching its decision, the jury considers both guilt and penalty-phase evidence. Such factors include the circumstances of the crime itself, prior criminal activity by the defendant, prior felony convictions by the defendant, whether the defendant was suffering from extreme mental disorders at the time of the crime, whether the victim was a participant in the crime, whether the defendant felt his conduct was morally justified, whether the defendant operated under extreme duress, whether at the time of the offense the defendant's mental capacity was impaired by mental disease or intoxication, the defendant's age, his role in the crime, as well as any extenuating circumstances.

If the aggravating outweigh the mitigating, then the verdict shall be death; otherwise the verdict shall be life without parole.

The prosecutor focused on the four innocent victims and the defendant's lack of remorse. In establishing Burns's aggression, violence, and lack of concern for the victims, the prosecutor repeatedly referenced Burns's intercepted kite.

In his summation, Norris called the crime "a bloodstain upon our American way of life." He continued, stating that the inhabitants of the van, given their intent, might as well have been chanting "Kill them all." "If you can imagine for a minute the van coming down in front of the Alexander house . . . having a chant coming down American streets: "Kill them all! Kill them all!'" "I suggest to you," he concluded, "that in the interests of justice that the same chant ought be: 'Kill them all! Kill them all!' Kill Horace. Kill Fee. Kill CW. They all deserve the death penalty for what they did in this case."

The defense argued that a defendant of "tender years," eighteen years old, in a bad environment, was under extreme duress due to his fear of the older CW, and that he rode in the van with no knowledge of what was intended.

Burns's attorneys further claimed that he should not be gassed based on the unreliable testimony of snitches and accomplices. They said his role was minor, that he should not die for the acts of Cox.

The defense concluded:

"Whatever your verdict will be in this case is a death penalty. The question is whether he dies immediately or whether he's given the opportunity to live a long time and think about this case on a day-to-day, around-the-clock basis. Life without the possibility of parole is a death sentence in effect."

The prosecution countered that the crime would not have occurred without Burns's participation.

The defendants, he concluded, "made their own decision. They earned it. . . . They killed them all."

––––––

One month after they returned their guilt-phase verdicts, the jury rejected the death penalty, imposing instead a sentence of life without the possibility of parole.

In pronouncing the jury's sentence, Judge Munoz stated, "I do not believe he should ever be released from prison. This was a vicious attack in the early morning hours. If not for the grace of God, there would have been six victims, not four."

One week later, on September 27, Horace Burns was admitted into the California Department of Corrections.

Two years after his admission to prison, on December 16, 1987, the Court of Appeals of California, Second Appellate District, affirmed Burns's conviction, denying each of his grounds for appeal. These included challenging the testimony of Ida Moore and Delisa Brown, the testimony of the jailhouse snitch, David Mangola, and the admission of Burns's jailhouse kite.

Burns would spend the rest of his life in prison. He was twenty years old at the time of his sentencing.

––––––

On June 20, 1985, following Burns's conviction and sentence, David Michael Williams, a Los Angeles high school teacher, wrote a "comment" for the *Los Angeles Sentinel*.

Several points are heart-wrenchingly obvious in Burns's letter. From the composition . . . replete with gang slogans, misspellings and assorted grammatical errors, it is clear that Burns is barely literate. Either he failed the schools or the school system failed him—maybe the truth is a combination of both.

He is glaringly unprepared academically; it is doubtful that he was able to enter the competitive job market after high school, if he finished his education at all. With such limited skills, he probably had few options other than to serve as a henchman for a drug syndicate, although this in no way excuses the heinous crimes.

. . .

In view of the above, it is particularly gratifying to see thousands of area high school seniors graduate this week. Because of their diplomas, their options are so much broader than the Burnses in this world, their futures loom so much brighter. . . .

As processions begin, our joyful tears for the marchers should be tempered with regret for those who do not. We must search for answers; we must retrieve the Horace Burnses that are willing to be helped.

And it is not enough to show interest in a restricted few. Our neighborhood is an African village where the young are children shared by all adults. If we are to benefit from the harvest, each member of the village must join in collective responsibility. The vigilant watch must continue.

Congratulations to the graduating class of 1985. We celebrate you as you walk, tall and stately. We anticipate your run, your swift race toward unprecedented success. We stand alert, ready to pick you up if you should fall.

There it was, Madee's life lesson all over again, her insistence on education, on literacy, on taking control over our lives. Give ourselves the maximum options. The only way we could ensure our own success was to make sure we had the ability to seize it. Instead of controlling his own destiny, Horace Burns let the streets control him. And the case was a microcosm of the problems plaguing the black community: absent fathers, overwhelmed mothers, failing schools, youth without options, those tiny minds, stuck in limited spaces, how they needed to grow, expand their future.

A whole world of Horace Burnses, and no Madee to guide them.

25

DO YOU KNOW
WHO THAT IS?

In november 1985, several months after the conviction of Horace Burns, the trial of Tiequon Cox began.

From the start, the Cox trial generated far more publicity. Cox was the accused shooter, and an enforcer in the gang.

Los Angeles Superior Court Judge Roger Boren, a former prosecutor and recent appointee of Governor Deukmejian, recalled that from the start the courtroom felt very tense. The combination of the emotions coming from the victims' large family, and the stoic, threatening demeanor of Cox, made it seem the courtroom could easily spin out of control.

This sense of tension was ratcheted up early in the trial process.

On November 22, 1985, Department 126, Judge Boren's courtroom was dark, with no proceedings held.

Next door in Judge Paul Bowland's courtroom four black males were seen by the judge casing it out. Judge Bowland relayed this information to Judge Boren.

On the same date, the Los Angeles County Sheriff's Department contacted Boren and told him that they had received word of rumors of an escape attempt, that members of the Rolling Sixties were planning to break out Tiequon Cox.

On the following day Judge Boren's courtroom had several undercover members of the Sheriff's Department stationed throughout the public gallery. Additionally, a magnetometer and a body scan were conducted upon entry. Finally, in the hallway that runs behind the courtrooms and leads to the judges' chambers, a deputy sheriff with an Uzi stood guard.

Also on the same day, during jury voir dire, Edward Cook, Cox's trial counsel, acting nervous and agitated, sought to meet with Judge Boren outside the presence of both his client and the court reporter.

Boren considered it a most unusual request, putting him in an awkward position.

————

Edward "Ned" Cook was an experienced public defender, having tried numerous cases, and ranked "Level 4," the highest degree in the office.

Cox's appellate attorneys, however, later questioned Cook's motivation for handling this case.

Cook, a Los Angeles native born in 1936 at St. Vincent's Hospital—where Madee worked up until her death—took the case because "Kermit Alexander had always been a hero of mine."

Cook described himself as an avid sports fan, and said he had cheered for me at UCLA and on the Rams. Cook in fact became so involved with the Rams that he once sat with team owner Georgia Frontiere in her box at a game. He gave her flowers.

Cook said he initially took the case because he thought it would be interesting. He later admitted that it became "somewhat of a nightmare." Cook also stated that he was always uncomfortable because he felt that I hated him for representing Cox, and he regretted the thought that my family viewed him as "the enemy."

As with Burns's attorneys, I never held anything against the man personally, and understood he was just doing his job. But given the nature of the case, his words on behalf of the shooter were hard to hear.

Based on the horror of the crime, and the strength of the ballistic and fingerprint evidence, Cook concluded from early on in the case that the only hope was to try to save Cox's life. In this respect he would later resort to a novel strategy.

As defense attorneys go, Cook struck me as a pragmatist, one who plainly saw that the emotions of the case were against his client, and that the physical evidence was overwhelming. He would essentially concede the guilt phase, and simply seek to stave off execution.

Throughout the trial it was clear to everyone in the courtroom that Cook and Cox barely spoke to each other.

———

It was only Judge Boren's second trial. His first was the *Twilight Zone* case, in which actor Vic Morrow and two children were killed when a helicopter crashed during the filming of the movie in 1982.

Boren's limited judicial experience, coupled with Cook's unique request, left the judge ill at ease.

When Boren stressed to Cook that under the law he was not able to meet without the reporter, Cook "hemmed and hawed," and then, in the reporter's presence, stated the following:

> MR. COOK: Your honor, first I would say that this does not constitute a conflict because any attorney representing Mr. Cox would be privy to this information. In our investigation of this case there—we think that there is some possibility that there may be an escape attempt in this case.
>
> THE COURT: Yes.
>
> MR. COOK: We would—we're against full shackles but I think there should be some—like a handcuff to a chair I think would be sufficient so the jury can't see.
>
> THE COURT: Okay.
>
> MR. COOK: I just think that's—
>
> THE COURT: For the safety of everyone then?
>
> MR. COOK: For the safety of everyone. As an officer of the court, I feel that it's my duty to—
>
> THE COURT: Okay.

MR. COOK: It's something, though, that should not be looked at lightly.

A defense attorney requesting his own client be restrained in court was highly controversial. Cox's appellate attorneys would later argue that it represented an egregious breach of the attorney-client relationship, and an example of Cook's ineffective representation.

Judge Boren felt that Cook was genuinely frightened, and the judge took the threats "very seriously."

Cox would have his hands and legs immobilized by a metal restraining device. Observers wishing to enter Department 126 were required to go through a metal detector.

———

Cook's request for restraints marked another step in the breakdown of the relationship between counsel and client.

Cook felt frustrated that Cox would not talk to him and provide aid in his defense. Cox, on the other hand, refused to trust Cook.

Those who knew Cox said that he felt "alienated," "hopeless," and "fatalistic" about his case.

Cox said he initially thought "perhaps my attorney will help me" but became highly suspicious when Cook told him that his codefendants were "singing like canaries." When Cook asked Cox if "you got anything you want to say," Cox became convinced that Cook worked for the DA and "that it was all part of a setup."

In fact, what Cook said was true. Both Horace Burns and Darren Charles Williams had talked to the authorities and implicated Cox. However, for Cox, talking would have surrendered his very self-esteem and dignity, his sense of control. Cox himself said that talking would have "been betraying myself, my brothers, my sisters, everything."

In the words of Cox's junior high school teacher, Donald Bakeer, "One child told me that whether Tiequon was guilty or not did not matter because he definitely 'would take the rap and never say that he was not involved.'"

———

On January 6, 1986, following jury voir dire and the impaneling of a death-qualified jury, the prosecution began its case against the accused executioner.

Even less than in the Burns case would the prosecutor spell out motive. Norris simply had to demonstrate beyond a reasonable doubt that Cox was the shooter, and that he acted intentionally and with premeditation, and he would meet his guilt-phase burden.

The prosecutor continually spoke with our family, assuring us he was confident of conviction. While he was compassionate and understanding of our grief, our anger, he pled with us to keep as calm as we could and let him handle the case. Aware of my personal quest for justice and sensing my rage, Norris had Detective Crews keep a close watch on me. His fears were real. It took all of my self-control not to jump the low railing and wring his neck.

My family and I were squeezed tightly into the small public gallery.

The proceedings were about to begin.

The jury was seated.

Judge Boren entered the courtroom.

Bailiffs were stationed throughout.

Sterling Norris stood on the left of counsel table, nearest the jury. Shortly he would make his opening statement.

The defense attorneys, Ned Cook and Joanne Rotstein, stood to his right. Beside them was their client, Tiequon Cox, shackled, dressed in L.A. County Jail blue, his large chest pushing the shirt outward, muscular arms visible beneath short sleeves.

Cook urged him to wear street clothes to court. Cox refused.

Cox stared straight ahead with no apparent emotion.

Jurors would describe him as "disconnected," "far away and distant . . . barely making eye contact with the jury."

Judge Boren recalled Cox as "enduring the trial," "sitting serious and sullen, but proud," giving off the air of "I'm not going to be broken."

When I looked at Cox I saw an insolent young gangster, caught up in his closed-off world, who couldn't care less about us, about society. He acted as if put upon, angry that he was forced to sit through these proceedings. As if we had done him some wrong.

As I looked at him in profile, he had light skin and long cornrowed hair. On his neck the letters *NH* tattooed above *RSC*, standing for Neighborhood Rolling Sixties Crip.

Suddenly he turned to face the gallery. I thought he was going to stare right at me, actually make eye contact. But he never seemed to see me. He looked right past my family and at his Rolling Sixties homies who sat nearby.

With a defiant look, he flashed his gang sign, right hand extended from his body as far as the shackles would allow, thumb, index, and middle finger outstretched, with the ring and pinky finger curled in. The fingers formed the Roman numeral VI for Sixties.

He turned back around and continued his forward stare.

I heard my sister Mary, who sat next to me, gasp. She grabbed my shoulder.

"Oh my God, Kermit. Do you know who that is?"

26

AUTUMN IN WATTS

I<small>T IS A</small> windy autumn day in Watts, sometime in the early 1970s. I am on the sidelines of a Pop Warner football game, watching my team, the Watts Wildcats. The boys playing are eight and nine years old.

My sister Mary and her husband, Caldwell Black, the team's coach, stand nearby.

As I watch the boys play, I automatically view the game from a technical standpoint. I constantly analyze which players show innate athletic ability and advanced skills. I try to project which ones have promising futures.

On this fall day, one player stands out. He is a running back on the Wildcats' opponent, from a team in South Central. I have never seen him play before. I'm immediately taken. He is faster, more agile, and more physical than the others, clearly on a different level. His combination of speed, flexibility, and pure instinct reminds me of a young O. J. Simpson. Properly coached, the boy's skills could take him into high school football and perhaps into college and even the pros.

He is electric. He shows early signs of style and grace.

However, as I watch the game, I see that the boy plays with anger and venom. He cannot control himself. He spikes the ball angrily upon scoring. When he runs the ball, and his blockers fail, he slaps them upside the head. At one point he yells at someone on the sidelines.

A flashback within a flashback, now to my childhood, and the team coached by the priest: my own father walking onto the field, pulling me physically to the sidelines, and sitting me down. The words still echo: "He doesn't play until he can control himself."

As I continue to watch the boy intermittently dazzle and implode, I can't believe that no one does anything.

Where is the kid's coach? I wonder. Where are his parents? Will nobody talk to him? This kid could really be something, but he can't control himself. He needs help.

From the sidelines I shout in frustration: "Somebody needs to do something. Somebody ought to help him."

Everyone agreed. No one did a thing.

———

Back in court I barely heard Mary's voice as it warbled through my head.

"That's the kid that was always in trouble in Pop Warner," she said, pointing at Cox. "Look at what he's done."

Like the family funeral, again a blue haze, an inability to focus or compute.

As I forced myself to look, recognition slowly registered. I super-imposed the image of the killer before me onto the child I saw on the field that autumn day. Cut the cornrows, remove the tattoos, the same light skin and piercing green eyes. Unmistakable.

Recognition turned past into present.

Words long gone were reborn.

"There's this player on the other team, he's known in the league, he's incredible, but a real problem child."

Even back in Pop Warner he had a reputation.

All of the guilt came crashing down. My community service, my work as a motivational speaker, my time as a probation officer. My whole life had been devoted to making a difference, to mentoring, to turning difficult cases around.

Kermit Alexander, NFL star who rose from the projects of Watts: Who had more street credibility? Who better to walk the walk?

But what had I done that day in Watts?

Now I flashed back to my night prowls on the streets of South Central, to the Holy Cross Cemetery, to the endless soul-searching as I tried to grapple with my feelings of failure.

This was deeper than missing the morning cup of coffee on the day of the killings. This was a fundamental breach in my life's meaning. I now understood my role in the tragedy. I could have helped the kid and didn't. I always preached, take control. I always held forth on the power of one little moment, one intervention. "A few minutes of time can change a life," I heard myself saying.

But for whatever reason, that day, my eyes went blind. I shunned the dirty work of engaging a toxic youth, for the easy one of analyzing his technical skills. I really sat up and paid attention when he carried the ball. I really dropped the ball when I failed to stand up and take him on.

I betrayed the moment. I neglected an opportunity. In street lingo, I "slipped," let down my guard.

And worst of all, Madee would have been beside herself. Oh, I could hear her. "Kermit, how could you?" she bellows. "Now go do something. Coach him. Befriend him. Help him out like you do all those other kids."

The game I always held up as an alternative to the streets isn't a magic charm that simply works on its own. You can't just let kids on the field and watch 'em go. It's what you do with them that counts, it's the lessons learned at play.

And there was my chance, and all I did was call out others. I was as bad as my old probationers. They always said it was someone else's fault: "Some other dude did it." The old refrain from county jail: "SOD," always Some Other Dude. Just like them, I pointed the finger elsewhere. Not my problem. Let some other dude deal with it.

There's no saying what would have happened, but at least I could have tried, at least I would have been true to myself, to the family creed.

Madee spoke up again, a voice from my youth. "Now Kermit," she always said, "on your way home from school, you do something good for somebody. That lady's house that you pass by every day on your way home, she's eighty years old. You put down your books and help her carry and unload her groceries."

My father again, "He doesn't play until he can control himself."

Stop it, I felt like yelling. Instead I cringed.

As I tried with Ivan—to assure him it was not his fault—some of my family now tried with me. How could I have known? There's no saying it would have made any difference. Of course I wasn't to blame. And as with Ivan it did no good.

Now *I* felt on trial, an accomplice. I was damned, at once sickened by the vile killer, yet yoked to him. Forever I would carry the guilt that I played a role in the making of a monster. I let him into our lives, allowed him to drag us back into the world I had tried so hard to escape.

I asked everyone else, where were you? Now I heard everyone ask, where were *you*? It's just like the old African proverb: point the finger of blame outward and you point three at yourself.

27

BORN OF THE SOUTH

THE COX FAMILY, like mine, was born of the South, both children of its plantations and its pain.

One of Tiequon's great-grandmothers went into labor and gave birth while "on the job" in the cotton fields. One of his great-grandfathers was convicted of quintuple murder over a gambling dispute and sent to prison for twenty years. Another great-grandfather was shot and killed on the streets of Dallas following a barroom brawl.

Health issues plagued the Cox family. Sickle-cell anemia, heart and lung problems, as well as grand mal seizures ran along the paternal line.

The family past also revealed persistent poverty and lack of education, early marriages with lots of children.

Seven of Tiequon's great-grandparents were African-American, one was Portuguese, likely the source of his light skin and eyes.

They came from Texas, Mississippi, and Louisiana. And they came west as part of the Great Migration, traveling to Los Angeles by segregated bus in the 1950s.

The dominant figure in Tiequon's maternal line was his great-grandmother, Annie Ellsworth—then known as Annie Scott, later as Joan Pickett—who settled in L.A. in 1919.

Ellsworth supported herself through domestic labor and as a nightclub entertainer. She married twice and carried on other relationships during the 1920s and 1930s. The affairs were typically stormy, involving alcohol, infidelity, and physical abuse. Her children reported that she took little interest in their education, with only one of the three finishing high school.

In 1944, Ellsworth began investing in property, purchasing a house in the Sugar Hill section of Los Angeles. While restrictive housing covenants, forbidding sale to blacks, affected most of L.A., the seller violated the law because Japanese internment had left a glut of housing on the market.

Ellsworth, ambitious to extend her holdings, felt the bite of L.A.'s housing policies and entered the litigation challenging their constitutionality. In 1948, the U.S. Supreme Court, in *Shelley v. Kraemer*, declared restrictive covenants to violate the Equal Protection Clause of the U.S. Constitution. Over the following decades Ellsworth accumulated real estate that would be worth over a million dollars by 1984.

In the same year as the *Shelley* suit, Tiequon's future mother, Sondra Lee Holt, was "born via a low forceps delivery," to Ellsworth's daughter, Audrey, and her husband, John Lee Holt.

Holt was described by relatives as irresponsible and unwilling to work or provide support. From the time his daughter turned three, he sexually abused her. "He waited until the house was quiet at night," Sondra recalled, "and then came into my bedroom when I was asleep. When he first started to rape me, I did not understand what was happening, but only knew it hurt and left me scared and confused."

By the time Sondra was six, her mother was addicted to heroin and committed to a state hospital. Upon returning from rehab, she continued to party and drink around the children, often leaving them with others. She dated a string of men, most of whom were drunken and abusive, often in Sondra's presence.

By age seven, Sondra, born with scoliosis, a curvature of the spine, required a corrective spinal fusion, leaving her in a full-body cast.

Psychologically damaged from abuse and the strains of surgery, Sondra struggled with school. She displayed borderline mental functioning and her intelligence was graded as "dull-normal." By her early teens she turned to drugs and alcohol as a way of escaping the violence and hopelessness of her home life.

Her drug habit landed her for much of 1963 and 1964 in the California Youth Authority, where she served time for possession. She was paroled in February 1965.

The following month she returned to the eleventh grade, where a school physician found her to suffer from mental illness, classifying her as "somewhat disturbed." Failing all of her classes, she dropped out.

In April 1965 she went to the doctor and learned that she was three months pregnant. She would continue to drink and use drugs throughout the pregnancy.

———

Tiequon's biological father, James Cox, was one of twelve children. Born in Texas in 1946, he subsequently moved to California with the family.

Throughout his life James suffered from grand mal seizures, caused by fluid pressing against the brain. He often blacked out and then later came to in the hospital. From a young age, he had problems with self-control and showed a sudden temper.

James met Sondra at a party when he was seventeen. Later that night, Tiequon was conceived.

As James later recalled, "I was in the county jail when I found out Sondra was pregnant with my child. . . . I was released from jail on July 31, 1965, and a week later I was in front of the preacher. My father picked me up from the jail and on the way home we stopped and he bought me a suit. That is how I learned I was getting married the next week. I think I was the last in my family to know that a date had been set."

James described Sondra as "a warrior" who "stood toe-to-toe with anyone, man or woman, and settled arguments by physical fights. She never backed down from a fight and didn't need much cause to get into one."

After their marriage they lived together for a couple of months, but by Thanksgiving of 1965 they separated for the first time. James left Sondra after she tried to shoot him. One week later Tiequon was born.

In the years following his birth, James would see him occasionally, after Sondra lost control, disappeared, or was institutionalized. James would take the boy to his great-grandmother's house.

During the first five years of Tiequon's life, Sondra was arrested ten times, the offenses including assault with a deadly weapon, resisting arrest, disturbing the peace, drunk in public, attempted murder, and assault and battery on a police officer. During this time she bore two more children.

One relative said of Sondra's relationship with her kids, "She loved them one minute, and hated them the next. She was both suicidal and homicidal. More than once, I saw her pull a gun on Tiequon, Demontray, and Edrina."

When Tiequon was three and a half, Sondra attempted to kill herself, and her children, by turning on the gas stove and lighting it. The police arrived and took her to the hospital to treat her burns. The responding officer described her as "confused, violent, homicidal, and hyperactive."

A year later, a four-and-a-half-year-old Tiequon witnessed his mother in a fight outside the house with her pimp. She screamed at him that Edrina was his and began strangling the girl in front of him. As onlookers pried the baby away, Tiequon was "hollering, yelling, and crying."

When Tiequon was five, Sondra turned up the gas on the stove and left the children alone. Tiequon took his siblings, one by the hand, the other in his arms, and led them through the rain to his nearby grandmother's house.

Of this period in Tiequon's life, a psychiatrist would later write:

Sondra was Tiequon's initial, primary attachment figure; the person who represented physical and emotional safety. Children like Tiequon are placed in an impossible bind by this type of negative and unreliable attachment: to survive, they must form an emotional attachment to a parent like Sondra, despite the parent's unreliability, despite the abandonments, and despite the abuse they suffer at the hands of the parent. The pain is enormously magnified, because it is inflicted by the very person to whom he had to turn to help him survive the pain. Abused children like Tiequon experience an excruciating conflict as they try somehow to integrate the fact that the abusive parent is both the source of their pain and their only hope for comfort.

In 1971, following another incident, the three children were removed from Sondra's custody. For the next five years they lived with their great-grandmother.

Her home was located on West Seventy-Seventh Street, a well-tended block of green lawns and trimmed hedges. Here Tiequon and his siblings received solid material support from their well-off great-grandmother.

Psychologically, however, the move from Sondra's to Ellsworth's was jarring, going from a home of chaos, violence, and unpredictability into a hypercontrolled environment.

Impressions of Ellsworth as a caretaker varied. "A wonderful little old lady" and a "fine law-abiding citizen," or "Wicked Picket" and "Shotgun Annie," based upon her reported habit of collecting rent at the barrel of a gun.

Ellsworth was described by relatives as "firm and rigid," "not an affectionate person, [she] did not give the children the care and attention they needed." Another stated that "Annie's house was not a loving, cheerful place." The home was further described as "grim, so much like a prison and I was so lonely that I could hardly wait to get to school." Lights could not be turned on at night without permission, nor could the bathroom be used, with the children told to go in a pot.

Ellsworth was said to have a temper, using physical beatings and threats of violence to impose discipline. Recalls a family member, "Annie was more than strict with Tiequon, Demontray, and Edrina.

She switched them with branches from the backyard trees for making noise in the house or letting the dog out."

Tiequon's uncle Roosevelt also spent time at Ellsworth's home and frequently disciplined Tiequon with "physical whippings or beatings." Family members also recalled that Ellsworth told Tiequon and his siblings "that no one in the family loved or cared about them or wanted them and that she was the only one who would take them."

During this time, Tiequon's friends described him as "depressed" and "empty," "as if he were only tolerating life." A second-grade teacher recalled him as "very quiet," "a listless learner." A relative stated that "as Tiequon grew older he seemed to care little about whether or not he survived. His friends and other neighborhood kids felt that he lived a sad and isolated existence."

————

Throughout his childhood, school was always a struggle for Tiequon. He entered the Western Avenue School in October 1970, when he was two months shy of five. School was already three weeks under way, and Tiequon was the youngest child in the class.

An educational psychologist with the Los Angeles Unified School District said that Tiequon "seems to have entered school before he was mature enough to learn. Immaturity seems to have hindered academic growth." His kindergarten teacher likewise commented that he had "difficulty adjusting to school." This was exacerbated by chronic absenteeism. Tiequon was present for twenty-nine days, absent for seventy-three for his first semester in kindergarten.

Despite such "difficulties," Tiequon was promoted to the first grade, where the problems continued. His first-grade teacher described him as "extremely immature—unable to do first grade work." She referred him for "EMR [educationally mentally retarded] testing." The teachers' "custom and practice is to consider a student to be extremely immature if he is easily upset and quick to cry." The high rate of absenteeism continued, with the first-grade teacher calling it "indicative of a highly unstable life."

Again, despite the problems, Tiequon was advanced to the second grade. While his life became more stable and his attendance improved dramatically while he lived with Ellsworth, his academic struggles continued. In the second grade, his teacher, referring to his standardized test scores, stated that they were "extraordinarily low and indicated he lagged far behind grade level." By the end of second grade he was considered a "very slow learner—nonreader, no number concepts." At this point it was recommended that Tiequon repeat the second grade, with his teacher stating: "In my entire teaching career, I have recommended that a student be retained to repeat the same grade level only two times. Tiequon was one of those two students."

The EMR was viewed by his teacher as a last resort, as it was "terribly stigmatizing for a student at such a young age. It can cause a child to be teased by his peers and, even if not teased, to lose confidence and self-esteem because he knows something is 'wrong' with him."

When he was given the Wechsler Intelligence Scale for Children (WISC), an IQ test measuring the child's capacity, his WISC was 95, and his full-scale IQ 94. Both put him in the average range of general intelligence. This suggested that there was nothing "internally wrong with Tiequon's brain" that was "causing his disabilities, but that a poor, chaotic or abusive home environment, lack of encouragement or help from home, or social problems were most likely the cause." He was found by an examining doctor for his EMR referral to have a "short attention span" and "lack of self control."

Moved on to the third grade after a second year of second, he tried hard, his teacher said, but "was slow to grasp new concepts." In the fourth grade his teacher expressed surprise that he "was not in a special education class," as he was "unable to read a complete sentence."

In the fifth grade he would shift between two schools, as his mother took him back for several months, before losing him to emergency foster care. Ellsworth was subsequently granted legal custody.

When he was eleven he ran away to his grandmother Audrey Martin's house. This house had neither Sondra's abuse, nor Ellsworth's restrictions. It was a "freewheeling," "hell-raising" place with parties, and strangers constantly crashing out. The social worker for Tiequon's brother, Demontray, classified the house as "unsuitable for placement."

He attended the Elysian Heights Elementary School for one month of sixth grade before returning to Ellsworth for the rest of his final year at the 74th Street School. Throughout this time he remained "academically below grade level in all areas."

———

Friends described Tiequon as "always in motion when we were in grade school, doing gymnastics on the way to school." A teacher said, "Tiequon played unusually hard and exerted himself vigorously physically on the playground."

Another elementary school teacher: "At the time I had Tiequon as a student, I noted that he was very aggressive on the playground. . . . He was easily offended. At the 74th Street School, disputes, disagreements, or name-calling were settled physically on the playground. It was important in that neighborhood for a kid to stick up for himself and fight. Otherwise, he might be constantly picked on and subjected to harassment. This was just the way disputes were settled."

When Tiequon reached junior high, he attended Horace Mann. Reports on his behavior conflicted.

The principal referred to Tiequon as a "very sweet, very quiet child," who "was reserved and withdrawn. He was the kind of kid you wanted to reach out to. He was not hostile."

At the same time, however, he was referred to the "Opportunity Classroom," for disruptive behavior. The Opportunity Classroom teacher recalled: "Shortly after I met him, I told my husband that I wished we could have him in our house for a while. Tiequon was emotionally needy and appeared to be someone lacking in affection. But he was also introverted and withdrawn." She remembered him leaning with his back against a wall, acting "guarded and watchful," carrying himself in a way that said "don't come near me."

At the time, Horace Mann Junior High had a notoriously poor reputation, described as a "violent snakepit," "downright dangerous," and a "battleground." A onetime student recalled, "Guns and knives were commonplace in the school. The campus security had no ability to maintain the peace." "It was a place to earn combat stars and stripes, rather than to do serious studying." Another reported, "The junior high school Tiequon and I went to, Horace Mann, was more a war zone or a gladiator school than a place to learn academics . . . at age twelve, my childhood was over."

In Tiequon's words, "When you walk up you're checking everyone and everywhere. When you'd be waiting for classes you'd keep moving and observing. It could cost you your life if you don't observe. The school was open ground." Tiequon said such conditions applied to the classroom as well. "You'd never let yourself be absorbed in what was going on in the class, you'd never let down your guard. You can't live like that. There are people just lying in wait for you to be slipping like that."

A peer from Horace Mann said that Tiequon was "challenged more often than others by kids in the neighborhood, in part because of his green eyes, light skin, and reddish hair. While being light-skinned might have been a positive thing in Caucasian neighborhoods, it was not an advantage in our neighborhood. That, plus having no parents who could or wanted to have him live with them, caused him to come up hard and he had to learn to protect himself early."

Donald Bakeer, a teacher at Horace Mann, commented that most of the male students "were afraid, had no one to turn to, and diverted energy away from school and learning into protecting themselves."

Previously, the *Los Angeles Times* reported, teachers at Horace Mann singled out the school as a security risk, threatening to strike because of "the severity and frequency of the violence," and said action needed to be taken to "protect them and their students."

Given this environment, only the least qualified and inexperienced teachers were willing to test their luck at Horace Mann. Thus teachers without skills held the children to very low standards, which in turn produced very poor work. Bakeer stressed that "Tiequon's teachers had very low expectations of him and therefore, Tiequon had low expectations of himself."

Further, a law required that half the teachers be white, in a school that was 90 percent black. The teachers, not from South Central, were often scared, and simply wanted to get through the day and move on to a different school as soon as possible. They therefore "tolerated behavior from the students that they would not have tolerated from their own children."

As a classmate of Tiequon's noted: "The majority of teachers at Mann were white, and many had given up on trying to teach us anything. Drugs and alcohol were widely available. Marijuana and PCP (usually known as 'sherm') were easy to get on campus."

In an attempt to buffer this environment, some at Horace Mann reached out to the students. Homeroom teacher Donald Bakeer, because of Tiequon's skills, made him captain of the basketball team.

Bakeer said that the gap between Tiequon's talent level and the next-best player was massive. This caused problems. Tiequon hogged the ball, refused to pass to lesser players or involve them in the games, and ran the show on the court, ignoring Bakeer's coaching. Bakeer eventually felt forced to remove Tiequon as captain.

Bakeer later reflected that this was very damaging to Tiequon, "and hurt him deeply." "The basketball team and our relationship were very important to Tiequon. Shortly after losing the position as captain he stopped coming to school. I then heard from other students that Tiequon was drafted into the Crips."

The assistant dean at Horace Mann focused on the lack of an appropriate father figure for Tiequon, stating that "a biological father or other adult male who could set expectations and a standard of conduct for his children was especially important for the boys in the community."

Tiequon's alienist would later conclude, "Tiequon began to find the nurturance, acceptance, and sense of belonging he needed from his peers. His community was full of similarly neglected, abused, and brutalized youths who came together to fill the vacuum left by the disintegration of their families and schools."

While accounts vary, a change was noted in Tiequon sometime between the sixth and eighth grades. Some in the neighborhood recalled that by age eleven he had already established a reputation as a tough kid who had the backing of an older group. Other sources indicate that the change occurred later, around thirteen years old. Undisputed is the fact that by age fourteen Tiequon was wearing gang clothing and colors and immersed in the gang lifestyle. He quit attending school in the ninth grade.

28

SO DRIVE

Back in judge Boren's courtroom, the prosecutor concluded his opening statement, and the first witnesses were called.

My family heard the evidence: the palm print, the ballistics, the eyewitness testimony of Webb and Driver, the neighbors from across the street. Then came the autopsy photos and Norris told us we might want to leave the courtroom. We did.

My brother Neal testified to having fought with the shooter, whom he saw from behind, holding a rifle. Neal described him as a black male, twenty to thirty-five years old, five feet, eleven inches tall, well built, with a dark complexion. According to Neal the man had some kind of blue object on his head, perhaps headphones, and wore dark blue pants.

Ivan testified regarding his quick glance at a black man holding a long gun. Ivan described the man as about five feet ten, twenty-five to thirty-five years old, with a dark complexion and short hair. Ivan also testified that the intruder had earphones on, wore a dress shirt with buttons, and also wore dark blue jeans.

Later in the case the defense would make hay of the survivors' descriptions.

———

Ida Moore and Delisa Brown testify to the van ride to our house, then the escape.

A minute or two after CW returns to the van, Cox comes running and jumps in. He holds a rifle.

As he pulls the sliding door shut, he says, "I just blew the bitch's head off, so drive."

All three men sit in the back. They tell Moore to floor it. She speeds toward Main, where she makes a right.

CW directs her to Vermont and Gage.

Other than directions, there is no conversation. Eventually CW tells her to stop at Jack's Vermont Club.

CW exits the van and enters the club.

He comes back out, tells Cox and Burns to come in. CW still holds the pistol, Cox the rifle.

Moore is told to ditch the van.

At 9 a.m., Brown listens to news of the killings on the radio and calls CW for instructions. He tells her to drive his Fiat to the Vermont Club.

Brown parks at the gas station next door. CW hands the rifle over a fence to Cox, who puts it in the Fiat's trunk. Cox drives the car, with Brown in the passenger seat, to Tenth Avenue. He takes a dark jacket from the backseat, retrieves the rifle from the trunk, and wraps it in the jacket. He disappears into an apartment complex, then returns empty-handed.

Cox then drives to his home and Brown goes with him. She watches him comb his hair and put on a shirt. He drives Brown to Moore's house, drops her off, and drives away.

Later on that same day, CW gives Brown twenty dollars. He wears new clothes and new jewelry.

CW tells Moore not to drive the van, that he will paint it for her. He warns Moore and Brown to keep quiet or he will kill them.

———

James Kennedy testified that on the morning of August 31, 1984, Tiequon Cox showed up at the apartment complex on Tenth Avenue in Hyde Park and handed him an M-1 carbine rifle wrapped in a black jacket.

First Cox told Kennedy to get rid of the gun, then he told him to destroy it.

Cox also told Kennedy to have his sister, Shanta, whom Cox was dating, wash the black jacket because it had gunpowder on it.

———

Perry Kendrix testified that in the early afternoon of August 31, 1984, he worked for Figueroa Automobile, and that Cox came to the dealer and bought a 1975 yellow Cadillac for $3,000 in cash. Kendrix saw Cox pull mostly $20 bills and some $100 bills from his pocket.

———

District Attorney Norris's closing argument highlighted the slaughter inside the house, as he called for the jury to remember the victims in their final hour, remember them as they were in life.

> The two boys, Damon and Damani, are lying just as they were sleeping before they were executed in bed.
>
> Obviously, Damani had fallen off [the bed] in the night, and was sleeping there in exactly the same place that he was sleeping when he was executed.
>
> Damon was lying just like you see the head there, just as if he were a sleeping young boy of eight. . . .
>
> And Dietra, likewise with the photo of Dietra, when you examine that—

At this point the district attorney is interrupted.

"Liar!" a woman yells.

It is Sondra Holt, Tiequon Cox's mother.

After the outburst, a bailiff tells Holt that she must leave.

As she is escorted from the courtroom, Cox glowers at the bailiff.

"They better not touch her," he says.

———

It is August 30, 1970. Tiequon Cox is four years old. His mother's pimp-boyfriend enters the house, catching Cox's mother in bed with a neighbor.

Tiequon and his two younger siblings are inside the house. From their room they hear a beating—whacks, thuds, their mother's screams.

Slamming the bedroom door, the boyfriend walks out of the house. A friend of the neighbor confronts the boyfriend and shoots him in the neck. He bleeds to death on the front doorstep.

———

Several months later, on December 15, 1970, Tiequon, just turned five, is outside playing. He visits a neighbor's house. What look like little red candies are scattered across a coffee table. The boy grabs a handful and eats them.

When Tiequon returns home, his mother, noticing that he looks sickly, forces him to vomit. The little candies were "red devils," a barbiturate. His mother runs next door and attacks the woman who left the pills within her child's reach, then returns home. Neighbors call the police.

There is banging on the door. His mother tells Tiequon not to open the door, but he does so anyway. His mother stands in the kitchen holding a knife. Tiequon crouches by her side. His little sister Edrina sits in a nearby high chair. An officer draws his revolver and orders his mother to drop the knife. His mother yells at the officers, calling them "motherfucking pigs," telling them they will have to kill her before she will surrender.

She finally drops the knife, but as they attempt to place her in handcuffs, she swings wildly, clawing and scratching, as they put her in a choke hold. When the police struggle to subdue his mother, Edrina is knocked from her high chair. Tiequon screams and tries to fight the officers as they wrestle his mother to the floor. A neighbor comes to pick up the children. His mother is taken to jail.

———

Early in the following year, 1971, Tiequon, still five years old, and his younger siblings are taken by their mother to visit their grandfather. Sondra and her father are drinking and begin to fight violently. Her father picks her up and holds her over a flaming gas stove, burning her face and hair.

———

Later that same year, Tiequon's mother goes over to her boyfriend's house. She finds him in bed with another woman and a fight breaks out. The boyfriend stabs her repeatedly in the stomach with a knife. She staggers home and collapses on her front porch, blood flowing from her wounds. Tiequon watches as she is taken away in an ambulance.

———

Back in the Criminal Courts Building in downtown Los Angeles, Cox was being led back to the holding cell on the fourteenth floor.

Memories of his mother's pain created in Cox an intense fear for her safety, as well as hatred and mistrust of the police and authority figures.

He came to "understand very early" that there was "something wicked about the presence of the police, something unjust," that they were "barbaric," "mean," and "cruel."

Now, as the bailiff placed Cox into the holding cell, he told him that he, the bailiff, was in charge of the courtroom. While in lockup, Cox said that if he were not in handcuffs he would "take care of the situation."

Based upon the bailiff's account, Judge Boren stated that he was going to replace the leg brace on Cox.

Boren called before him the bailiff, who stated:

As I was taking the defendant downstairs I explained to him . . . that his mother was creating a disturbance, and that I would ask her or anybody else to leave the courtroom if I felt that it was necessary.

And he said he didn't give a fuck; he didn't give a fuck about me; he didn't give a fuck about anything.

And as he was leaving the courtroom he said he didn't give a fuck about the deputies that were here. Gave them the same type of stare that he gave me after his mother was ejected.

And he says, "Well, I don't want to talk to you. I don't want to hear what you have to say."

The judge then allowed Cox to speak. It was one of the few times he ever spoke during the proceedings.

COX: Okay, when the man addressed my mother, he didn't have to come off so harsh to her. We will see tomorrow if I have this brace on. I let them put this brace on. I cooperated. Ain't no more cooperation with the brace.

JUDGE BOREN: Does that mean that you are going to cause—

COX: I am going to cause problems about this brace. I don't like wearing this brace. Whatever I have to go through, I will go. I don't like wearing this brace. There is no need for it. As long as I am not provoked, I am all right. When I am provoked, then I let it go.

JUDGE BOREN: I am going to order that the handcuff be removed. Leg brace will remain today, and will not be put on tomorrow, unless something else comes to light.

Well, I assume, Mr. Cox, that when you talk about "provoked," you mean more than deciding something is just merely offensive to you?

COX: What the DA says, that doesn't bother me. I mean, the deputies and how they act, and show respect, that is what I mean. When I am provoked; one of them causes me problems, or something that disturbs me.

JUDGE BOREN: They have very serious responsibilities here with respect to security, that they take very seriously, and I—I have to take very seriously . . . so I hope you understand that.

COX: I understand they don't have to kill me but one time.

Following this hearing, the prosecutor concluded his closing argument, stating that the four dead family members, all shot in the head, exhibited a clear intent to kill on the part of the accused.

Norris stressed the importance of timing, that after Cox killed Mrs. Alexander, CW, who was in the house, was "either startled or shocked, or whatever, but that he departs." At this point there was the pause in the shooting testified to by Lashawn Driver. It was then that Cox walked back down the hallway, into the front bedroom, and began shooting again. Driver, "the only witness really standing outside there," saw CW come down the driveway, as he had left the house before Cox got into the front bedroom. Venus Webb likewise positively identified Cox as the last man coming out.

> Now, let me suggest what Cox is. Whatever these two other folks are: Horse, he's standing outside holding the van; and CW has the information of setting it up and so forth and so on. Cox is the killer. He's the one that they get to do the job right.

As evidence of Cox's lack of compassion, Norris stated:

> On the day that he kills these four people, on the day that he kills the two kids, the eight-year-old, and the thirteen-year-old, not only does he go down and continue his operation on 10th Avenue, but he goes to Kendrix's used car lot. . . .
>
> And if the [three defendants] should have those Nazi storm trooper uniforms on, then this man over here, Mr. Cox, ought to wear the skull and crossbones because he was the executioner.
>
> . . . it is Mr. Cox who is the most culpable of them all. Had it not been for Mr. Cox, would any of these four people not be alive today? Let me suggest that Horse and CW didn't have the guts or the horrible mentality to go in and pull that trigger in a way that Mr. Cox did.
>
> Let me suggest to you that the entire people of the county of

Los Angeles, any American is in danger when that reign of terror such as Mr. Cox can get out and walk into a house.

This is walking into a house of innocent people. Walking into a house that could be yours, walking in and murdering everybody in the entire house. That's the kind of execution-murder that we're talking about.

Now, Mr. Cox, when he walked in there, when he got out of that van and he took [the rifle], he had a choice and he made a decision when he got out of that van and he walked in and when he walked in and pulled the trigger three times on Ebora. . . .

Give Mr. Cox what he earned on that morning and taking those lives of those four people. Give him what he earned. Give him the four convictions of first degree murder and the finding of special circumstances. . . .

[I]t is now your duty to do that, to do that for justice, not only for the victims, but, above all, for justice.

Thank you.

THE COURT: Any argument, Mr. Cook?
MR. COOK: Submit it.
THE COURT: Submitted? All right.

————

As we awaited the verdict, I could not stop brooding over the fact that the only thing that triggered feeling in the otherwise detached Cox was the fear of harm to his mother.

The sentimental breakdown seen in even the most hardened thug is universal when it comes to their mothers. An ex–gang member in a recovery group reflected, "It was a trip, seeing all those great gangsters crying like kids. You know, they be going through the program hard as a rock, but then they break down when they start speaking about their moms."

I knew the feelings well. I understood them. I shared them. I had seen them a thousand times. Especially in the black community, where for boys without fathers their mothers are all: core, anchor, and guiding life-force.

But never will I understand how a young man so protective of *his* mother could so heartlessly murder mine.

Forever will the words ring in my ears: "I just blew the bitch's head off, so drive."

29

DON'T CRY

In 1984, TIEQUON COX was an eighteen-year-old member of the Rolling Sixties. While his official entry into the gang remains murky, it likely occurred sometime between the age of eleven and thirteen.

From a young age, Cox was taken under the wing of the original generation of the Rolling Sixties, most of whom were five or six years older.

According to legend, the Rolling Sixties formed at Crenshaw High School on Halloween of 1975. They were an offshoot of the original West Side Crips, formed under Tookie Williams five years earlier. This splintering and factionalizing of the Crips would only accelerate over the coming years and would profoundly affect the futures of Tookie Williams and Tiequon Cox.

One of the first generation of Rolling Sixties was an individual with the gang name of Big Fee. Big Fee mentored the young Cox in the ways of the streets, and as his protégé, Cox became Little Fee.

The origins of the name "Fee" are also clouded. Some say it came from number twenty-six on the periodic table of the elements, iron, thus Big Iron and Little Iron. Others claim it comes from the prefix of feline, Big Cat and Little Cat. A third theory is that Fee refers to money, the taking of a fee for a service. Cox said "Fee" referred to getting paid.

Little Fee (sometimes "Li'l Fee"), because he hung out with the older generation, quickly gained respect on the streets. Cox began referring to this peer group as his "family," recalling that as "a young boy these people gave me special attention," because they saw "good material" in him and "protected" him. "They might walk you home at night," and "do things that people do for each other when they care."

Cox said they "respected each other," and "were loyal." As to those with whom he was close, Cox said they "were like older brothers" to him, "they took a special interest" in him, and were there when he "needed them." "It was just understood," Cox said, "you were young and inexperienced and you needed someone to look after you."

The need for someone to "look after you" on the streets of South Central, Cox said, was made clear to him at an early age. When he was ten, he recalled standing in front of his house as a group of Bloods physically assaulted his mother. He remembered feeling so helpless as he watched, unable to protect her.

By the time he turned eighteen, in December 1983, Cox was known as a "muscle man" of the gang, though he would later claim this was "not my choice." Cox's image on the streets was also bolstered when he became one of the first gang members to tattoo his neck.

During the spring and summer of 1984, following his release from CYA, Cox gained a reputation on the streets as an "enforcer."

His own attorney would later state, under oath, that members of Cox's family told him that Cox had killed a dozen people.

On January 21, 1986, the jury, after deliberating for just two hours, convicted Tiequon Cox on all four counts of first-degree murder, and found the special circumstances to be true.

In the penalty phase, Norris put on evidence of Cox's prior crimes.

It is April 7, 1981, at Hyde Park Boulevard and Eighth Avenue. Cox is fifteen. He and two others beat thirteen-year-old James Love, and fourteen-year-old Gerald Penney, in the face with a broom handle. Two dollars, a gold chain, and a comb are taken from Penney. Cox takes sixty cents from Love's pocket. Cox punches them both in the face several times.

On the same day, twelve-year-old Preston Taylor gets off the school bus and waits to cross the railroad tracks in Hyde Park. Cox comes across the street and punches him in the face, knocking him to the ground. Cox asks if he has any money. Taylor says no and Cox digs in his pockets, taking a dime. Cox then kicks the boy as he lies curled up on the ground.

A man walking down Eighth Avenue tells Cox to stop. Cox threatens him with a broom handle.

It is midafternoon, May 18, 1981. Rosalyn Lebby drives her brown Pontiac to pick up her eight-year-old son, Kareem, at the Hyde Park Elementary School. Her "average little black poodle" rides in the back.

She parks in front of the school and her son climbs in the passenger side. His door remains open.

At this point a green Nova pulls alongside. Two young men get out of the car and approach Lebby. Tiequon Cox walks to the passenger side holding a silver gun and gets between the open door and the car. The other man comes around to the driver's side. He orders Lebby out of the car. She asks for her dog and her purse. The second man tells her to leave them. Cox, holding the gun, tells Lebby, "I got your ass."

Lebby's son sits in the passenger seat looking at his mother. She tells him to get out of the car, then takes his hand and runs across the street.

The two men drive her car around the block toward Crenshaw, then circle back into a nearby driveway. Lebby returns to her car, attempting to retrieve her dog. Cox gets out and walks toward her with the gun. He says nothing, but stares her down in a fashion that says "back off." Lebby turns around and returns to the school.

Officers in the Southeast Division Patrol Unit pursue Lebby's stolen car. They first sight it at Sixty-Ninth Street and Seventh Avenue. As the car heads south, the officers notice two occupants. As they pull alongside, in a marked car, the passenger jumps out and runs into a backyard.

The driver, Cox, tears off, leading police on a half-hour chase, reaching speeds of eighty to ninety miles an hour: "Southbound on Crenshaw over to Manchester, westbound on Manchester to Prairie, around the Forum, Hollywood Park, into Hawthorne, back over onto Normandie, down Century, down into Gardena through several small residential areas . . . then back up north to the exact same location where the original pursuit [began]."

From that point he takes another circle, following the same general course that he took the first time.

Along the route, Cox causes several accidents, colliding with a car at Manchester and Prairie, slamming into parked cars on Fifth and Florence, finally smashing head-on into a telephone pole on 78th and Western. At this point he runs from the car, north up Western. An officer chases him, fights with him, subdues him, and takes him into custody. A loaded chrome-plated revolver is recovered from the wrecked car.

For this crime, Cox is sent to California Youth Authority in July 1981. He would spend the next thirty-three months at CYA, known on the streets as "Gladiator School."

———

Upon entering CYA, Cox was told that it would provide a stable environment where he could complete his education and "learn usable skills in order to divert him from a path of gang violence."

Upon entry, Cox was fifteen years old and one of the youngest wards. He was five feet seven, weighed 136 pounds, and was far behind his age and grade level academically. His initial evaluation labeled him as "gang-oriented" but stated that "he did not appear delinquent in his behavior."

In December of 1981, he was transferred to the facility at Paso Robles in the Santa Lucia portion of the Coastal Mountain Range. Cox's first impressions were that the place was "hostile, dangerous, madness." Wards were housed in large dormitories. There was no privacy. No opportunity to let down one's guard. He saw other boys slashed with razors and homemade knives. He saw them beat on each other. He saw a boy get his teeth kicked out. There was no help to be had. He quickly realized the rules of survival: trust no one, rely only upon yourself, be vigilant, watch your back.

At Paso Robles, Cox was constantly tested, challenged to defend himself; this was simply the way of YA. Show weakness and your food and possessions are taken, you will be picked on, dominated.

In describing Cox, one of his counselors stated: "He was quite small and thin compared to the other wards, had unusual green eyes, and had an engaging, genuine smile, which I saw only after many months as his counselor." In an effort to be able to better protect himself, Cox began an intense weightlifting regime. By March 1983 he had gained thirty pounds of muscle.

A counselor at Paso Robles found Cox to be making progress, "from a gang-identified, impulsive kid" into an "honor ward."

In the spring of 1983, Cox was moved to Chino's Youth Training Center (YTS). At Chino, wards were housed in cells, not dormitories, the fences covered with razor wire, the furniture bolted down. Cox's progress was again noted as positive. He received no negative behavior reports.

By the end of August 1983, Cox, age seventeen, was moved to the Preston School of Industry. Upon entry Cox witnessed a ward "get cut up bad with a scalpel." For Cox, "Paso Robles was bad, Preston deadly."

Despite positive references to his development, at Preston two problems continued to dog him: gang identity and his habit of fighting to solve problems.

He spoke, however, of changing his life on the outside, of not returning to the streets. He continued attending school at Preston, receiving B's, C's, and a GED. He continued lifting weights and by January 1984 had put on another fifteen pounds of muscle. At this point he was recommended for parole.

On March 18, 1984, Cox walked away from CYA.

———

Cox said that upon release he had hopes. These lasted "for at least days or weeks." He thought about a college athletic scholarship to play baseball. He wanted to reunite the biological family and get his younger siblings out of foster care.

But he said the dreams quickly died, captured by the hopeless reality of the old streets: the graffiti, the debris, the enemies, the police, the testing and challenges, the "madness" of South Central. Now eighteen, he carried a reputation, and rival gang members sought revenge, while the police harassed him as a hardened criminal. Over the following six months he was repeatedly stopped and detained.

Cox felt "I still needed to do a lot of growing up, but I just could not turn my back on my brothers who needed me."

————

Back in the penalty phase in the Criminal Courts Building, the defense attempted to humanize Cox in an effort to save his life. They also sought to show that his upbringing, schooling, and environment made him what he was.

Donald Bakeer, Cox's eighth-grade homeroom teacher at Horace Mann Junior High, drew close to Tiequon, feeling him in need of a "male support image."

Bakeer wanted Tiequon to live, he cared for him, and considered him "a victim of the environment, system, whatever." For Bakeer, Tiequon "never really had a chance, didn't really make a decision. It was the environment at that time that decided for the kids."

Tiequon's great-grandmother, Annie Ellsworth, eighty-five at trial, mentioned that it was Tiequon's twentieth birthday as she testified.

Ellsworth said that since "Ti" was born, she had raised him. She put Ti in the Boy Scouts, and his brother Demontray in the Cub Scouts. She bought all three children bicycles and clothes and gave them an allowance. When Ti was fourteen, he left for her daughter's house, after Ellsworth had disciplined him for failing to pick his little brother up from school. Ellsworth said she laid down laws of the house, and that Ti may have found her too strict. After serving his time at CYA, the authorities told Ellsworth that Ti wanted to come and live with her. She had a detached room for him where he could stay in the rear of the house.

Since Ti had been in custody on this case, Ellsworth said he had called her daily. In one call he told her, "Grandma, regardless of what happen, I want you to know I never hurt nobody in my life." He also told her that if he had stayed home with her and listened to her he wouldn't have been in the predicament he was in now.

She concluded her testimony, "Oh, my God, I want him to live. Because he is so young. He is so young. And I know he isn't guilty." Audrey Martin, Tiequon's grandmother, wanted him to live "[b]ecause that's my grandson and I love him."

Demontray Cox, seventeen at trial, testified that when he was twelve or thirteen, he and Tiequon ran away from their mother's house because she was drunk and abusive, hitting Tiequon and throwing a vase at him. The three kids then lived with their great-grandmother, but Tiequon again ran away, because she was "too strict on us, keeping us in the backyard and stuff." Demontray described her as "pretty tight," but felt she "wanted what was best for us kids."

While growing up, Demontray saw Tiequon's father, James Cox, a few times. When asked if James Cox was his father, Demontray responded, "I don't know, really."

Demontray wanted Tiequon to live, because "He's my brother and I love him," "I don't believe he did it," and "He's too young to die."

Tiequon's fifteen-year-old sister, Edrina, testified that the kids were taken from their mother, but well cared for by their great-grandmother. She said Tiequon had been a nice brother and she wanted him to live.

When Edrina began to cry on the stand, Tiequon spoke out from the counsel table, "Don't cry. Don't cry. Be strong."

30

LET HIM DIE ON
THE ROCKS

In a capital case the prosecution and defense get two arguments each. Norris went first, followed by Cook and his co-counsel, Joanne Rotstein.

When speaking of our family, Norris stressed how our mother endured the challenges of raising eleven children to adulthood, only to be "rewarded for her good work by being blown apart by Mr. Cox." He continued: "I think that is much more telling than what Mr. Cox may ever suffer."

Norris further dismissed the idea that the gangs and environment made Cox do it. Regarding the arguments that "all the kids are into it," and "there but for the grace of God go I," the district attorney responded that all the other kids "didn't walk in and take the life of four innocent people . . . it's Mr. Cox. Whether it is the gang; whether it is him, it is all part of that evil intent you have to have in order to do something like this.

"Imagine for one minute being there . . . on that hot August morning . . . and you picked up the body of Ebora, of Dietra, of Damon and Damani . . . and you saw the blood on your hands, and you knew that across the way is the man that killed all four of those people, Mr. Cox, I don't think there is any hard question what the proper penalty is, and that is death for Mr. Cox."

Joanne Rotstein argued:

The question in the penalty phase is whether or not Tiequon Cox is to be executed in the gas chamber at San Quentin.

The law didn't require that you actually make a factual determination on a verdict form as to who the actual shooter was.

Now in the guilt phase it was clear that Tiequon Cox was involved in the murders. You had his palm print on the footlocker. You knew he was in the house. The crime itself was not contested by the defense.

We didn't put on any evidence and we didn't argue. At the penalty phase now we're asking you to make a determination, make a factual determination as to who the shooter was, who pulled the trigger in that house.

As Rotstein argued that Cox was not the shooter, my sister Joan was overcome with emotion: "Goddamn it, he was the shooter. Goddamn it. I don't know why you're saying what you're saying. You know he did it."

Rotstein continued that the description by Neal and Ivan of the man with the rifle as having dark skin was consistent with CW and not with the light-skinned Cox.

And we know [CW] gets back first, because Ida and Lisa also see him return to the van first.

But why does he leave first?

Because he panicked. He's in a struggle with someone that's still alive [Neal], and he panics, because perhaps he's afraid that someone saw his identification, his face, what he was wearing.

Well, when does Cox leave his print on the footlocker?

After the man in control of this entire operation, after the man that orchestrates this entire incident leaves, Cox goes into the bedroom; leans down on the footlocker, and leaves his palm print.

He picks up the rifle that's knocked aside during the struggle.

Now, there is certainly evidence of CW's domination of the entire incident. CW not only dominated and controlled this escapade over to the Alexander house, but he dominated Ida.

Rotstein concluded by arguing that punishment and the protection of society would be accomplished through life without the possibility of parole, which would ensure that Cox would never get out of prison.

Cook likewise argued that CW was the shooter, based upon the descriptions, then focused on Cox's upbringing and the influence of gangs. He concluded by focusing on the weight of the decision facing the jury:

It is like you are going back there, like you are in a monastery by yourself, and you have to make this decision in your own heart.

Who gave you the power of life or death?

Think of how you got on this case. You are obviously . . . all on the jury registration list, so you are picked for a certain time and you are drawn by lot to come into this courtroom.

And then, after going through a long process you are the twelve people chosen.

Does this qualify you to decide who's going to live or die? Does this make you God . . . God's instrument in here taking a life?

If you are judged you are going to be judged as an individual.

You are not going to have the other eleven jurors with you and say, "Well why did you give this kid death when he probably wasn't the shooter, and he wasn't the shooter; when he really didn't have a chance anyway."

We are talking about an eighteen-year-old kid here. Can you be one hundred percent sure if you say death, and Tiequon takes that long walk to the gas chamber, and is choked on this gas, that you did the right thing?

Let's just assume Tiequon was standing at the edge of a cliff, and Judge Boren said to one of the jurors, it can be anyone of you twelve, or all of you individually . . . now if you want him to die, you go over and push him off the cliff, and let him fall two hundred feet and die on the rocks down there.

————

On February 18, 1986, the jury, after two days of deliberation, recommended that Tiequon Cox be sentenced to death.

Members of my family and our friends in court sobbed, "Thank you, Jesus."

Cox remained impassive as the verdict was read. When he left the courtroom, he kicked over a chair in anger.

Members of my family bowed in relief, and Geraldine, Damani's mother, collapsed. I carried her from the courtroom.

None of us had any doubt. The defense simply tried to exploit any ambiguity in the split-second descriptions given by my traumatized, just-awakened brother and nephew, neither of whom saw the shooter's face in the dim morning light.

Further, the sequence of events recounted by Neal contradicts the defense claims. Neal said he wrestled with the shooter, causing the gun to drop to the floor. The shooter then picked up the rifle and hit him in the head with it. The only reasonable explanation: the same person who fired the rifle, picked up the rifle, hit Neal in the head with the rifle, and fled the house carrying the rifle. That person was Tiequon Cox.

Further still, it wasn't CW who said, "I just blew the bitch's head off."

For Judge Boren, the wrong-shooter defense entered his "binder of red herrings," theories based upon mistaken eyewitness identifications that just didn't add up.

For Sterling Norris it was "a very justified verdict." "Cox has to be one of the most vicious criminals I've handled."

————

I got Tiequon Cox. We shared a past: southern kin, South Central kids, filled with both talent and rage.

I felt sympathy for the boy. He was traumatized by his mother. He barely knew his father. I pitied his little brother and sister who looked up to him, his great-grandmother who tried to raise him.

Our lives crossed. I wish I had acted. But others tried and got rejected.

His great-grandmother provided a stable home with resources. She enrolled him in Boy Scouts and sports programs. She expected responsibility, that he walk his kid brother home from school. She restricted him when he let her down. Her leash was tight. If that explained crime, every southern son would live behind bars.

Likewise, the caring teacher who saw potential and provided guidance and opportunities was cast aside.

The environment was bad. I knew it well. But no one made him join the gang. No one forced on him the role of assassin. The majority of the neighborhood shuns the gangs. He embraced the gang and shunned other options.

And what about sympathy for the children of August 31, never allowed to awaken? How about Ivan and Neal, traumatized for life? What about Gerald Penney, James Love, Preston Taylor, Rosalyn Lebby and her little boy?

He chooses his victims, picks easy targets. The fights are never fair, the odds never even. He proves himself by preying on the defenseless while he is heavily armed.

Tiequon Cox is no Horace Burns. Here there is no *Tiequon v. Fee*. This one is united. It's simple. He just doesn't care. If it stands in his way, down it goes. Never open up—Rolling Sixties till the end.

I pity the child. But the man destroyed my family. I have sympathy. I carry guilt. But it's tough to kindle mercy for one who shows others none.

————

On April 30, 1986, Judge Boren sentenced Tiequon Aundray Cox to death, finding the jury's decision justified given the overwhelming evidence.

Judge Boren said that Cox "would kill again without provocation" if given the opportunity, and called Cox "one of the most dangerous killers" he had ever encountered. While motive was not spelled out during the trial, Boren stated that Cox committed the "cold-blooded" murders "in all likelihood for some kind of financial gain."

> It is the order of this court that you shall suffer the death penalty and that said penalty be inflicted within the walls of San Quentin State Prison in California in the manner prescribed by law and at a time to be fixed by this court in the warrant of execution on all counts.
>
> You are remanded to the care, custody and control of the Sheriff of Los Angeles County to be by him delivered to the Warden of the State Penitentiary at San Quentin, California within ten days from the date thereof.

————

I had numerous contacts within the San Quentin correctional staff. Over the coming years they would keep me informed of Cox's activities in prison.

During the Cox trial, Norris only hinted at the motive. Following the case he said that in the upcoming Williams trial, he would show that the killers received $60,000 for the contract killing of an entire family. But Norris declined to say why or by whom the murders were ordered.

31

THE GRAY GOOSE
TO THE AC

O<small>N</small> MAY 7, 1986, Tiequon Cox is transported from Los Angeles County Jail to San Quentin State Prison.

He is handcuffed, shackled, and chained to the floor of the "Gray Goose," a California Department of Corrections (CDC) bus. After driving up Highway 101 from Southern California, the bus turns onto Sir Francis Drake Boulevard and approaches the prison.

San Quentin Point is a promontory in Marin County. The weather is typical of Northern California: breezy, about sixty-five degrees.

The Gray Goose enters San Quentin at the West Gate. San Francisco Bay is on the right-hand side. Windsurfers dart across the choppy surf. A flock of pelicans glide low over the water. A ferry heads into Larkspur Landing, northbound from the city.

San Quentin is the oldest prison in the state, opened in 1852, just two years after California entered the union. The first inmates were housed on barges moored off the point. They were criminals from San Francisco's Barbary Coast days. Turned into a land-based facility in the 1860s, at the time it stood as California's largest public works project.

To this day, San Quentin retains its nineteenth-century character, more the Victorian-era fortification than a modern institution. The front entry resembles a castle, the gate slams shut with a medieval clang, and the original hospital façade within, which reads "1885," seems a relic from an Old West ghost town.

The prison is famous for its mess hall murals, painted by a Mexican-American inmate, Alfredo Santos, in the 1950s. Done in sepia tones in the Depression-era public works style, they trace California's history from its first settlers through World War II. Said to be made of shoe polish, and rumored to be haunted, the murals feature a woman's eyes that follow you wherever you go, a B-52 bomber that shifts perspective, and a cable car that changes direction as you walk past.

Like its murals, the prison's past residents provide a tour through California's history. Housing Wild West bandits like Black Bart, Prohibition-era gangsters such as Machine Gun Kelly, and 1960s radicals George Jackson and Huey Newton, the prison is now home to the latest generation of gangbangers and serial killers. Notably its gas chamber has seen the deaths of the red-light bandit Caryl Chessman in 1960 and Barbara Graham in 1955. It has stood dormant for the past twenty years.

As the bus carrying Tiequon Cox comes to a stop at a fork in the road within the prison, a low structure, known as the "boneyard," is on the left. This is where inmates are granted conjugal visits. After a short distance, the bus makes a right at the receiving warehouse.

It continues past the warehouse, then makes a left and arrives at the sally port at Five Wall. On the right is the exercise yard and baseball field. Dressed in blue CDC uniforms, inmates walk laps, do pull-ups, push-ups, stand around talking, politicking, scheming.

The bus drives along the field. It now passes by the "dungeon," an isolation unit resembling an ancient torture chamber. Inside it is dank and pitch-black. Iron rings hang from the ceiling, once used to suspend prisoners by their upraised hands, a reminder of the strappado used in the Spanish Inquisition. The dungeon was last used for solitary confinement in the 1940s.

Passing the dungeon, the Gray Goose finally comes to rest in front of R&R (receiving and release). Inside R&R the restraints are removed. Cox is subjected to a full unclothed body search. He is directed to lift his arms, open his mouth, lift his testicles, then bend over and spread his buttocks while giving several deep coughs. This is to ensure that the inmate is not "kiestering" anything in his anus, such as a knife, a shank, a "bonecrusher."

Cox is next placed in a cage and provided with his initial issuance, or "fishkit": boxers, a T-shirt and flip-flops, blue denim pants, and a blue chambray shirt. He is photographed and fingerprinted, then required to place a full handprint on the back of his sentencing document, which reads CONDEMNED.

He is checked to make sure there are no bruises or injuries and then given his medical clearance.

As a newly arrived condemned inmate, he is taken to the Adjustment Center, or AC, San Quentin's highest-security facility, a level 4, or supermax, structure. Within the Adjustment Center he will be assessed and assigned either a grade A or B condemned status, which will determine his housing.

The staff in the Adjustment Center sends two particularly large correctional officers for Cox's initial entrance. He is again placed in restraints, then walked across the lower yard, up the ramp, in front of the dungeon, and into the AC.

Upon arrival he is placed in a first-floor holding cell in the middle of the tier. The restraints are removed and he is again subjected to a full-body search. He is then dressed in boxers and a T-shirt.

A sergeant administers the initial interview. "You respect us, and we'll respect you. Otherwise things can go sideways." Correctional officers refer to this as the "come-to-Jesus conversation."

Again, the prisoner is placed in restraints and taken to his initial cell, first floor, south side.

The condemned prisoner will remain in the AC for at least thirty days after the initial assessment. He is then addressed by the warden, a second "come to Jesus." "We need you to 'program,'" the warden says. This means to fall in line and follow prison procedures. "You need to follow all of the protocols and not cause problems." The warden pauses to see that his words are sinking in, then concludes, "We have a no-warning-shot policy."

After his initial stay in the AC, Cox is assigned an "A" grade, which means he will leave the Adjustment Center and join the mainline population.

He will be transferred to the Condemned Unit housed in East Block. At just over twenty years old, Cox is the youngest member of California's death row population.

———

On Tuesday, November 4, 1986, Californians went to the polls. Incumbent governor George Deukmejian—unlike the nail-biter of 1982—won an easy rematch against Mayor Tom Bradley. Deukmejian ran a tough-on-crime law-and-order campaign in which he declared himself "the leading advocate for crime victims in our state." Deukmejian also aligned himself with other popular issues involving crime and punishment in California.

At the time, the death penalty experienced record-high approval in the state, with 85 percent of those polled expressing support. Deukmejian promised voters that if they reelected him and ousted three liberal justices opposing capital punishment, he would appoint judges reflecting the public will.

By a large margin voters gave the governor his wish. Chief Justice Rose Bird was removed from office. Appointed chief by Governor Jerry Brown in 1977, Bird became a lightning rod over her opposition to the death penalty. In what came to be known as Bird's "box score"—with sixty-one reversal votes in the sixty-one capital cases that crossed her desk—the chief justice failed to uphold a single death sentence. Also removed from the bench were Brown appointees Joseph R. Grodin and Cruz Reynoso, both of whom routinely voted with Bird in reversing capital convictions. Grodin was voted out by a margin of 57 to 43, Reynoso 60 to 40, and Bird an overwhelming 67 to 33. Before the November 4, 1986, election, no justice had been removed since the state constitution's amendment in 1934.

From the start, the campaign for Bird's ouster was hypercharged, with Deukmejian railing against her at nearly every campaign stop. Since her narrow escape on the 1978 ballot, conservatives eagerly sought her removal. Bird, on her part, highlighted her "backbone" and "integrity," stressing an independent judiciary's duty to cast votes in line with principles of justice when faced with mounting and hostile political pressure. Bird went after President Reagan's attorney general, Edwin Meese III, calling him a right-wing "bully boy" who was out to get her. She castigated Governor Deukmejian, claiming that he was impatient for executions and wanted to turn the Supreme Court of California into a "house of death" for his own political gain.

But the face of the campaign became Marianne Frazier, the mother of a murdered twelve-year-old girl. In television commercials Frazier sat next to a framed picture of her daughter and asked voters to remove the justices who had overturned the killer's death sentence. A political consultant active in the effort to remove the three liberal justices stated, "Too much attention has been paid to the needs of the criminals and not enough consideration has been given to the victims and the general public."

Following the ouster, Governor Deukmejian elevated conservative justice Malcolm Lucas to chief, and appointed conservative associate justices to fill the slots vacated by Grodin and Reynoso. It was the first time since the Great Depression that a Republican governor had the opportunity to appoint a majority of the California Supreme Court. Death penalty supporters and law-and-order advocates felt they finally had the court to enforce their will.

————

One month after the election, on December 7, 1986, Tiequon Cox was returned to the Adjustment Center for a conspiracy to assault staff. After yelling obscenities and threats at the yard gunman, Cox instructed another inmate to start kicking prison staff in order to create a diversion. At that point Cox stated that the rest of the inmates on the yard should rush the security fence and overtake the correctional officers.

This incident foreshadowed one of the most infamous in San Quentin's history.

32

AN AMERICAN TRAGEDY

Dᴜʀɪɴɢ ᴛʜᴇ ᴄᴀᴘɪᴛᴀʟ trial of Darren Charles Williams, "CW," the prosecutor for the first time revealed the motive behind the killings.

While much of the testimony was familiar from the first two trials—Ida and Delisa placed CW as the shot caller, Lashawn Driver identified Cox and Williams as coming from the house—Williams's statement to RHD detectives provided the linchpin for the prosecution.

On February 28, 1985, Detectives Crews and Miller followed Williams's father as he picked up his son in Richmond, California. Williams was then arrested, taken into custody at the Richmond police station, and interrogated. The tape-recorded interview lasted fifty minutes.

It was played for the jury in open court.

Williams spoke in a low, soft voice.

He flew up to the Bay Area from Los Angeles. He borrowed the money for the flight from his mother. He was in the Bay Area at the time working with "disturbed kids and people."

"I want to know who set you guys up, who you were supposed to hit," Crews said. "You said you were telling me that this girl that's crippled was shot at some business establishment. And she's suing the owner of the business establishment."

Williams hesitated, then said, "That's what I heard. I think something like sixty thousand dollars to whoever did it."

"Sixty thousand to—to shoot her? Did you ever see any of that money? You're shaking your head."

"I ain't never seen none of it—"

Crews cut Williams off.

"Horse is going to take a deal and end up doing a few years in the joint. That little shitbird's been sitting in county jail talking to everybody. He fuckin' talked to Kee-Kee. Kee-Kee's talked to us. He fuckin' talked to a guy in there who's doing federal time, getting ready to go to federal time. . . . He says, 'Hey, I'll go and testify that Horace Burns told me this.' And what do you think that Horse is going to do? Horse didn't do anything. Horse just sat in the van."

"I didn't do nothing," Williams said. "I know I'm going to do some time. I know that."

"Sure you're going to do some fuckin' time."

"I wasn't there."

"You keep saying no, I wasn't there, and what you're doing is you're stopping yourself from getting any possibility of a—a chance or to a deal. What I'm saying is we can talk to the DA and you assist us in this investigation, you won't get the death penalty. The more you cooperate, the better it looks in his eyes when it comes time for sentencing. So the judge, you know, if he's got a hard-on for you because four people were killed and two happened to be little kids, what's he going to do. And this thing about being in jail at the time, that ain't going to fuckin' fly. We checked you every way loose before we went out and got the warrant. You weren't in custody anywhere in this God's country."

"I was in jail. I got out that morning. I wasn't there."

"Okay, CW, okay, CW. Are you going to help me with trying to find this guy, you'll give us the name?"

"I don't know his name. I only know where they went to go get the stuff."

"Okay, where is that?"

"On Gage and Vermont at the Vermont Club."

———

From the jukebox, James Brown's "Sex Machine" blasts.

"Get up. Get on up."

Loud voices and a low ceiling of cigarette smoke hang over the club. Dice are slammed on the bar. The crack of pool balls cuts through the music.

"Get on up. Stay on the scene."

Off the dance floor, in the shadows, the tables are full. Two men go over a horse racing form. Others slam a round of shots. A woman wiggles in a man's lap, then inhales deeply. He wipes a bit of white powder from under her nose. He laughs. She giggles. Before the jukebox a mass of people dance.

"Like a sex machine. Get on up."

A man weaves out onto the floor, carrying drinks, Johnnie Walker Red, Chivas Regal, Seagram's VO.

It is close to midnight.

"The way I like it. Is the way it is."

A young woman named Valarie Taylor is celebrating her twenty-first birthday. She dances, takes another drink, continues dancing.

"Right on. Right on. Get on up."

And she dances some more.

The music pulses, the lights are dim. The pool balls crack. The dice slam. The voices grow louder, drunken, frantic, high.

"Like a sex machine."

Glasses clink. A man arrives at a table with a pitcher and fills four glasses. Cheers. The glasses clink. From the bar the dice slam.

"Get on up."

The dance floor throbs.

Crack. Slam. Smoke. Yells.

Crash at the bar. Broken glass. A fight. Two men throw haymakers.

"Right on. Right on." The music continues.

A pile of bodies writhes.

"Knife!" someone yells. "He's got a knife!"

A thud and a crash, as a chair shatters. A table is overturned. Another chair flies into the pile.

No more pool, dice. No more laughter.

Yells, screams. Broken glass.

"Get on up."

A deafening boom. A gunshot.

Screams, and a rush for the door.

"Shake your moneymaker. Shake your moneymaker."

Amid broken furniture, broken glass, puddles of ashes and spilled drinks, a young lady lies on the floor, motionless.

"Shake your moneymaker."

Smoke hangs above her. A lit cigarette lies at her side. It fizzles on the wet floor.

The bar empties. Outside screams, commotion, the sounds of people running.

The jukebox is cut.

The young woman lies still. She tries, but she can't.

A couple crouches over her.

A woman sobs.

On the floor the blood begins to pool.

Again she tries, but cannot move her legs.

———

"You don't know the guy's name?"

"I didn't have nothing to do with it. I didn't have nothing to do with picking up the money."

"How much did they get paid for it?"

"I think sixty thousand dollars."

"Sixty thousand dollars? What did those—what did those two guys do with sixty thousand dollars?"

"I don't know. I know Fee took and bought a new car around then."

"We know you ran out right when the first shots went off. And you may have been on your way out or whatever before the first shots went off. I want to know."

"See, just being there ain't going to cause me to go to jail, is it?" Williams asked.

"I don't know. You know, the DAs look at this, you know, a funny way. If you can prove to us that you changed your fuckin' mind and you were on the way out of the fuckin' house and wanted nothing to do with it before the second shots were fired, that's a completely different ball game, you know."

"See, I real—I don't really know what, what—I think they were supposed to go in and get the girl and bring her out, and I don't know what happened then."

"Oh, by the way, you did hit the wrong house."

"Yeah."

"You were two houses away."

"Well, see, I don't know what it was about. They went in because, see, like back then I was on cocaine and I was going through a lot of changes. Fee and Horse was selling cocaine then and Ida and Lisa and me, you know, we were smoking pretty tough then."

"Did you go into the house at all?"

"I didn't—I didn't even go into the house. I got up to the porch and turned around."

"You're saying you never went into the house."

"See, as I know it—"

"It don't really make any difference whether you went into the front porch or into the house because you didn't pull the trigger is what I'm trying to tell you, Darren."

"Yeah, but I just—I just can't, you know, at night and stuff, I can't even sleep, just—"

"Oh, I can imagine. I can imagine. I believe you. Suddenly I believe every word you're telling me. That's got to be one hell of a nightmare to wake up to every night."

"Well, they talked about it on the way over there quite a bit about how much money they'd make and what they were going to do."

"Well, see, the thing is, like I told you, you're helping yourself. And the more information we get to get this Jack, it helps you a hell of a lot more, every goddamn word we can get to Jack on."

———

Crews testified that while a background investigation was conducted on Jack and the Vermont Club, no one from LAPD ever talked to Jack.

Crews went to the Los Angeles Police Commission, because any establishment that sells liquor, has pool tables, jukeboxes, music, dancing, must be cleared.

He went to the Vermont Club, located at 6209 South Vermont, and checked back through the ownership records. In the 1970s, Jettie Young held the license, and it was called Jet's Place.

In 1980, the location was purchased by a man named Ossie James Jackson, who held it through December 1984. Background records showed Jackson to have prior arrests for gambling, bookmaking, and various other vice-related matters. He was known as "Diamond Jack" and the owner of the Vermont Club. He lived at 6207 South Vermont, the apartment above the club.

Crews interviewed a young lady named Valarie Taylor who lived at 136 West Fifty-Ninth Street, two doors west of the Alexander house at 126 West Fifty-Ninth Street.

The prosecution put into evidence as Exhibit A a copy of the lawsuit that was filed by Valarie Taylor against Ossie Jackson and Jack's Vermont Club on April 4, 1984, six months after she was shot and paralyzed in the club.

The complaint asked for general damages of $1 million, medical and related expenses in the amount of $30,000, and future medical and related expenses in the amount of $100,000. Finally, lost wages and lost earning capacity in the amount of $1 million, for a total of $2,130,000.

Included in the exhibit was an answer to the complaint, which in general terms denied the allegations. The answer was filed on September 5, 1984.

A used-car dealer, from El Monte, California, Cesar Rodriguez testified that on September 1, 1984, the day after the murders, CW came to his lot with his wife, Cheryl Howard. CW paid $1,500 in $100 bills for a Datsun 280Z. The $100 bills came from a big wad that CW pulled out.

Lisa Brown told the police that she heard that CW spent over $40,000, but now he was broke.

———

Williams's defense stressed his crack cocaine addiction, and its effects on his personality.

Dr. William Vicary performed a psychiatric evaluation of Williams, who said he smoked half an ounce a day in 1984, and dealt the drug to support his habit.

During this time Williams lost about forty pounds, because cocaine, a stimulant, acts as an appetite suppressant.

Other effects included hyperactivity, anxiousness, irritability, and aggressiveness. Williams sometimes went several days in a row without sleep.

The doctor testified that "if you have been using it on a regular basis over a long period of time, it causes mental deterioration . . . significant impairments in your judgment, your impulse control, and your overall social functioning."

Williams stated that he became "more and more socially isolated, more suspicious, more frightened of other people, even sometimes paranoid, thinking that people were following him."

Williams said it was his heavy cocaine abuse that caused his erratic and uncharacteristic behavior.

———

Sterling Norris argued that Williams was guilty beyond premeditated murder; he was guilty of a "mass execution."

Lisa Brown, Norris said, heard one of them say that "we are going to kill everyone in the house."

"And CW and Fee came walking toward the Alexander house, and in a matter of minutes they walked away again," and "four dead bodies were left. Get a first-grade pupil," Norris said, and then "what was the intent?"

In emphasizing CW's role, Norris continued with the Nazi analogy: "CW is Himmler, Goebbels, or Hitler himself, in relation to commandeering this operation. He arranged it, engineered it, of the Nazis he is wearing the commander's hat. He puts Fee into Ida's house, into the van, and into the Alexander house. He's the man, he summoned everybody.

"They are arranging this thing. And what do they need? They need the executioner. They need Fee. CW is the commander and Fee and Horace his foot soldiers."

It was CW who set "this mission in motion." "CW was the one anxiously moving about the van, hunched up front, looking at the piece of the torn brown paper bag with the address written on it. CW told Horse to stay in the van to keep the girls from driving away when they heard the shots."

As to the motive:

"That morning none of the three had a cent, and then within twenty-four hours both were buying cars with cash, peeling the money off from large wads, and who knows how much additional money was there. CW had new clothes, and doled out money to Ida and Lisa.

"Can you imagine killing four people and then walking in and taking the money and counting out the dollars for how many for Ebora, how many for Dietra, how many for the two little kids? That was their blood money that they got for this execution.

"I will have to grant all three of them, they are the bottom part of humanity."

And never, Norris said, did CW show any remorse. First, not there, then when confronted with the evidence, he was just in the van along for the ride. Then he said, "It could be Little CW, I mean it don't have to be me."

He kept lying and changing his story, trying to avoid culpability.

"Tiequon Cox would never have walked in that doorway . . . never would have executed Ebora, Dietra, Damon, and Damani. You can call Mr. Cox a rabid dog. Then what is the man that sets the rabid dog loose?"

———

Williams was defended by an African-American father-and-son team, H. Clay Jacke and Jacke Jr. Jacke Sr. was an experienced criminal defense attorney who practiced into his eighties. Junior would later be appointed a Superior Court judge in Compton by Governor Jerry Brown.

The two Jackes argued that CW was not "the brains" behind the crime. "The brains," they argued, "walked out of this courtroom in an expensive suit the last time she testified."

It was Ida who set up the crime for money to feed her crack habit, then "maliciously" lied on the stand to gain immunity.

Ida and Lisa were spiders, who "weave a very intricate web so they can move about silently and feed on their prey." Ida had the gun in the van "ready to take action." Ida had driven the neighborhood for twenty years and wouldn't have needed CW's simple directions that morning. From start to finish Ida and Lisa did far more than Horse.

CW did not kill anyone. Other than a mangled bullet that couldn't be conclusively linked to any firearm, every intact bullet came from the rifle fired by Cox. CW did not go past the porch, and if he did, he quickly ran out. Therefore, they argued, CW had no intent to kill, and if he ever did, he abandoned it when he fled the house. They pled with the jurors not to let emotion cloud their vision as finders of fact.

The police coerced a confession from CW, threatening him with the death penalty. Mr. Norris was dangerous, because he was "above average as a prosecutor," and as the old adage goes, "Any ordinary prosecutor can convict the guilty, but it takes a brilliant one to convict the innocent."

They concluded with CW's community service, working with "disturbed kids and people," calling the crime "contradictory to his mental setup." "Who could work with kids," they asked, "and then come in and help someone put a slug in the head of two small children? That is repulsive. I don't see how that could have happened."

———

Norris, dismissing the Ida as Ma Barker theory, concluded:

Now that multimillion-dollar lawsuit is the reason and the motive. CW's statements verify that. He wants to put it on Horse and Fee.

The evidence tells you that is not so, it is he who set it up, he who had the connection, and he who made the money transactions, got the rest of them the money.

Defense counsel at one point made an argument here that this is a great tragedy that this happened, that the four of these people are dead. And I think when you look at that, the greatest tragedy would be to let any of these three escape for their acts on that August day of 1984. . . .

They came down on an American street and annihilated a whole family. Now, that is an American tragedy.

———

Williams was convicted on December 15, 1986, on four counts of first-degree murder with special circumstances.

On June 2, 1987, the jury, after taking three votes, recommended death in the gas chamber.

Sterling Norris told the press that the verdict was deserved. Although it was unclear whether Williams fired any of the shots, he was the "go between, who was hired for $50,000 to $60,000 to arrange the killings."

Press reports from the day after sentencing stated: "Prosecutors believe that the Alexander family members were murdered by mistake, after the contract killers went to the wrong address. The individual believed to have masterminded the killings has never been charged, but the investigation remains open, Norris said."

Defense attorney H. Clay Jacke Jr. said his client should have been spared the death penalty.

"I thought that his prior activities in the community were such as to have entitled him to the benefit of the doubt," Jacke said. "He had worked with kids, and with youth movements and disturbed children and had gotten all kinds of awards."

As for my family, we were relieved, both with the verdict and the fact that, nearly three years after the crime, the trials were finally over. And with Williams, as with Cox, we had no doubt.

Williams's entire defense mirrored his taped interrogation. Everyone but him, SOD, always Some Other Dude: not CW, but Little CW, Cox, Horse, Ida, Lisa, the coercive detectives, and the dangerous DA. And even if it was him, it wasn't *really* him, because *that* him was *so* high, because *those* drugs made him "uncharacteristically" act like some other dude.

CW's defense also lacked logic or consistency: He never left the van, but if he did he only went on the porch, unless he went into the house, in which case he didn't fire any shots, nor did he intend to kill when he entered the house, but if he did, he stopped intending when Cox started shooting, and he ran out the door. Ida and Lisa clearly lacked clean hands, accomplices not angels. But this in no way cleared CW, whose own words proved his guilt.

CW's child care struck me as a farce or a front. Rolling Sixties Day Care. To the extent it was true, it smelled of the same hypocrisy of Cox and his mother, a gangster protecting his own while destroying others. Scraps of Tiequon's humanity earn him our mercy, CW's service calls for our grace. The jury may consider the killers' finest hours, but must put emotion aside when it comes to the victims. Consider the children he served; ignore those who died by his hand.

———

The Burns case shined a light inside the "death van" and pierced the violent world of the Rolling Sixties. Cox's trial showed the making of a killer. Williams's case revealed the motive.

After the Williams conviction, my family knew definitively that we were hit by complete accident. This brought at least factual clarity.

As Los Angeles County District Attorney Ira Reiner wrote:

> We know from the admission of [Darren Charles Williams] that the killings were the result of a businessman hiring these three to kill a woman in a wheelchair only two houses from the Alexander house; the woman was paralyzed as a result of an incident in the businessman's restaurant. She had filed a lawsuit for several million dollars. They picked the wrong house and killed four uninvolved persons.

But despite this courtroom closure, cosmically, I was left adrift. The convictions restored no meaning to my life. In fact, following the trials, I felt more confused than ever.

They hit the wrong house. What a symptom of a world gone mad. Armed thugs fearlessly invade a family home at daybreak, the home Madee could not bear to leave, the one that overwhelmed Gordon, brought him to his hands and knees to kiss the floor in thanks. Twenty years ago it symbolized our arrival, now our demise.

Back on an autumn night in '83, a fuse was lit in a nightclub on South Vermont. Unknown to us, this set in motion a chaotic chain of events that would lead a killer to our home. Had anything broken that chain—the fight in the bar, the filing of the lawsuit, Jack's connection to CW, CW's relationship to Cox, Madee's refusal to move, my having overslept, CW's misreading of the address—destiny would have been altered. Every detail had to align, fall just so, to produce this tragedy.

By the cruel ways of fate, a succession of mistakes crashed through our door that hot August morning.

Some kind of evil had been unleashed.

And deep within, I wondered if I was a cause.

Was the source to be found on that field in Watts years before, or did it all start when Valarie Taylor danced?

33

TO REIGN IN HELL

On july 29, 1987, a year after Tiequon Cox's arrival, Darren Charles Williams joined him on "East Block Condemned." Unknown at the time, this would remake the face of death row.

Prison is a secret and insular world, marked by its own internal codes. Death row is a subculture deep within this subculture, defying even the norms of the general prison population.

The major prison gangs operating nationwide in both the federal and state systems all started in California during the radicalized political atmosphere of the late 1960s. Formed out of the anticapitalist, black power rhetoric of the Black Panther Party, George Jackson founded the Black Guerrilla Family while in Soledad State Prison. The Black Guerrilla Family, or BGF, sought to unify black inmates throughout the California prison system. Touting Maoist economics and a militant radical ideology, the BGF became feared not only within California's prisons, but, due to its reach, outside prison walls.

With even violent felons serving short prison terms in the late 1960s and early 1970s (for example, during this time seven years was the average term served for murder), members of BGF were consistently being cycled in and out of the prison system and then spreading the word on the streets. And with the ability to communicate with the outside, even incarcerated inmates could exert their will on the streets through a network of drug dealers, hit men, and cronies.

At the same time that the Black Guerrilla Family formed, other races started their own prison gangs for purposes of unity, protection, and profit. White inmates organized under the banner of the Aryan Brotherhood, while Mexican inmates, depending on their region of origin, aligned with the Mexican Mafia (Southern California), Nuestra Familia (Northern California), or the Texas Syndicate. While all of these prison gangs adhered to notions of racial solidarity, they would ultimately operate as surprisingly sophisticated organized crime syndicates, with one overarching goal: monetary gain.

Cashing in on narcotics sales, the organized prison gangs often betray racial solidarity in the name of profit. Smuggling drugs and money in and out of even maximum-security prisons, death row and supermax life-term inmates control extensive drug networks worth millions of dollars. Via visitors, compromised guards, attorneys, and outside supporters, the drugs, money, and cell phones flow.

As many ex–prison gang members will confess when they "debrief," telling the authorities what they know upon renouncing membership, the loyalty in prison gangs is as porous and situational as in the street gangs where many cut their teeth. If the profits and control of the high-ranking "made" members of the prison gangs are compromised, a hit is ordered. At this moment the veneer of racial solidarity shatters. Many foreswearing membership found the prison gang a violent, paranoid, and brutal façade. While the image of blacks versus whites versus Mexicans rides the surface, most prison gang assaults are committed against members of one's own race. Race is trumped by profitable narcotics networks. It is therefore not race so much as challenges to control that trigger violent retaliation.

While such prison gangs and their progeny infect the California prison system, death row runs by different rules. On East Block, where the majority of California's death row inmates are housed, only a small number of condemned inmates are known to have traditional prison gang affiliation.

On death row, condemned inmates with gang affiliations retain their street gang loyalties. East Block death row inmates are allowed four to five hours of yard time four days per week. There are six yards, each forty feet long by twenty feet wide. Concrete walls twelve feet high, topped by ten feet of metal fencing and crowned by razor wire, surround the death row yards. Armed guards patrol elevated walkways overlooking the yards. Painted numbers line the concrete walls so the exact location of shots fired at prisoners can be calculated after a shooting. Until the late 1990s death row inmates were allowed to lift weights in the yards.

The yards are separated by metal wire fencing. This allows inmates in adjacent yards to communicate, but not physically interact with each other. The yards are segregated according to affiliation and statuses. One yard is for Bloods, two for Crips, one for the "unaffiliated," another for pedophiles.

In 1987, after CW's arrival on death row, he and Cox ran Yard Two, "the Rolling Sixties Yard." They ruled in tandem, said a prison guard. Cox-Williams was a "two-headed monster." Stanley "Tookie" Williams, founder of the West Side Crips, in prison for a quadruple homicide committed in 1979, ran Yard One.

In 1988 Tookie Williams sought to unite all death row Crips under one organization, the "Blue Note Crips," to be run by him. As the number of Crips serving long sentences increased in the 1970s and 1980s, various efforts were made to fuse and politicize the gang behind bars. Titled either Blue Note or Consolidated Crip Organization (CCO), the agenda included literacy, an immersion in black history, African roots, the Swahili language, and the classics of power politics: Sun Tzu's *The Art of War*, Machiavelli's *The Prince*, and *The Autobiography of Malcolm X*. Discipline, power, respect, and control were paramount. Aspects of radical Islam also found their way into this philosophical jumble.

In October 1988, Tookie Williams's agenda clashed with that of Cox and CW. Through the grapevine of East Block Condemned, Tookie got word to Cox that CW was planning to put out a hit on Cox, an attempt to break the bond between his rivals. Cox and CW huddled, deriving a plan.

On October 23, while "out on yard," Tiequon Cox concealed a shank, a homemade jailhouse weapon. When Tookie Williams left his yard, Cox stabbed him in the back of the neck.

The incident was seen as a blessing by death row staff. For Tookie Williams not only intended to bring all condemned Crips under his wing, but sought to do the same with the Bloods. In the unique internals of death row, Bloods and Crips may unite, or at least lay down their arms, posing together for photos or politicking on death row yards. Thus prison guards feared a consolidation of condemned black gangsters and welcomed the rift.

The feud also marked a changing of the guard. The Rolling Sixties were the new generation. According to one prison official, "the Sixties were like the Black Guerrilla Family on steroids." Freed from political positions, or delusions of representing a civil rights agenda or community action group, the new gangs ran without restriction. Moral codes and ideologies were abandoned. "Power to the People" became "I don't give a fuck." And as the suicide bomber is made more lethal with no concern for survival or escape, the lack of goal or vision frees the new-breed gangster to rage uncontrolled. And if "civilians" got in the way, too bad, "collateral damage," or as Horse said, "just something that happened."

The stabbing landed Tookie Williams and Tiequon Cox in the AC. And in the upside-down world of the gang, it made Cox a celebrity. Sixties on "the row," in the general prison pop, and back in Hyde Park cheered their young star who dared take down the king. Despite killing women and children, this cemented his legacy, OG to the max.

Like Satan in *Paradise Lost*, Tiequon Cox would rather "reign in Hell than serve in Heaven."

34

I CANNOT FORGIVE
THE CHOICE

As TIEQUON COX mastered death row, I struggled to keep it together.

In a way we shared lives again. We were both outcasts. Tiequon Cox was locked up in San Quentin. I became a loner and drifter.

With all the defendants behind bars, there was relief, but no joy.

I felt justice served. The shooter and the one who planned the hit had earned the death penalty, and Burns, for his role, a life behind bars.

But nothing could bring back the departed. And nothing could bring back my old life. I had gone from professional athlete to professional victim. I was now defined by the murders. I was drained by them. I felt old.

It was ironic. Every day as the trials plodded I couldn't wait for them to end. Boring, procedural, passive, questions, answers, interruptions, waiting, recess, waiting, deliberations, jury questions, more waiting. It was claustrophobic, shut in that hot courtroom with the killers, uncomfortable with much of my family, listening to the killings replayed day after day. But for the last three years the trials became an obsession. And they provided a goal: do what we could to get the killers convicted.

Now what? Now that they were finally over, I had no idea what to do with myself. I sure didn't miss going to court. I just didn't know how to fill the void.

I tried coaching some youth teams here and there, and worked a series of mindless jobs. I had no motivation. I no longer saw possibilities. I just couldn't visualize a future, or anything that could bring peace or contentment. I couldn't imagine deliverance. Much of the time I spent brooding, cycles of anger, guilt, and sorrow.

In the early nineties, I moved to Riverside, California, to be near my father, who was seriously ill. Madee was taken without a chance to say goodbye. I wasn't going to let that happen again.

This period of time, the 1990s, became my lost decade, consumed by alternating bouts of listlessness and rage.

I was lost, stuck in an existential crisis in which nothing made sense. My lifelong pillars were gone. I fought the constant urge to call Madee. I wanted her advice on how to cope with her murder. Nor could I pray or find solace in God. The trust was gone. How had He allowed this to happen?

Likewise, if I thought of actually achieving anything, I looped back to how I would share it with Madee—again an impossible set of thoughts.

And my family, the sense of anchor and camaraderie, was gone. The scars over the accusations of my role in the murders had never healed. While the family sat together at trial to face down the killers, this was just short-term unity against the common enemy. Once the trials ended, so did the contact.

My marriage disintegrated as I grew ever more distant and unreachable. After divorce, I seldom saw my kids.

I was walling myself off from everyone.

In the coming years, if I did see my family it was through the DA, Sterling Norris, as he briefed us on the ongoing appeals of Cox and Williams, told us how to get copies of their trial transcripts, updated us on the state of the law, and on strategies going forward.

———

On May 2, 1991, the California Supreme Court affirmed Tiequon Cox's conviction and death sentence.

The court dismissed issues based upon faulty jury selection, including the claim that the prosecutor used peremptory challenges to eliminate jurors reluctant to impose the death penalty.

As to the guilt phase, the court ruled that the trial judge erred in allowing Cox to be physically restrained. They found the error, however, to be harmless, as it did not cause the jurors to prejudicially view the defendant. The court further held that Cox's counsel, Cook, was justified in bringing the situation to the judge's attention, and that it did not constitute a conflict of interest between counsel and client.

The California Supreme Court also rejected arguments that Cook was ineffective in his representation of Cox by failing to challenge the jury venire (pool), and bringing evidence of Cox's gang affiliation before the jury. Further, the court found that allowing "gruesome" autopsy photos of the victims to go before the jury did not constitute judicial error. Finally, the court rejected the argument that Cook's failure to present a guilt-phase defense or to even make an argument was "tantamount to a guilty plea."

Likewise, the court rejected arguments regarding alleged penalty-phase errors, including prosecutorial misconduct when he asked the jury to remember the victims in life, thus generating unwarranted emotional sympathy. Lastly, the court refused to find the imposition of the death penalty in this case disproportionate, considering Cox's "involvement in the offense and his background and character."

———

In the early morning hours of Tuesday, April 21, 1992, Robert Alton Harris sat strapped in the chair inside San Quentin's gas chamber.

Outside the prison's east gate a large crowd gathered. Megaphones, poster boards, buttons, and signs broadcast conflicting messages on capital punishment. Biblical verses of vengeance and forgiveness, Old Testament versus New, were exchanged.

A multiagency task force was assigned to ensure order. The Coast Guard responded as a boat approached Point San Quentin blasting death metal music. The prison was on lockdown. This was to be California's first execution in twenty-five years.

Inside the octagonal green gas chamber, Robert Alton Harris was unstrapped and led from the tank as the U.S. Court of Appeals for the Ninth Circuit imposed a temporary stay.

In 1978 Harris was convicted of murdering two teenagers in San Diego. He carjacked them in a fast-food parking lot, then shot them in a canyon. After taking their wallets, he parked the car and ate their sandwiches. He later used their car when he robbed a bank. By pure chance, the police officer who arrested Harris for the bank robbery was the father of one of the dead boys. At the time, the officer had no idea that the bank robber had just murdered his son.

In the morning of the day scheduled for execution, Harris said goodbye to his friends, fellow death row inmates, and to the guards who had watched him for the past fifteen years. In the afternoon, he hung out in the prison visiting room with his attorneys and some family and friends. By evening he was moved to the death watch cell, thirteen paces from the gas chamber.

Like many inmates on death row, Harris had had a traumatic childhood. He suffered from fetal alcohol syndrome. He was a premature baby due to beatings his father gave his mother while pregnant. After birth he was routinely abused, on one occasion punched so hard while in a high chair that his head slammed against the wall and blood spurted from his ear.

At 8:15 p.m. Harris was served his last meal: "21 pieces of extra-crispy Kentucky Fried Chicken, two large pizzas without anchovies, a six-pack of Pepsi, some jellybeans and a pack of Camel cigarettes."

Shortly before midnight the Ninth Circuit issued its third stay, this one claiming that the gas chamber constituted cruel and unusual punishment, in violation of the Eighth Amendment.

At three in the morning the U.S. Supreme Court overrode this stay, stating: "This claim could have been brought more than a decade ago. There is no good reason for this abusive delay, which has been compounded by last-minute attempts to manipulate the judicial process."

Two Supreme Court justices dissented. Harry Blackmun and John Paul Stevens wrote: "In light of all we know today about the extreme and unnecessary pain inflicted by execution by cyanide gas, and in light of the availability of more humane and less violent methods of execution, Harris's claim has merit."

Following the U.S. Supreme Court's order, San Quentin staff began the execution protocol: friends and family members of both the condemned and the victims, along with members of the media, were moved into the death chamber.

At 3:49 a.m. Robert Alton Harris was led the thirteen paces from the holding cell to the gas chamber. He was strapped into the chair, at which point he gave "a thumbs-up sign" to the guards. The phone rang and five minutes later Harris was unstrapped and led from the chamber.

Just prior to 4 a.m. the Ninth Circuit granted its fourth stay of execution in the last twelve hours.

The U.S. Supreme Court again reversed the Ninth Circuit, stating: "No further stays . . . shall be entered by the federal courts except upon order of this court."

At 6 a.m. Harris was again strapped into the chair. Again he gave the thumbs-up symbol. Looking through the glass of the death chamber, Harris saw that his brother was crying. He mouthed the words "it's all right." Looking at Detective Steven Baker, whose son he had murdered, he mouthed, "I'm sorry." Baker nodded, but said the apology was "fourteen years too late."

As a member of the press described it:

"At 6:05, the gas was released into the chamber. Harris leaned his head back. A short time later his head fell forward, then lifted slowly back. His eyes were closed and his mouth slightly open. Then his head pitched sharply forward. He started to convulse.

"At 6:09, he took two large gulps of air, seemed to gasp, then coughed. He began drooling. His body jerked.

"Two minutes later, he was still drooling, his body was still going through spasms, though the spasms were smaller. They were his last noticeable movements."

At 6:21 a.m. "a porthole in the door separating the witnesses from prison officials opened and a piece of paper was handed out. A correctional officer read a notice from Warden Daniel Vasquez that Robert

Alton Harris, No. B66883, had been legally executed on April 21 and had officially died at 6:21 a.m."

The warden then read Harris's final words: "You can be a king or a street sweeper, but everybody dances with the grim reaper."

––––––

The execution gave Tiequon Cox and every other death row inmate a foretaste of their future.

The execution gave me a preview of what awaited my family.

It was a microcosm of what was to come in California's death penalty wars: lengthy delays, protests, hand-wringing, last-minute stays, continued legal wrangling over the means by which the condemned would be executed.

The case also highlighted a fundamental issue regarding the right of the state not just to execute, but to punish.

Central to the debate was how to weigh the effects of the brutal background of the condemned with their individual responsibility for the horrors they inflicted upon innocent victims.

As my family and I carefully followed developments in the ongoing saga of capital punishment, I learned how truly hard it was to get the death penalty in California. Of the inmates who would be put to death in the coming decades, guilt was never in question and the facts of each case were extreme. As the district attorney told us, the best argument for the death penalty is the behavior of the killer.

In refusing to grant Harris clemency, Governor Pete Wilson stated, "As great as is my compassion for Robert Harris the child, I cannot excuse or forgive the choice made by Robert Harris the man."

––––––

One week after the execution of Robert Alton Harris, the streets of South Central Los Angeles exploded. The spark in 1992, as in Watts in 1965, was the stoppage by local law enforcement of an intoxicated black motorist. While the 1965 conflagration was ignited by rumors of police mistreatment of Marquette Frye, the 1992 incident was sparked by the videotaped beating of Rodney King a year before.

On April 29, 1992, when an all-white jury in Simi Valley acquitted the officers of all charges, residents of South Central responded initially with street protests, which quickly devolved into violence, looting, burning, and overall mayhem. When order was finally restored days later, the damage was considerably worse than in '65. This time, fifty-four were killed, over two thousand injured, and property damage totaled over $2 billion.

As in the Watts Riots of 1965, legitimate grievances were shoved aside as gangsters, vandals, and looters hijacked the protest. Instead of focusing on inequality and underemployment, footage of burning, destruction, and violent assaults streamed into living rooms across the country. Seared into the public mind was the image of gang members pulling Reginald Denny from his truck, crushing his skull with a brick, and then dancing over his body as he bled in the street. Finally, legitimate problems such as underdevelopment were only exacerbated as the community at large suffered from the ruinous acts of a destructive few.

In the aftermath of the riots, profound changes swept through L.A.'s gangs, the LAPD, and the community of South Central. As a result of the incident both Chief of Police Daryl Gates and Mayor Tom Bradley lost their positions.

Politicians, police, and residents all feared that these riots, like those of Watts more than twenty-five years before, would unleash a new and more violent wave of crime.

35

THE DREAM

As l.a. smolders, and the death penalty machinery grinds on, not a day passes that I don't replay what should have been.

The date is August 31, and I sit with Madee, as she finishes her cup of coffee.

Her grandsons, Damon and Damani, play in the other room, yelling, roughhousing. Sounds like a pillow fight, actually more like Damon harassing Damani, trying to wake him up.

"Hey, you guys," I say half jokingly, "you better watch it, you know how Madee is about her house."

"Uncle Kermit!" Damani protests, pretending to be too old for such horseplay. "I'm not doing anything. He won't let me sleep."

Thwack.

"Okay, Uncle Kermit," Damon laughs, "we'll calm down," followed by "take that," and the sound of a thud, a fall, then more wrestling and laughter.

"I'm serious," I say. "She's about to come in there and bust you up with a shoe."

A door closes. Footsteps approach the kitchen. Madee looks toward the hallway. I follow her gaze.

"Morning," Dietra says, entering the kitchen.

Madee and I both look at her, don't even need to say a word. We both know what the other's thinking. How beautiful she looks. "The baby," ready to get married and fly the nest. The last of Madee's brood.

And Madee, she starts to tell me of all those plans she has now that she has finished raising her family. "Kermit," she says, "I'm going to devote even more of my time—"

The sound of the screen door swinging shut interrupts her.

"Now who's that?" she says, again peering toward the hallway.

"Just me," Daphine says. "How's my baby Damon doing?"

"Fine, just fine," Madee says.

"No more of them nightmares I hope."

"Nope, content as can be."

More sounds of boys thrashing about in the bedroom, thuds, crashes.

"Hey, come on now," Daphine scolds. "Knock it off in there."

"Oh no!" Damon yells. "Mama, I don't have to go home, do I? I'm not going to school. I'm not leaving," he declares.

"Darn straight you're not," Madee says, loud enough for the boys to hear. "He's with me today, Daphine. I already told you, we're headed up to the Coliseum to collect pins."

"Yeah!" Damon cheers.

Daphine laughs, pulling up a chair. "Where are Neal and Ivan?" she asks.

"Oh," Madee sighs, waving her right hand toward the rear bedroom. "They'll sleep till noon if nobody wakes 'em. Neal doing them equations all night long." She shakes her head. "And Ivan, he never turns the TV off. 'Just one more,' he always says. And I tell him, 'Ivan, you've watched those same highlights a dozen times.' And you know what he says? 'So what.'" She laughs. "It's not like the score is going to change when you watch it for the fifth time."

We all laugh. Then Daphine's tone turns serious. "Any more thoughts about moving?" she asks Madee.

Madee shakes her head and purses her lips. "Daphine, when the good Lord tells me it's time to move, *then* it's time to move."

Daphine looks at me, rolls her eyes.

"Until then," Madee says, "I've got work to do." She pauses, reaches for her toast. "In fact, you can help me. Grab that peanut butter," she says, pointing toward the cupboard. "Get that bread."

She motions to the counter. "And start fixing some sandwiches for those kids you know'll be hanging around here later."

We all laugh. It's still real clear who's in charge.

On the stove, my favorite is cooking. Red beans and rice, southern-style. I can't wait.

I open up the pot to see how they're doing. Not too far along.

"Kermit, be patient," she scolds. "You know better. I just put them on."

I knew it was coming. I did it just to tease her, get that reaction. It works every time.

"Kermit," she continues, "I'm so proud of you, going to be on TV again, working for UCLA."

"That's right, and—"

"That reminds me," she interrupts. "I'm going to wear those blue earrings today, show my Bruin pride." She pauses, then laughs. "Even if we are going to the Coliseum. You know what else—"

The phone interrupts her.

"I wonder who that'll be?" she says, smiling as she reaches for it.

But it doesn't stop ringing.

Her kitchen fades away, as does my dream.

The phone is my own, I pick it up.

"Kermit," the voice on the other end says. "Sterling Norris. Got a minute? Good. Here's what's going on."

Back to reality. Back to the courts, procedures, death row.

36

A SUPERHERO

On July 13, 1994, the Ninth Circuit Court of Appeals denied a class action lawsuit brought by Darren Charles Williams (CW) and other death row inmates. The suit argued that San Quentin's policy of refusing the inmates' conjugal visits violated the Eighth Amendment prohibition against cruel and unusual punishment. In dismissing this claim, the Ninth Circuit held that "[c]onjugal visits are inconsistent with the principles of incarceration and isolation from society," concluding that ". . . there is a valid rational connection between a ban on contact visits and internal security of a detention facility." The court also rejected the argument that San Quentin's refusal to provide a means of preserving sperm for purposes of artificial insemination violated the constitutional rights of the condemned.

———

On February 23, 1996, William Bonin, the Freeway Killer, was led the thirteen steps to San Quentin's death chamber. When the curtains were parted, observers looking through the glass saw a man strapped down to a gurney shaped like a crucifix. Needles with tubes were inserted into his arms.

In 1993 a federal court ruled the gas chamber cruel and unusual punishment, referring to execution by gas as "torturous, painful, and cruel," that lethal injection was "more humane."

Inmates called it "the Big Jab."

From behind the execution chamber walls the chemicals were released: sodium thiopental (also called sodium pentothal) put Bonin to sleep and pancuronium bromide ceased his breathing. Finally, potassium chloride stopped his heart.

As reported by the *Orange County Register*, Bonin "died quietly Friday in the execution chamber . . . without any outward signs of the pain and torture that were hallmarks of his murders."

In 1980, Bonin in a ten-month crime spree kidnapped, sexually abused, tortured, and then strangled twenty-one boys in Southern California.

Victims' family members and death penalty opponents drew different lessons from California's first-ever death by lethal injection.

For family members, Bonin's death was too easy, failing to provide the measure-for-measure based upon the suffering he had caused his victims. They stated, "He should have gone through a little bit more pain," and "It was too peaceful."

Prosecutor Bryan Brown remarked, "He had it easy compared to his victims." Brown noted none of his victims received a last meal of pizza and ice cream, nor the services of a chaplain.

Other family members made similar comments about the tranquility of Bonin's passing: "I didn't get to see the fear in Bonin's eyes, and he didn't get to see the hate in mine." Another, disappointed in the tranquility of the killer's passing, said, "I will now have to stab him in my dreams."

Death penalty opponents worried that the antiseptic quality of the proceeding would make it more palatable to the general public and therefore speed the way for more executions. This in turn, opponents feared, would make executions in California more routine and accepted.

———

On August 21, 1997, thirteen years after CW was convicted of orchestrating the murders, the special circumstance finding, required for his death sentence, was reversed.

The California Supreme Court held that the trial court "omitted from the jury instruction the requirement of a finding by the jury that defendant acted with an intent to kill."

Under the law of special circumstances, without the intent to kill more than one person, the multiple-victim special-circumstance language is eliminated, and therefore there can be no death penalty conviction.

Feeling that the retrial thirteen years after the murder would be too much for the family to endure, Norris chose not to retry Williams on the special circumstances. This meant that Williams would be removed from death row and placed in the general population.

It was a stinging defeat for District Attorney Norris.

He now held out hope that justice would at least be served for the shooter.

———

On October 25, 1998, a fight broke out on death row's exercise Yard Two.

Five members of the Bloods, who had been let onto the yard, acted in concert attacking Cox.

Four 37mm wood rounds were fired before all inmates complied with the orders to get down. Cox and a Rolling Sixties confederate got back up and rushed their assailants.

Four more 37mm rounds were fired, two from the yard gunner and two more from another responding guard.

The following day the tier officer escorted one of the Bloods involved in the altercation to the shower. As he walked by Cox's cell, Cox speared the inmate between the cell bars, striking him in the right shoulder. The spear was four feet long and sharpened to a point.

This incident earned Cox his seventh trip to the Adjustment Center.

Cox's previous offenses included fighting on the group exercise yard, conspiracy to assault staff, and inciting other inmates. On two occasions he was found with "an inmate manufactured weapon." A cell search turned up a pair of dismantled sunglasses, "one of the temple arms . . . melted down exposing the metal within." Likewise, an X-ray search of his legal material revealed a black plastic shank four inches long and five-eighths of an inch in diameter that was sharpened to a point.

Cox also was sent to the AC for refusing to allow guards to handcuff him to search his cell.

Another citation stemmed from Cox leading the Condemned exercise yards in cadence while chanting: "Can't Stop, Won't Stop, Will Not be Stopped, Machine, Machine." This was an old George Jackson, Black Guerrilla Family maneuver, prohibited as a "paramilitary exercise."

Finally, Cox had two counts of "behavior which could lead to violence."

In the first, he and CW "took an aggressive stance" toward a sergeant in the East Block Condemned Visiting Room. "Cox ripped off his shirt and threw it on the floor and appeared threatening toward staff."

In the other incident, this time in the AC, Cox told an inmate that if staff "try to strong-arm us we will all go off," followed by "If they start fucking with you let me know, we will all get down."

The other inmate replied, "You know that."

Cox then yelled down the tier: "Is everyone down with that!"

Unidentified inmates replied, "Yeah, we are down!"

Cox then threatened the officer: "You have been jumping on too many kooks. You are going to run into a real motherfucker soon . . . blood will spill around here."

———

When a death row prisoner violates prison policy, correctional officers have only one recourse: the AC. With the dungeon shuttered it is the last stop short of death.

In the Adjustment Center the inmate is granted fewer privileges. It therefore provides what little leverage guards hold over the condemned.

In the AC prisoners are allowed only two to three hours of yard time, three days a week. This is compared to the four to five hours afforded the mainline condemned population. Also, the yards are smaller, individual, and isolated, other than one limited AC "group yard."

On the East Block yards, inmates can work out on exercise equipment and play handball and basketball. Thus an incentive for condemned inmates to "program" is the continued opportunity to socialize, politick, and exercise communally.

Phone, visits, and other privileges are also restricted in the AC.

———

Shortly after noon on July 18, 2000, Cox, Roscoe Tuilaepa, and Noel Jackson huddle in group Yard Three, "the Crip Yard," in the AC.

Paul "Roscoe" Tuilaepa, a Samoan Crip from Southern California, regarded as one of the strongest and most dangerous men on death row, was convicted in 1986 of multiple murder in a Long Beach nightclub. After committing robbery, on the way out the door, Tuilaepa blasted three victims with a shotgun. Tuilaepa later earned a lifetime stay in the Adjustment Center when he "got loose," viciously beating several guards, kicking one into a coma. In this one incident Tuilaepa "retired" three correctional officers. Due to inmates like Tuilaepa, who maxed out on the bench press at 590 pounds, weights were removed from California prisons in the 1990s.

Also present with Cox and Tuilaepa was Noel "No No" Jackson, a Rolling Sixty convicted of a contract killing in 1984. Michael Niles, a basketball star at the California State University, Fullerton, who played for a year with the Phoenix Suns, hired Jackson to kill his wife, because she "messed with him when he was playing basketball" and sent his brother to prison. On December 13, 1984, Jackson murdered Sonja Niles outside her home in Riverside County. Niles promised to pay Jackson $5,000 for the hit. He planned to get the money from his wife's $100,000 life insurance policy. At trial Jackson and Niles each pointed the finger of guilt at the other, claiming he had fired the fatal shotgun blast to the victim's head. Niles's jury rejected the death sentence, giving him life without parole. Jackson was sentenced to death.

Cox, Tuilaepa, and Jackson cut a hole in the group yard's chain-link fence, using haircutting shears. Tuilaepa was the first through the hole. Cox, Jackson, and two others followed, making it completely off the yard and reaching a walkway used by correctional staff to escort handcuffed inmates to and from the AC.

A guard carrying a portable alarm sounded a red alert. Sixty guards from throughout the prison responded.

A second guard grabbed a 37mm gun that fired wooden blocks. He aimed it at the inmates from a nearby building. A lieutenant ran to the back of the unit, while another stood with his stun gun "at the ready." The prison was ordered locked down, trapping the inmates inside the walkway away from most staff. To the guards' surprise, the inmates then charged.

As Tuilaepa closed in on a guard, a volley of wooden bullets struck him in the left shoulder blade, knocking him facedown to the ground. The discharge from the gun produced a huge booming sound, leaving a thick haze of blue-gray smoke. Cox and Jackson stumbled over the fallen Tuilaepa. All five inmates were then ordered back through the hole in the fence line and told to crawl on their stomachs to the back of Yard Three, "where they could be secured and observed in a controlled area."

Cox, identified as the leader of the takeover attempt, refused to submit, yelling and swearing at Correctional Officer Vernell Crittendon. Crittendon ordered Cox to get down on the ground, warning him that the rifles were not going to fire wooden blocks. Facing the muzzles of a dozen trained rifles, Cox finally complied.

Shaken by the event, one officer stated, "This type of thing shouldn't be happening. The inmates came very, very close to holding one of us hostage. They're condemned men. They have zero to lose."

The incident was erroneously reported as an attempted escape. It was in fact a concerted effort to take over the Adjustment Center. Located well within the prison complex, and surrounded by layers of barriers, the AC stands nowhere near an exterior wall. The three inmates sought not to escape from, but to break into, the AC.

Tuilaepa revealed their intentions after the failed attempt: "We just wanted to kill every guard we could get our hands on."

To Officer Crittendon, the intent was "to create a scene of bloody chaos and mayhem." The motivation: expression of rage. The desire: to spill as much hated correctional blood as possible.

To Crittendon, Cox was the face of the operation.

When asked what Cox hoped to gain, Crittendon said Cox would have walked from the Adjustment Center covered in blood. Shot and killed he would have been martyred. Wounded he would have been lionized. In either case he would have shown the world, "This is what Rolling Sixties are." He sought to become "a superhero."

For all at San Quentin, the attempt came too close to the events of thirty years before.

———

The date is August 21, 1971. George Jackson, Black Panther and founder of the Black Guerrilla Family, pulls a gun and begins taking hostages in the Adjustment Center. At gunpoint, Jackson seizes cell keys from a guard and begins unlocking doors and releasing inmates.

Three guards and two white inmates have their throats slashed by razor blades inserted in toothbrushes. Jackson flees the Adjustment Center and runs into the main courtyard within the prison. From thirteen towers, thirteen gunners put Jackson in their sights. He is killed with a shot to the neck.

For correctional staff, the courtyard where George Jackson died is a reminder of the darkest day in San Quentin history. On-site, a memorial stands to the guards killed in the line of duty.

For black militants the courtyard is a shrine, the site of a martyr's death.

———

Tiequon Cox's takeover attempt of the Adjustment Center earned him an indefinite stay within its walls. It also led to changes within the AC: no more communal exercise yards, only individual pens or "dog walks," where inmates walk laps alone, one hour per day.

Following the takeover attempt, Tiequon Cox was considered the most dangerous man on death row.

37

THE WILDERNESS

IT IS EARLY in the new millennium. I am sixty years old, and have hit my low point. My life is dark. I exist only in the wilderness.

I am directionless and unable to find any meaning in an absurd world. I have hit the kind of nihilistic despair I see so often in the lost youth of our inner-city streets.

I am single. My marriage ended in divorce due to neglect. I trust no one, my family least of all. I am no longer a star, just an outcast. God is probably out there somewhere, but not here for me. This is oblivion.

Nothing makes sense. For no particular reason I am always on the move, a nomad. I feel a victim of chance, no longer master, controlled by external events.

What I feared for a decade has now become reality. I find nothing to live for. At least after the crimes, as I hunted, I had a mission. At least during the trials there was a goal. Again, now what?

An ex-star without an income, my NFL money is almost gone. Like so many former athletes I chase new dreams, get-rich-quick schemes, overnight moneymakers sure to throw me back into the good life. Always they fall short, people wanting to use my name, or thinking I'm loaded, seek to enlist me into their new "can't fail" enterprise.

For the past several months I crisscrossed the country by car. For a while I tried to dull the pain and kill the time by playing endless rounds of golf. There was even a period of time when a friend at a golf course let me sleep in the maintenance shed on the grounds. Now golf has become too expensive, and boring. Even on the course I couldn't leave myself behind. The damn guilty mind followed me wherever I went, all the time chattering, blaming, refusing to let me live. Ever more I find myself spending nights in my car. I am turning into a real transient, golden boy gone to rot, Kermit Alexander—hobo.

Not a nomad in a romantic or freewheeling sense, for my mind is constrained. I operate in a narrow mental prison that confines my thoughts to guilt, suffering, and self-pity. Not a wandering free spirit—a shackled hobo.

As I trudge about the country, I catch the flu. Sleeping little and living the homeless lifestyle, the flu turns wicked, then into pneumonia. My head feels as heavy as an anvil. All I want to do is sleep.

I end up in Oklahoma. Another new opportunity. It feels just like the last new opportunities and the old new opportunities before that. Again, the venture involves a Thoroughbred horse racing syndicate. Why not? It never worked before. It's bound to this time.

I treat myself to a motel room. Sick, coughing, unfocused, and clouded, I attend meetings. I don't really understand the venture, other than that it sounds far too good to be true. Another bust. More time and money wasted. Debt looms.

Now I am really wallowing in it. And I know it. It's pathetic, and I can't stop it.

How have I come to this? I truly have nothing, and nothing helps. No diversions pick me up—can't concentrate to read, TV is boring and depressing, no job to throw myself into. Booze just makes me tired, can't even get a buzz on. No life, no family, no direction, no money, bad health, bad attitude. Bad.

I recently had a nice girlfriend, a great girlfriend, long term, steady, but I messed that up, sabotaged it really, wouldn't ever let her get close, drove her off. Boy it could have been good, was good, and damned if I didn't twist her mind and push her away. Just never could let down the guard and open the gate. In fact, the closer we got, the more I messed things up, caused a rift, must have done it on purpose, to punish myself, an irrational way of dealing with guilt, worthlessness. Finally, she said, "Enough." Moved out, moved on.

I let my family down, failed to intervene, failed to show up, failed to protect. Failed. So why do I deserve a family? Why do I deserve to be happy?

Well, I'd succeeded, I'd stripped myself of everything meaningful, and made myself miserable. Well done. Everything I had ever wanted to be, I was not. Every way I had always wished to view myself, I could not. Guilt, like the flu, had developed into a kind of chronic mental pneumonia. This is what I've earned. This is what I deserve.

How did anyone ever shed guilt? And such layered guilt. I saw the half-finished coffee cup, the kettle, with the burned beans, young Tiequon on the football field. My sisters. My family. My first wife. My girlfriend. All ruined. I was cursed.

As I lie there on that bed in that Oklahoma motel room, I simply fester. It is early evening and the sun has set. I cannot motivate myself to get up and turn on a light. Light? I deserve darkness. I don't move.

I'd heard people say it before: "I was so depressed I just could not get out of bed." I always thought, how weak, sure you can, just do it. Just get up. Easier said . . .

Wind whips the drapes. A passing truck's lights flicker the room. The wind dies, the drapes hang still. The darkness returns.

This is my fate, to lie sick in a transient ball of self-pity in a roadside motel in the middle of the prairie. I deserve it all. The fever, the bronchial cough, the delirium, they suit me.

I drift off into a fitful fever-ridden sleep, tormented by voices snaking in and out of my head, weird words try to form, some memory of a condition I had seen in the paper, sick people unable to experience pleasure, autopilot automatons, unable to engage in healthy relationships, what was it, anaconda, anatomical, no that wasn't it, the word won't form, but keeps looping. Then biblical verses, words, phrases, taunts of wandering, wilderness, loss: "whoever brings back a sinner from wandering will save his soul from death," "He pours contempt on princes, and causes them to wander in the wilderness," "my sheep wandered through all the mountains," "and your children shall wander in the wilderness forty years," "forsaken." "Lost in the woods of error."

Overheated under the covers, I squirm, plead through the waters of sleep for the silence of peace, for the voices to quell. Hot. It feels like dozens of people share the room, hide in its corners, shout from its shadows. They are with me, of me, mock me: Exodus, Leviticus, Deuteronomy, Numbers, Old Testament, Old School, the Old South. I'm back in the South, Jim Crow, white hoods, dumped in the swamp, disappeared in the bayou, "some wandered in the wilderness," "some wandered in desert wastes." Hot, I try again to surface. Drowning. My father, fighting in the South Seas. A cup of coffee, burned beans, a frying pan upon her chest, the flashing lights, the gurneys, the morgue. "Some wandered in a solitary way." I drive. I drive. I drive. "So drive." I wander. I drive in a tunnel, a tunnel rat, a tunnel of blood, an artery, from node to infected node, 126 West Fifty-Ninth, to the police station, the morgue, UCLA, LAX, Daphine's, gray, hot, sun, cars. I cannot rest, I cannot sleep. I cannot wake. They won't stop, they won't shut up. "Some wandered in desolate wilderness." Why didn't he move her, why didn't he show up, why didn't he help that kid? Why didn't he? Why didn't he? Why didn't he? More voices, more judgment, more Old Testament. "Not worthy," "Faint and weary," "Wretched." "I need to go to the hospital." A dark closet, a stab of light, he peers out. "There's nothing worse than an empty house." "Eternal rest grant unto them." "I wasn't responsible, Uncle Kermit. I wasn't responsible." "Stop it, Ivan!" I yell, flailing beneath wet, sweat-soaked sheets. "Stop it, Ivan." "Fled into the wilderness," "in captivity," "dreary." A helicopter, a ghetto bird, an M-1 carbine, a fever, a frenzy, the train off the tracks, never arrives, a broken dream, a dream out of reach, "Why would they mess Mom up?" Mess, mess, mess, "an uninhabited, and barren desert." Mess, mess, mess. "Do you know who that is? Huh? Who that is? Huh? That's that kid that was always in trouble, now look what he's done." "A serpent in the wilderness." "Some wandered in desert wastelands." Forgotten by forty, a stray at sixty, the prairie, the plains, a nomad, a vagabond. "Lost in the woods of error." The wind rattles the blinds, the wind beats against the motel, a truck rumbles past, shakes the room, lights, angles, sharp lines cut the walls and ceiling, then back to black. "Spent with hunger and thirst, as well as by the fatigues of the journey." "I just blew the bitch's head off." "Lost," "alone." Blood on his hands, the blood will flow, a superhero. "Bitch's head off." "So drive. So drive." "My sister can finally rest." I try to wake, I try to sleep. I sleep by the graves. "Alone in the wilderness, fled into the wilderness." "Better to reign in Hell," "faint and weary," "wretched."

———

"Kermit," a different voice says. It is familiar, but not in a good way. It is not the good, fun, reassuring Her. It is familiar. It is the scolding, disappointed, commanding Her. It is righteous and sure. Unlike the fever chorus, I know this one well.

"Stop feeling sorry for yourself. This is embarrassing."

I am disoriented, medicated, and delusional. I cannot make out the source of the voice. But I know it well.

"This is really pathetic. You should be ashamed of yourself."

I cannot move. I lie frozen on the motel bed. The feeling is claustrophobic. I'm underwater, struggling for the surface.

"Get back to who you are," the voice demands: "Protect. Provide. Stop wallowing in your own self-pity."

"Madee!" I cry out.

"If you don't change your ways right now," her voice continues, "you won't last another year."

"Madee!"

"You weren't raised to quit. Die or get on with it."

"Madee!"

38

THE LAND OF HIGH MOUNTAINS

At sunrise, in January 2004, our plane came in for a rough landing in Port-au-Prince, Haiti.

The runway in Port-au-Prince was potholed, and the airport unlike any I had seen before. The sole terminal could best be described as a mess, filled with smells, music, chaos, extreme heat and humidity, and even more extreme despair and desperation.

I had always been curious about Haiti and wanted to visit and see if all the stories surrounding the mysterious island were true. One side of my family had Haitian roots, and voodoo lore and rituals hung in the background of my early childhood in Louisiana. My grandmother, whom we called Mamee, would speak Creole, and to this day I can still understand bits of it when I hear it spoken. In going down to Haiti I felt I would learn something about my heritage.

Haiti also played a pivotal role in black history. In 1804, Haiti, then a French colony of black slaves, gained its independence, making it the first and only nation of slaves to do so. This fact makes its two-century descent so tragic, born of such courage and promise, only to land in despair. Recently Haiti has been tagged with several nicknames, none of them good. Haitians jest they are the only country with a last name: "Haiti, The Poorest Country in the Western Hemisphere." Novelist Graham Greene, who set *The Comedians* in

Haiti, termed it a "Nightmare Republic," and "a shabby land of terror." Greene said of Haitians, "they live in the world of Hieronymus Bosch," and of their living conditions, that it was "impossible to exaggerate the poverty of Haiti."

I was in this strange land, not just to explore my roots, but for something immediate as well.

It had to do with my girlfriend, Tami Clark.

Tami is beautiful, blond-haired and blue-eyed. But most important, she is someone who truly fights to make the world a better place. Like Madee, everyone is welcome in Tami Clark's world—no one is a stranger. The daughter of Baptists, Tami grew up in a religious household split between California and Texas. From her earliest memories, the family was always involved in some kind of church-based charity work. They volunteered at the Casa de Esperanza (House of Hope), an orphanage in Tijuana, Mexico; worked at a soup kitchen, the Path of Life, in Riverside, California; or spent Thanksgiving at the Union Rescue Mission in Los Angeles. Tami and her aunt prepared travel packs, containing soap, shampoo, and lotion, and just passed them out from their car to needy people they saw on the street. Tami didn't just talk a good game about people needing to help others; she and her family truly walked the walk.

After attending Baylor, a private Christian university in Waco, Texas, Tami returned to Southern California, where, in the early 2000s, she became involved with Compassion International, a relief organization that included recording artists and radio stations. Their cause was to bring some aid and relief to Haiti.

After my period of wandering ended in Oklahoma, I too returned to Southern California. My goal was to resurrect my relationship with Tami. I tried to be more open and honest, less angry and brooding. For the first time I spoke about all of the problems I had with my family.

At the time, Tami found it impossible to connect with me. She was heavily involved with her church, but I still could not embrace God. She could not give herself to me at that time. I just carried too much pain.

She then left for Haiti without me.

———

I first met Tami Clark in 1991, when she was doing charity work in Mammoth Lakes in the eastern Sierras, just south of Mono Lake. She needed a grand marshal for a Fourth of July parade. Her friend Efren Herrera, a former placekicker for the Dallas Cowboys, recommended me, telling her that I was an experienced public speaker with a long history of volunteer service. I accepted, because it gave me something to do, and it felt like a vacation.

As soon as Herrera introduced us, I felt a spark. Tami later told me she did, too, but she also sensed tension in my handshake. She said it had electricity in it. It felt strained. Her heart whispered, "Come here." Her head screamed, "Run like hell!"

In the months following the event, Tami got a divorce and moved to nearby Temecula, California. We went on a date. Then another. We had a lot in common. We shared a commitment to charity work, she too was an avid sports fan, but most of all, she could make me laugh, something I did far too little since the murders.

I remember an early phone conversation we had, when she mentioned that she had been flipping around the channels on TV and stumbled upon the movie *Brian's Song*, about the great friendship between two Chicago Bears, Gale Sayers and Brian Piccolo. Tami loved the Chicago Bears, going back to a loyalty to Bears linebacker Mike Singletary from her days at Baylor. Baylor's mascot is also a bear.

After watching footage of me diving through the line and tearing up Sayers's knee, she asked, "Was that you?" "Yup." "Then we're through." She hung up. This had always been a sore spot for me, and I thought she was serious.

I called her back and tried to explain. I had apologized to Sayers, I said. Sayers knew the hit was clean. Sayers returned to the field in 1969 and gained over a thousand yards. Sayers was fine, he was later inducted into the Pro Football Hall of Fame. As I went on, she started to giggle. "I was just kidding, you know. Boy you're easy," she said, laughing.

Then we both laughed. I really laughed hard. What a fool, falling for that, but I had just not been in the habit of laughing for some time. I was out of practice, but boy did it feel good. It also let me know who I was dealing with, and I liked it.

Tami said that making me laugh became a mission for her. She told me how much fun she had with me, but that I didn't do a very good job trying to hide my sorrow. The turmoil would just bubble up, and then I would shut down.

The next year, 1992, we moved in together, but my walls and distance never allowed us to get truly close. She knew my issues were related to August 31, 1984, and its aftermath, but whenever she asked, I withdrew, then exploded. She also knew I was estranged from my family as fallout from the killings, but again I kept her an arm's length away, giving a virtual Heisman stiff-arm whenever she cut too close. When questions about my mother, my family, the relationships and dynamics neared the live nerves, I would first answer generically, next get evasive, finally turn hostile.

It put her in an unwinnable situation. She wanted to help ease the trauma. But she couldn't and I wouldn't let her try. I had not come to terms with what happened, never knew what role I played, and didn't know how to go forward. I trusted no one, least of all myself.

Tami, needing to know more, started doing research on her own. She went to libraries, scouring the microfiche, asking people outside my presence to tell her what they knew, knowing that her private investigation would set me off.

Then finally, one day, as we drove on the freeway to visit her parents in Anaheim, she pushed the issue.

"Every time we go somewhere," she said, "somebody asks me about your family."

I opened my mouth to interrupt. She held up a hand to stop me.

She said she could feel the tension coming off me, filling the car.

"Just listen," she said. "One day when you're ready, could you just tell me what really happened?"

This time she wouldn't take the generalities or evasions I threw up to block her. This time she was going to press until I blew up or broke down. I would do both.

Feeling cornered and out of control, I slammed the accelerator, gunning the car close to a hundred miles an hour. Tami swore I was going to smash into the upcoming barrier and kill us both.

She asked for it.

"Kermit!" she screamed.

I tore the car off the freeway, onto an exit, and peeled out into an empty lot. I jammed on the brakes, jarring us to a sharp, lurching stop.

"Just don't say a word." I glowered. "You want it, I'll give it to you one time, and that's it. Don't interrupt. Don't ask questions."

Tami was shaking, and under her breath said only, "Okay."

In a menacing voice, I continued, "Because I've never told anyone this story, never talked about it with anyone except my family, and this may be the last time I ever do."

Four hours later, tears streaming down my face, I was done. It was like lancing a wound, releasing twenty years of venom. It didn't cure me, didn't dull the pain, but it released some pressure. Drain the puss and the infected limb may heal. The immediate and violent purge was temporarily relieving, but the underlying guilt and cycles of rage would live on.

Finally, in 2001, after nearly ten years of living together, Tami couldn't take the tension and moved out.

———

In 2003, when she returned from her first trip to Haiti, I took her to a special spot of ours and asked her to marry me.

Lake Perris is in a valley in the mountains of Southern California. For months I helped her train in these beautiful parklands for a 250-mile charity bike ride. For hours we talked on a particular bench. I was forthcoming, open, ready to commit.

Now I would finally take this vital step in the healing process. I was ready to allow someone into my life. I would place a ring on her finger.

As we sat on that special bench, filled with magical memories, I asked Tami Clark to be my wife, Mrs. Kermit Alexander.

Her answer: "No."

I couldn't believe it.

After this journey back from the depths. "No?" Really? Really. No. She was turning me down? For years she had waited for me to propose.

"No." The words echoed.

She said she was just not ready to give herself up to me. True, she said, for years she had waited for me to propose, but I had always kept her at a distance. Just because I finally had an epiphany, and I was ready to commit, didn't mean she could just wash away years of pain. She did not trust that I had come to terms with my own life, and that I would not continue to hold my secrets from and inflict my moods upon her. You have to trust to be trusted, and as far as she was concerned, I still did not.

And furthermore, she told me, something had changed in her life.

As she spoke, I watched a new light cross her eyes.

Uh-oh, I thought, someone new.

Yes, she said. She met him in Haiti. His name was Clifton.

———

Clifton was an orphan, age of five or six. He suffered from extreme malnutrition, his belly distended, his hair falling out. He had scabies, his nails wouldn't grow, and his teeth were decayed. Calcium deficiencies led to broken bones. He looked like an old man in a little boy's body. Haitian doctors didn't give him a year.

When Tami asked the mission's director about the little boy, he said, "Oh yes, everybody meets Clifton," referring to the boy's engaging personality.

"So he calls all women 'Mom'?"

"No," the director said, "never heard that one before."

And then Tami knew something was up. When he first saw her, he ran and jumped into her arms, cooing, "Mama."

When Tami's trip was up and she had to leave the orphanage, Clifton cried and refused to let go. When she swore she would return, he wouldn't look at her. She had broken his heart. She turned out to be just like all the others: come, tour, do a few days' good deeds, then leave. No one ever really came back. Not to Haiti.

———

After clearing customs, Tami got us a driver. After exiting the airport, we drove through miles of tent cities. Infamous cites, such as Cité Soleil, one of the worst slums in the world. The "housing" consisted of sticks and boards, with a plastic milk container cut in half and filled with wax serving as the light. Dirt, mud, and refuse surrounded the living quarters. It looked as bad as any footage I had ever seen of the slums outside Mumbai, India, or the notorious hillside favelas of Brazil. Some of Haiti's slums were so bad that armed UN peacekeepers refused to go in.

"Kermit," Tami kept stressing, "I've worked with poor folks my whole life, but nothing prepared me for this." The crushing heat, coupled with the stench of poverty flowing from open sewers and decomposing garbage, made us both claustrophobic and nauseated. Add to this the danger posed by the marauding gangs, and the constant sight of girls pregnant following their first cycle made one want to run, to escape. Tami kept telling me that on her first trip, she doubted whether Haiti was a place she could function, much less make a difference. But, she said, this was where differences had to be made. This was where you had to face it, where you couldn't look the other way.

But God, the sights almost forced you to look away, only once you were inside it, there was nowhere else to look.

Port-au-Prince, the nation's capital, with more than two million people, is surrounded by steep mountains. The water flows down a public irrigation system and pools around the settlement. In the slowly moving water, pigs and oxen defecated, and a man washed his motorcycle. Downstream, a woman scooped the water in an old tin can and used it to prepare a meal. Others bathed in it. We kept waiting for a tropical breeze. When the wind blew, it was just a belch from a sewer.

I was stunned; the squalor and the poverty were amazing, like nothing I had seen. I couldn't believe people were allowed to live like this. Residents of the poorest ghettoes in America would be middle class under Haitian standards. Put up against Haiti, Watts felt like Shangri-la.

After touring the tent villages, we left Port-au-Prince and drove to the town of Titanyen, ten miles to the north. Due to road conditions, the drive took an hour and a half. The traffic was wild, a mass of weaving, swerving, stop-and-go chaos. Traffic lights and stop signs were more approximation than regulation, causing people to slow down, sort of.

As we continued to plod northward, we hugged the Caribbean coast, with the hillside falling off to the sea to our left. For the length of the drive, the horn honking was incessant, and of all different styles, long and drawn out, short beeps, intermittent bleats and blasts. We were told this was a kind of "language of horns," with the different sounds encoding messages grasped by all local drivers. What's more, since the roads were so rutted and potholed, traffic in both directions weaved and bobbed, sometimes veering off the road onto the dusty shoulder, causing a flutter of chickens, children, and travelers, other times slicing across the road into oncoming traffic, causing counterswerving on the other side, in an ongoing game of chicken.

Add to potholes, horns, and ruined roads the constant stops caused by "tap-taps," or Haitian taxis. Cars and small trucks that had been opened up to hold as many people as possible, they were painted bright circus colors with inspirational sayings or identifying monikers, "Jesus Saves," "Praise the Lord," "Exodus," "Hollywood," and "No Problem." The name "tap-tap" derives from the custom of tapping the floor loudly with your foot when you want the car to stop so you can get off. As we slowed and then stopped behind a packed tap-tap and watched a man, laden with bags of produce, defy physics and squeeze in, we asked our driver, "How many people can fit into a tap-tap?" The driver paused. We watched the man disappear into the sea of travelers. The driver's answer, "One more."

As we continued north on the endless ten-mile drive, the roadside was in a state of constant commotion. Women balanced baskets upon their heads. Mules, chickens, and very stray dogs with very long breasts dodged each other. At speed bumps or particularly impressive potholes, children rushed up to the traffic, hawking mangoes, sugarcane, and *pistaches*—a kind of peanut hybrid. Behind the kids, open-air markets bustled, with melons, tubers, roots, and nuts set out in wooden lean-tos covered by thatched roofs.

Somehow the chaos had a strange rhythm to it. A *blan*, Creole for foreigner, would either crash or lose their mind on these roads, likely both. But for natives, it had become normal. They could negotiate this landscape the same as we drive a U.S. highway. You just get in a groove and you go.

As we drove on, we crossed dry desert washes, cacti barriers, plantain trees, and rows of sugarcane. The sky above was overcast and humid. Mountains were a constant to our right, stretching east toward the Dominican Republic. A muddy coastline extended west, before blending well offshore into the turquoise waters of the Caribbean.

As we approached the town and the orphanage I had a strange feeling of peace, something I would not have expected to find in Haiti. I felt close to Tami, sensed a new chapter unfolding.

We drove through the gates to the Mission of Hope campus. As Tami had promised, when you enter through these gates, you can "feel the hope."

Twelve hundred children in uniform attended school. The classrooms were small boxes with cinder-block windows. The students were orderly and attentive.

I felt a long-gone sense of purpose returning. Just look what even small amounts of American money could do: make massive differences in the lives of Haitian children. It was at the Mission of Hope that Tami heard her calling and began pondering how she could help Haiti.

After touring the mission, we took a road up into the surrounding hills. We got out of the car and gazed out over the Caribbean. At last, a breeze. Still hot, humid, muggy, but the air was fresh.

I breathed deeply. The mission, the valley, the fields stretched to the sea. The sky above, an overcast gray, tranquil, it all felt surreal.

For the first time in years they weren't inside my head, following me wherever I went. Tiequon Cox, Sterling Norris, my family pointing their fingers of guilt, CW, Judge Boren, Los Angeles Superior Court, for once they all felt so far away. I couldn't imagine them coming up here to get me.

A gust of wind blew from the sea. No stench, a real sea breeze.

Tami said the heat and the wind reminded her of Amarillo, and her grandmother's home. She told me about windmills spinning under a big Texas sky.

———

Haitian poverty results from an unhappy history of corruption, upheaval, and violence.

In 1697, in the Treaty of Ryswick, the island of Hispaniola was partitioned, with the western third, Saint-Domingue, going to the French, while the eastern portion, Santo Domingo, went to the Spanish. Saint-Domingue would rely on African slave labor to produce coffee, sugar, and indigo for export.

In 1791, inspired by the French Revolution, with its message of liberty and equality, Toussaint-Louverture, known as the Black Napoleon, led a slave revolt. After more than a decade of fighting, the guerrilla warfare and yellow fever combined to defeat the French. In 1804 Saint-Domingue became the first and only independent nation to be run by its former slaves. The nation changed its name to Haiti, from the Taino Indian word *Ayiti*, meaning "Land of High Mountains," or "home or mother of the earth." Throughout the nineteenth century Haiti would relive its violent birth: coups, revolts, assassinations, and chronic indebtedness were the norm. Fearing that the chaos and instability caused both economic and security risks, and thus left it vulnerable to European incursions, the United States occupied Haiti from 1915 to 1934.

Following the U.S. departure, Dominican dictator Rafael Trujillo used a border dispute as a pretext for genocide. In the 1937 Parsley Massacre, Trujillo institutionalized *Antihaitianismo*, the claim of Spanish Dominican superiority over Haitian blacks, and oversaw the murder of between ten and thirty thousand Haitians.

Following a period of multiple elections, revolutions, and coups, dictatorial order was restored to Haiti in the late 1950s under the authority of François "Papa Doc" Duvalier. The regime relied upon voodoo mysticism and random terror to subjugate the populace. His rule enforced by uniformed thugs—the Tonton Macoutes, dressed in sunglasses and dungarees, and *cagoules*, their faces hidden by masks—Papa Doc ruled Haiti until his death in 1971. His nineteen-year-old son, Jean-Claude "Baby Doc" Duvalier, continued his father's rule until his ouster in 1986. Following the thirty years of stabilized Duvalierist terror, Haiti returned to repeating cycles of failed elections, coups, dictatorships, and revolutions.

After a military takeover in the 1990s, U.S. president Bill Clinton intervened in an effort to restore democracy and free elections. The early 2000s saw elections marred by fraud and intimidation. At the time of our arrival in 2004, a coup was under way to oust President Bertrand Aristide for the second time.

The constants of uncertainty, debt, and violence have crippled Haiti's development and infrastructure. A satellite photo of the island, showing the Haitian-Dominican border, reveals the environmental toll. The Dominican side is forested and green, while the Haitian side is parched and desolate. Deforested, and devoid of natural defenses, Haiti is left vulnerable to the Atlantic hurricane season, suffering casualties unheard-of in its Dominican neighbor. The shelter is less, the soil weaker, the flooding intensified, and sources of fresh water and power depleted.

————

After Tami and I returned to the orphanage at Mission of Hope, she began looking for Clifton.

She disappeared inside the mission. I waited outside by the car.

I then saw a little boy peek his head around a corner, then dart from behind a wall and tear past me. He looked like a little escapee trying to run away from the orphanage. He rushed toward a group of kids playing soccer.

I don't know why—I had never seen a picture of the boy and didn't know what he looked like—but I just knew it had to be him.

"Clifton!" I called out.

The boy screeched to a stop. He turned around and looked at me, and just as fast, ran and jumped into my arms.

That was it. So natural, something meant to be. And he stayed in my arms, chattering away, grinning up at me, as if he'd known me all his life.

And talk about presence, that intangible "it" quality, that boy had it. And he was calling out to me. A reason to live, held in my arms, babbling, my future, found on a dusty soccer field in an orphanage in Haiti.

And that was *the* moment, the first glimpse of a second chance. The path was lit. I could see a way out of the Valley. Shed the ghosts of Watts in the Land of High Mountains.

And Madee was there with me. But this time she didn't need to say a word.

39

WE CAN'T DO THIS

On december 13, 2005, thousands of miles from Haiti, rapper Snoop Dogg held a free outdoor concert in Northern California. It was nighttime and a light rain fell, but the thousands of fans didn't seem to notice.

The performance was held outside San Quentin's east gate, in support of clemency for Stanley "Tookie" Williams. It was the date set for his execution. Supporters felt he had reformed, and therefore his life should be spared.

Following the death penalty's return, this was the greatest drama surrounding an execution since Robert Alton Harris.

Tookie Williams, Crip pioneer and prison badass, bodybuilder supreme, spent the last ten years recasting himself as reformed, redeemed, a new man. The new Tookie's mission: to keep youth out of gangs, to broker treaties between rival factions, and to promote a "peace protocol." He began publishing books for young readers promoting an antigang message, *Gangs and Wanting to Belong, Gangs and Drugs, Gangs and Violence, Gangs and Your Neighborhood.*

Whether this transformation was real, whether it did anyone any good, and whether it was enough to save Williams's life depended upon the source. Not surprisingly, as with every issue dealing with capital punishment, opinions fell into polarized camps.

For supporters of Williams, here was a changed man, someone who saw the light during his long stay in prison. He genuinely cared about his community and was doing something to help. Who would have more street credibility to reach young minds than a man like Tookie Williams—tough, street-smart, from the hood. Testimonials poured in regarding the effects of Tookie's books. A Swiss national legislator, as well as anti-death-penalty activists, nominated him for a Nobel Peace Prize and a Nobel Prize for Literature.

While Williams never admitted to the crimes, a murder of a man in a botched robbery and the killing of a couple and their daughter a month later, he did apologize for his role in organizing the Crips. Supporters pointed to both his potential innocence as well as his story of redemption as reason to spare his life. Celebrity activists included Jesse Jackson, actor Mike Farrell, South African president Desmond Tutu, former California state senator Tom Hayden.

Law enforcement officers, prison guards, and those opposed to Williams's clemency saw the record differently. For them, the evidence of guilt was overwhelming, with Williams making statements regarding specifics of the crime that only the killer would have known. They cited his unwillingness to admit guilt as proving a lack of remorse and an inability to take responsibility for his actions. Additionally, many questioned the sincerity of the conversion.

Williams's critics further pointed to his unwillingness to debrief, or tell officials all he knew of the workings of the Crips both in and out of prison. Prison guards stated that when he entered the exercise yard, the sea parted and cronies wiped down his bench and table before his arrival. In other words, he still ruled his gang in prison, where underlings rolled out the "blue carpet" in his honor.

Finally, many questioned whether Williams even wrote his books; they claimed that Barbara Becnel, a sometime coauthor, actually ghostwrote everything, including his full-length memoir, *Blue Rage, Black Redemption*, which charts his saga from Crip to antigang activist.

For San Quentin spokesman Vernell Crittendon, Becnel was the driving force behind Williams's message, and Williams was ultimately a kind of walking contradiction. Crittendon felt Williams did want to be seen as a force against gangs, but was motivated by the desire to save his own life. Williams did want to reduce violence on the streets, but was unwilling to give up the prestige and benefits that Crip gang status bestowed upon him in prison. Williams wanted to renounce the gang but bask in its glory. Finally, Crittendon saw the ultimate undoing of Williams's redemptive quest as the unwillingness to admit responsibility for the homicides.

Once his appeals were exhausted, Williams asked for clemency. This was Governor Arnold Schwarzenegger's second request since taking office in November 2003. But the execution of Donald Jay Beardslee, early in 2005, presented none of the complications of the current case.

Prison spokesman Crittendon termed Beardslee's execution— with no issues of guilt, no extenuating circumstances—the most clear-cut of the new era. Beardslee confessed to murdering two young women, garroting one in Lake County, shooting another in Half Moon Bay. The most memorable moment: when a reporter from the *San Mateo Daily Journal* collapsed and had to be rushed away from the death chamber by ambulance. Otherwise, proceedings were described as "very unemotional."

"He's gone," the prosecutor said following the execution. "Go home and hug your daughters. And hope like hell that a predator like him never gets hold of them."

Williams's case, unlike Beardslee's, was complicated by the global media coverage, the redemptive angle, and the fact that Williams insisted upon his innocence.

Ultimately denying clemency, Schwarzenegger stated: "Clemency cases are always difficult, and this one is no exception. After studying the evidence, searching the history, listening to the arguments, and wrestling with the profound consequences, I could find no justification for granting clemency. The facts do not justify overturning the jury's verdict or the decisions of the courts in this case."

After the execution team experienced some trouble getting the needles through his oversized arms, Stanley Tookie Williams was declared dead shortly after midnight.

————

In 2005, while the Tookie Williams redemption saga wound down, we took another trip to Haiti to visit Clifton.

After meeting Clifton, I had tried again with Tami. This time she said yes, and in May 2004 we were married at Lake Perris. We took our honeymoon in Haiti. Our first goal as a couple: adopt that little boy.

I was open again to God and woke up early each morning to express thankfulness for this new opportunity and to pray: "I hope I don't miss anybody today. . . . I can't miss someone and have them turn into Tiequon Cox. Please, Lord, don't let me miss Clifton. Please don't let me miss anyone again."

There was no way I would betray this moment, miss this chance. This time my eyes were open. I would not slip.

In addition to working to get Clifton into our home, we also wanted to make a bigger difference in the lives of the people of Haiti. Tami's memory of the windmills in Amarillo spurred the idea of what would become "Operation Windmill," an effort to bring a desperately needed clean energy source to Haiti. The windmills would generate power and pump water. This was also a vital step in weaning the Haitians off charcoal use. The charcoal came from trees, which led to chronic deforestation and environmental distress.

The process of adoption was brutal, mired in endless bureaucracy, paperwork, fits, starts, denials. It called for superhuman patience. But I welcomed the opportunity. I could once again help, and with a purpose came a sense of control, something lost for twenty years. During 2004 we took a half a dozen trips to Haiti, where we visited Clifton, and advanced the windmill project.

Between trips we also bought a house in Riverside. It wasn't modern or fancy, but it had three bedrooms, a pool, a horse stall, and a big yard surrounded by palm trees. We couldn't wait to get Clifton into his new home and begin our life. We pictured him exploring all the rooms, looking in wonder at his new surroundings. For a boy from an orphanage in Haiti, we hoped a home in California would feel like paradise.

In between our Haitian trips, Tami served as the catalyst, reuniting me with my estranged family. The process was slow and painful, but positive. Once I could finally forgive myself, I forgave others.

The vengeance had been burned out of me. I had been brought back to life.

———

After two years in the adoption trenches, we were met with deflating news.

Clifton, we were told, was not available for adoption.

To allow Clifton's adoption, the people at Mission of Hope informed us, would be against the very mission of the mission, which was to raise educated, stable young people, imbued with Christian values, who would remain in the country and begin to build a self-sufficient and stable Haiti.

I sure couldn't argue with the message. But I sure wished they had told us that earlier.

While crushed, we both knew we had to continue to be a part of the child's life. Every month we sent him money, bought him clothes, and covered his medical expenses.

Clifton continued to call Tami "Mom," and began introducing me to everyone as "my dad."

During this period we were flying to Haiti every few months. The problem was, whenever we left, Clifton sank into depression, so bad that he wouldn't eat and often became quite ill.

Finally, the director said to me, "I have to ask you to stop coming, because he falls apart after you go. It has put his health at risk."

———

Throughout the first decade of the twenty-first century, Tiequon Cox was confined in the Adjustment Center at San Quentin Prison.

During this stay, Cox gave up all personal belongings. He forfeited his television and refused to take a mattress. When a guard asked him why he didn't want his TV and mattress, Cox replied that possessions became attachments, which correctional staff could then take away from him, thus placing him under their control.

This was Cox's effort to assume complete control of the most controlling environment. It was this single-minded commitment to nihilism that made Cox so dangerous. He had absolutely nothing to lose, he was free of all possessions, attachments, values, and restraints. No religion, no belongings, no future.

By taking control of his death row experience, Cox had made it part of his fantasy, a Rolling Sixties world taken to its ultimate extreme. Even in the inverted world of death row, he was the nth degree. It was Cox in the AC they would talk about on the streets. It was the warrior of the row to whom the songs would be sung. They could bring the fire, but they couldn't break Li'l Fee.

Others within the staff noticed that Cox never seemed to sleep. The light in his cell burned around the clock. And there he'd be, sitting on the floor, back propped against the cell wall, legs stretched straight in front of him, peering at you through squinted eyes. "If you just gave him a sombrero," one guard said, "he would have looked just like a Mexican worker taking afternoon siesta."

During his decade in AC, Cox delved into yoga, meditation, and martial arts. But most of all he just sat there, "staring straight ahead, like a man in a trance, like some kind of monk."

With the weights confiscated and yard time reduced, Cox became inventive in his routines. Pass his cell at 2 a.m. and there he was working out. Endless sets of push-ups, sit-ups, burpees, one-legged burpees, lateral burpees, and extreme burpees, all involving squats, kicks, leaps, and jumps. The workouts were reminiscent of George Jackson, known for his AC fingertip push-ups—part of the mind-body steeling process.

Cox was described as having no body fat and being cut like a gymnast. One guard was struck by the flexibility of such a large and muscular individual, continually repeating, "He'd be exercising in his cell and he could kick straight up, just kick straight up." Another practiced move: he'd stand on one leg, with one foot on the ground, and another placed flat against the wall. Guards surmised that this was a kind of training, just in case he ever "got loose." The raised foot would be at a perfect height to take out a short female guard, just plant a hard kick in her face.

"Preparation and opportunity," that was the key for people like Cox, said the guard. "Be prepared and just wait for that opportunity to strike."

———

After crushing us, the mission director subsequently told us that given Clifton's state, he ultimately thought it would be best for him if we went through with the adoption after all.

What a roller coaster.

This new news brought momentary joy, until I realized we had simply been returned to where we had just been before. But compared to being told that the adoption was impossible, merely being returned to the world of an endless theoretical adoption felt like a victory.

But the adoption policies in Haiti, to the extent there were any, were inscrutable, and ever changing. We kept trying.

When we next returned to Haiti, we once again got what we expected: more surprises. This twist dramatically complicated our plans for adoption.

When we left the Mission of Hope to deliver provisions to other orphanages, Clifton wanted to join us. He would be our guide, he said.

After entering the Good Samaritan Orphanage, to the north of Titanyen, we saw Clifton begin to play with four other children. It was another humid Haitian afternoon, and the kids were in a cracked cement yard.

They were high-fiving each other, laughing, roughhousing, and tumbling about like a litter of puppies. They ranged from four to twelve years old.

At first we didn't want to disturb him, then finally couldn't resist any longer.

"Clifton!" we shouted. He smiled and began to come toward us. "Who are your friends? Introduce us."

Clifton's impish grin began to light up his face. He smiled at his playmates and said something in Creole. They snickered. We looked at each other and shrugged.

He then looked back at us and in a thick accent, in broken English, responded, "These are not my friends, these are my brothers and sisters."

"This," Clifton said, "is my sister Manoucheka," pointing to the oldest girl. "And Jameson," he said, touching the oldest boy. He then introduced another boy, Zachary, and a little girl, Semfia.

We went dumb, couldn't say a word. Smiling awkwardly, trying not to look at each other for fear of revealing our shock. Now what? Break them up? Leave others behind?

Jameson then stepped forward and asked us if we would take a picture of the four of them together with Clifton. Jameson said they all really wanted to have something to remember Clifton by, since we were taking him away and they would never see him again.

Oh boy, that did it, when he said that, Tami and I both broke down. We tried our best to hold it together in front of the kids. They had already been through so much, the last thing we wanted to do was confuse and upset them more. But that did it. Both of us kept wiping away the tears.

My head spun. An expectation existed, a plan stood in place. I felt so sure adopting Clifton was the right thing, for him, for Tami, for me, for us. I would exorcise the ghosts of past failures. Haiti had come to stand for solace, my rescue. Tami and I had been bonded through this wonderful little boy. But this changed everything.

I looked at Tami, her head downcast in an effort to hide the tears.

I then looked over at the five kids. They had stopped playing. They just stared at us.

Jameson, nine, raised an arm partway, pointing at my camera.

"Well," he said. "Can we get one picture?"

A leaden sky hung overhead. Mountains loomed in the background.

"We can't do this," I said.

40

WE TAKE THEM ALL

"I FOUND HER. I found her," the girl says. "Hurry. I know where she is."

At this point she begins to run. We follow. We cross a ravine. Faster and faster the young girl tears through the streets. In the heat and humidity, we can barely keep up as she runs ahead.

"This way, come on, hurry," she says again. "She's this way, come on." The girl picks up speed, dodging potholes, debris, a chicken, a broken-down car. Several times we nearly fall as we follow her.

We are in a district known as Delma 33. We follow the girl into the depths of Port-au-Prince. She continues over dirt, rubble, between fences, behind yards. Finally she slows, leading us onto a narrow path squeezed between two buildings.

As we emerge from the path, we arrive at an old brick-and-mortar church that looks like it was struck by an earthquake. Much is in ruins. It seems abandoned.

"Here," the girl says. "She is in here."

We look around in the dimly lit, desolate interior but can make out nothing through the heavy interlocking shadows.

Despite its decrepit state, the church retains a sense of mystery and gravity.

Finally, Tami draws my attention to a waiflike creature. She lies still on a mat in the corner of the church. She looks twice her age of forty-two. A scarf covers her head.

She has suffered several bouts of malaria as well as lesions of the brain.

She is homeless and lives in the church.

The woman begs us to pray for her. She cries that she is possessed by evil spirits.

As we kneel about her and say a prayer, we cannot stop staring at her.

Then Tami says to me, "Oh my God, Kermit, look at her face."

———

Back at the Good Samaritan Orphanage, Tami had asked me, "Kermit, how can you say that?"

I turned to her and held her, then said, "We can't break them up."

"But—" she began.

I interrupted: "We either take them all or we don't take any of them."

"I know," she said. "They're still invested in each other."

"Yup," I said, "we take one, we take them all."

"I know," she said again.

"Then we take them all."

"Are you serious?"

———

Now we stand in the old church. We have decided to pursue not one, but five impossible adoptions. The visit to this church is a step into the maze.

"What?" I whisper, having no idea what Tami is getting at.

She continues: "Look, Kermit. You can see the faces of all five of the children. Her face is like a mosaic of her kids."

It is uncanny; despite the fact that the children all look different, there is a kind of composite of all of them within the mother's withered features.

Looking away from the face momentarily at the contours of the old church, I grow nervous. This is the moment we have come here for, to gain her blessing for the adoption of her five kids. Without this, any future moves will be futile.

Because she is the mother of the five children, by law we need her consent. The entire process will be arduous enough as it is, but this first hurdle must be cleared. We have no idea how she will respond. Before asking her permission, we decide it best to get her some medical care and hopefully revive her somewhat.

After concluding the prayer, we bring her to a hospital and get her an IV. She is desperately malnourished and dehydrated.

Once cogent, she responds.

She is beside herself with joy. She cannot believe her good fortune. Her children will be saved, she says, removed from Haiti. Given her desperate condition, she has obviously been incapable of properly caring for them. She happily consents to the adoption.

———

After weeping for joy at this successful step in establishing a new family and starting a new life, I found my mind drifting back to that courtroom twenty years ago, again swearing I would not let past mistakes recur.

Testimony regarding Tiequon Cox's mother rang in my ears. She was on drugs, half-crazed, a delusional alcoholic who was in and out of institutions, incapable of providing her kids with any type of normal home.

Now, in Haiti, as I looked at this sad woman, suffering from the ravaging effects of malnutrition and disease, and compared the possible fate of her orphaned children with that of Cox and his siblings, I knew that my mission was to save these kids. My resolve was steeled. I would provide these kids with a second chance, as they would for me.

"Protect. Lead. Act."

This was it, the real deal, gritty, dirty, hard to look at. No theory, nothing abstract, no talk of doing good deeds from remote locations, saving the world from the comfort of an armchair.

This was the street-level world of Port-au-Prince, filled with sores, sewage, and stench. And I had learned, the hard way, that if you really wanted to make a difference, this was the world into which you had to dive. The more you wanted to look away, plug your nose, close your eyes, and run, the better you knew you were in the right place, the spot you were needed most. Hospitals, orphanages, shelters, the hardest to take, filled with cries, anguish, and pain. This is where I had to be.

Years ago in Watts I had unknowingly turned my back, failed to act, with a desperate kid who couldn't control himself. It's one thing to talk a good game, give speeches in front of children made to sit at desks and behave. It's another to actually deal with the malcontents, misfits, and down-and-outs in the real world, those kids who won't look you in the eye, and when they do, their eyes are filled with hate and mistrust. The kid to whom you say, "I want to help you," and who answers, "Fuck you," is the kid on whom you can't turn your back.

I saw it now with true clarity, no delusions. I knew that taking five Haitian orphans into our home would be anything but easy. I had plenty of experience with large families and their incessant conflicts. It would be at times trying, brutal, frustrating, and heartbreaking. That was life. I was ready. The grand irony, with five children to care for on the horizon, I felt free, released from the dark shackles of guilt.

When I had prowled the streets of South Central years ago I was looking to kill; now in Haiti I was looking to heal. Action can overcome curse, help alter the hand of fate.

———

When we returned to California, we remapped the living arrangements for our home in Riverside. We planned out the house, which rooms would be for the children. We decorated their rooms. Over and over, we replayed that day when the five Haitian kids would together enter their home. What would their reactions be? Would they even know what refrigerators, dishwashers, and washing machines were? How would they react to their own pool, shower, and bathtub?

While we tried to keep ourselves busy, the wait was excruciating. While we had both been through legal and bureaucratic battles in the past—home purchases, divorces, insurance companies, courtrooms— nothing had prepared us for this. This even made a capital jury trial seem simple and easy to understand.

Aside from the intricacies typical of any adoption, the complications here were fivefold, due to the number of children, then infinite, due to the impenetrable nature of the Haitian government. Moreover, whenever the process seemed to move forward, it was derailed by a hurricane, a coup, a disputed election, and postelection riots.

During this time, Clifton remained at the Mission of Hope, where he was well cared for, but we moved the other children from Good Samaritan to a safer and more stable environment at the Haitian Academy Boarding School, a twenty-acre campus located near Titanyen in Cache-Cache Dougé.

To stay busy, and make money to support the costs associated with the upcoming adoptions and the constant trips to Haiti, I took a job as a community services officer at nearby Riverside Community College. Tami continued with her work at a nonprofit that fought against child abuse. She also started her own business, making gift baskets for real estate agents to present to new home buyers. We had a barn, storage, and office space built out back in the yard of our new home. This served as the headquarters for her business. It took off quickly, and within a few years Tami had several employees and hundreds of clients.

To occupy our time, we constantly planned ahead for our life after the adoptions. This made the adoptions feel more real and seem more imminent. We bought a van and a long dining room table to accommodate all of the incoming hungry mouths. We kept tinkering with the rooms, imagining the day the beds would be filled with little bodies.

As we worked and waited, I dreamed of once again having a full house, chaotic with life and activity, a house like the one in which I was raised.

Madee's words, "There's nothing worse than an empty house," started to take on a more hopeful air, growing less sinister, and more prophetic.

I actually began picturing her with the kids, how she would interact with them. She'd watch over me, help me raise them.

Finally, after decades, a future to look toward once again. We had a new home, our finances were solid, the kids were on the way, and my siblings were making their way back into my life. And this time it wasn't just to talk about executions, appeals, and district attorneys. My family was warm and supportive about the adoptions and helped me through the ordeal. They couldn't wait to meet their new nieces and nephews.

————

One month later, on February 21, 2006, two hours before murderer and rapist Michael Morales was to be executed, U.S. District Court Judge Jeremy Fogel granted a stay, ruling that California must conduct the execution in a manner that does not violate the Eighth Amendment's ban on cruel and unusual punishments.

Fogel ruled that San Quentin's gas chamber was never intended to serve as a site of lethal injections administered by poorly trained staff in a dimly lit compartment. This, Fogel said, risked leaving inmates conscious but in pain, thus violating Eighth Amendment prohibitions. Instead, the judge said, the sodium thiopental, the drug that puts the condemned to sleep, would have to be injected directly into the vein by a licensed medical professional. This put the state of California in a bind since licensed medical doctors are prohibited from engaging in executions.

————

Over the next two years the news out of Haiti was disheartening.

The Atlantic hurricane season of 2008 was one of the worst on record. The island was battered by Hurricanes Faye, Gustav, Hanna, and Ike. Collectively they thrashed Haiti's naked mountains, leaving major cities underwater.

On top of that, in 2008 a spike in food and energy prices led to riots and an overthrow of the prime minister.

These continued shocks to Haiti's stability made us fear the adoptions might never go through.

————

Two years later, on January 4, 2010, I turned sixty-nine.

Now, six years since I had first met Clifton, the adoption proceedings plodded, no end in sight, a constant repetition of lost paperwork, coups, riots, and natural disasters. I had to keep myself from slipping into the mind-set that whether it be criminals, bureaucracies, or Mother Nature, the world conspired against me.

Then, one week later, on the afternoon of January 12, 2010, everything changed once again.

Tami was driving her car on Interstate 15, in the process of making arrangements for our annual Super Bowl party. She was listening to the radio when a special bulletin interrupted regular broadcasting.

When she heard the report she felt ill, and nearly drove the car into the median.

My phone rang. Tami was crying. She told me to turn on the TV.

41

NEWS THAT DEMANDS
A CHAIR

Haitians call it "news that demands a chair," meaning "you better sit down for this."

Some referred to it only as *bagay la*, meaning "the thing," refusing to give it a name, for fear *that* would bring it back.

It was described as an "acute-on-chronic crisis," and just further evidence that the nation's history was "written in blood."

I assumed the worst.

As I saw the images, I felt sick, then fell to my knees in prayer.

At 4:53 p.m. local time, on January 12, 2010, six miles beneath the earth's surface, the Enriquillo–Plantain Garden fault zone separating the North American tectonic plate from the Caribbean plate ruptured for the first time in two hundred years. The seismic activity along the fault line placed the epicenter near the town of Leogane, within ten miles of Port-au-Prince. The result was a magnitude 7.0 earthquake.

Buildings collapsed, zombies stumbled about under a layer of gray dust, panic-stricken wanderers prayed for their lives, cars crashed, rush hour shook to a halt.

I kept studying the rubble, searching for familiar faces.

My head thundered.

Tami returned. We hugged, then sobbed.

The street cracked, poles fell, bloodstained children shrieked.

We wanted to look away. Impossible. We stared. Brutal.

It was six years since we began the adoption of Clifton. Six years, and another dream was just out of reach, another arrival halted, busted. I was cast back into the Valley.

———

Hourly news coverage showed in graphic detail the dead, the injured, the starving. Huddled children were forced to eat "cakes" made of mud. Rancid sewage engulfed communities, threatening an epidemic to come. Ramshackle housing, which often crumbled before it was completed, collapsed to rubble and dust. And the reports were repeatedly interrupted by aftershocks, which brought down more buildings.

With each broadcast the death toll rose: 10,000; 30,000; 60,000. Because Haiti's vital records are so approximate, an accurate total will never be known, but most estimates placed earthquake-related fatalities at somewhere between 200,000 and 300,000. An earthquake of nearly identical magnitude hit the San Francisco Bay Area in 1989. The death toll was sixty-three. The population of greater Port-au-Prince is two million, the Bay Area over seven million.

With alternating masochism and hope, we were glued to CNN. We didn't sleep or eat, just sat watching in shock.

Building codes didn't exist, and less than 10 percent of buildings approached modern standards. Worse, Port-au-Prince was an unplanned city that grew pell-mell with no consideration as to land use.

The National Palace, along with every government building but one, lay in ruins. The statue of Toussaint-Louverture stood. He was covered in dust, and as always, with his back to the palace, something locals claimed an ill omen. For centuries the nation's founder refused to face his creation.

On the second and third days after the quake, stories of medical horrors started to hit the airwaves. And due to minimal communications and a crippled infrastructure, it was impossible to split rumor from fact. A wave of stories covered amputations done to ward off gangrene, followed by reports of hastily done and unnecessary amputations.

This was followed that evening by rumors that slum gangs, called Chime (the downtrodden), roved through the devastation, heavily armed, terrorizing, and raping. Port-au-Prince was already known as the kidnapping capital of the world—following the quake the numbers of the "disappeared" exploded.

Collapsed floors, pancaked buildings, people covered in a fine powder roamed the streets. Forty percent of federal employees were listed as injured or killed. Coming out of Port-au-Prince, a new syndrome was reported to the world, *psychose béton*, or the phobia of concrete. Sufferers developed symptoms similar to post-traumatic stress disorder: terror, paranoia, and sleeplessness.

———

When I learned of the symptoms of post-traumatic stress disorder (PTSD) affecting the people of Haiti, I heard my own diagnosis. The disorder was me.

It was brought on by "learning about unexpected or violent death . . . of a family or child," and involved "intense fear, helplessness, or horror," the "persistent reexperiencing of the traumatic event" through "recurrent and intrusive recollections . . . or recurrent distressing dreams."

Symptoms included persistent anxiety, anger, irritability, an exaggerated startle response, and hypervigilance, an "abnormally increased arousal," a constant "scanning of the environment for threats." Sufferers felt out of control and devoid of support, reporting "painful guilt feelings about surviving when others did not," engaging in acts of "phobic avoidance" of anything linked to the original trauma. This response ruins relationships and leads to "marital conflict, divorce, or loss of job."

It was all me. The intrusions, the guilt, the avoidance, the anger. The unwillingness to open up, and the flights of rage when forced. I shut myself in and locked others out. When my father was in the service they called it shell shock. Now I called it my life.

———

President Clinton was on TV coordinating relief efforts. UN secretary-general Ban Ki Moon appealed for aid. Clinton hammered a message of hope. Haiti's moment of crisis must be its moment of change. He launched his program: Haiti would "Build Back Better."

Since his honeymoon in Haiti in 1975, the poor island nation held an emotional place in Bill Clinton's heart. He and Hillary had flown there repeatedly, and they described themselves as a "Haiti-obsessed family." Clinton was the first sitting president to visit since Franklin Roosevelt. And when the earthquake hit, Clinton said he took it "personally and emotionally," while Hillary became "physically sick."

Following the quake, Clinton, the UN special envoy to Haiti, along with fellow former president George W. Bush, led the long-term recovery effort. Clinton, who thinks constantly of Haiti's future, expressed his hopes that one day it would be the next South Korea, become another "miracle economy."

Two days after the quake, Clinton was in his Harlem office leading a high-powered team of philanthropists and nongovernmental organizations in his effort to "Build Back Better": fixing roads, planting trees, growing fruit for export, and expanding recycling efforts. Clinton's words from the Harlem meeting: "The Haitians have the first chance they've had to escape their own history."

Once again I was hurled into historic events I wanted no part of. The Watts Riots, the tragic crime, now, on the world stage, the worst earthquake in recent memory.

Orphans Manoucheka, Jameson, Zachary, and Semfia were among the poorest and most vulnerable of the poor. All were just outside the epicenter near Port-au-Prince. Clifton, as far as we knew, was still at Mission of Hope.

There was no phone service and four days after the earthquake we still couldn't get any news regarding the children.

I felt all of the old wounds reopen. The brief solace of salvation was extinguished by the familiar pall of darkness that had marked my last twenty years. I had that helpless, meaningless feeling, the numb anger that comes with being overwhelmed when events tear out of control. This time it wasn't an unknown gunman at daybreak, but Mother Nature in the late afternoon. I couldn't blame this one on myself, but that didn't still the pain.

Was this what the last six years would come to? More than twenty trips to the island, exhausted savings, spent emotions, and what would we have to show—the corpses of the kids we'd promised to rescue.

For days, Tami tried everyone in Haiti she could think of. But the lines were down. For days we didn't sleep.

Worldwide, the Haitian diaspora moaned, in Manhattan and Queens, Miami, Boston, and Montreal, in France, Jamaica, and the Virgin Islands. They talked to each other, some talked to Tami, but they were as information-starved as us. No one could get through. But rumors, speculation, fears, and apocalyptic scenarios spread like disease. And no one could blame their pessimism, certainly not me. If you were of Haiti, you couldn't help thinking the worst. I did.

At this point, I really didn't know if I had it in me to withstand another trauma. I feared it would simply override my system, short-circuit me the way the first tragedy nearly did. It took twenty years to overcome August 31. I wasn't up for another twenty from January 12. That was a sentence I wouldn't serve.

I couldn't stop imaging funerals. I sketched them in my mind. I dreamed them. I obsessed over them and counted them: one, two, three, four, five, followed by a sixth: mine. My obituary: "Former NFL star, sixty-nine, dies of guilt."

I could only think, if those five kids die, that will be the end of me, I will be the only man to die twice.

———

As Haiti fights through the rubble, and Tiequon Cox sits in his death row cell awaiting the decision on his federal appeals, two conflicting developments mark California's ongoing death penalty wars.

First, a petition to abolish capital punishment is launched. If enough signatures are collected, for the first time since 1978, Californians would vote on the death penalty. If passed, the referendum would convert more than seven hundred death sentences to life without parole. The measure is backed by the American Civil Liberties Union and other groups, who argue that capital punishment is primitive, unfair, cruel, unusual, and costly. Opponents, who include law-and-order advocates and victims' rights groups, contend that the death penalty serves as a deterrent, brings justice and closure, and affects only a tiny fraction of the most heinous killers, who have all been proven guilty beyond a shadow of doubt.

The second development is the completion of San Quentin's new lethal-injection-only facility. It is stark, white, modern, and medical. It is capable of administering either the three-drug protocol or the single injection of sodium thiopental. It contains no chair, only a gurney onto which the inmate is strapped.

Prison staff report that if the referendum fails, the new chamber will be activated, and condemned with exhausted appeals executed at a quickened pace.

In an effort to keep Tiequon Cox out of the new chamber, his attorneys have argued that he suffered from post-traumatic stress disorder. The diagnosis is part of the larger claim that Cox's attorney, Edward Cook, provided ineffective assistance of counsel by failing to accurately portray, during the penalty phase of the trial, the psychological horrors to which the young Cox was subjected.

The appeal claimed that because Cook had been ineffective by forgoing a guilt-phase defense, calling no witnesses and merely stating "submit it" for argument, he therefore forwent a proper penalty-phase defense.

Cook responded that he felt there was no chance to make any argument during the guilt phase, since the evidence was overwhelming. Cook therefore placed all of his efforts into saving Cox's life. Cook felt the best chance of this was by surprising the prosecutor with the wrong-shooter argument.

In the world of capital appellate defense, attacking the trial attorney for ineffective assistance of counsel is a common tactic. Here the impetus of the federal attack was Cook's failure to show Tiequon in an appropriately sympathetic light, given his abusive childhood. They stressed that while Cook presented the basics, he did little to expose the true horror of Tiequon's upbringing and convince the jury to save the young man's life. Had this been done, Cox's attorneys argued, there was "a reasonable probability" that "the result of the proceeding would have been different."

In support of this argument, a clinical psychologist, David Lisak, asserted that "[d]uring the first twelve years of his life, Tiequon experienced well over a dozen incidents in his home and family life, so far outside the range of human experience, that each one alone meets the psychiatric criterion as a precipitator of PTSD." Lisak stated, "By the time of Tiequon's incarceration in the California Youth Authority at the age of 15, and his release at age 18, he had witnessed or been aware of so many gunfights, deaths, and maimings in his community of South Central Los Angeles that he would be classified as having endured moderate to heavy combat if assessed using criteria developed for the classification of adult Vietnam combat veterans."

In Cox's interviews with Lisak, Cox stated, "I never learned to have any goals about my future. I never had a positive sense of the future. I was never given that type of vision of the future." Cox continued, "I've seen people beaten up, beaten to death, robbed, get shot, run over and crushed. It makes you numb after awhile. You have to become numb to it or it will destroy you." He estimated that more than thirty close friends had died in gang disputes, and he assumed that he would be killed.

As a coping mechanism, he became hypervigilant and hyperprepared, both traits he would hone during his life in prison. Describing his life on the streets, he would "peer out the windows, check the bushes, look over the cars on the street, check the rooftops." He "listened for clicks, fast movements, car engines accelerating, doors slamming. These are all dead giveaways," he said. "So you learn to tune out the common sounds. You must, because if you miss a beat you might be dead."

———

As the days dragged on, Tami kept trying every number in Haiti she could summon, every contact she had ever made. For days, no luck.

Then, finally, she got through, reaching a key contact by phone.

Had he heard anything from any of the ministries?

He said it would take him a few hours to contact the ministries and that he would call her back.

Oh God, more waiting, nothing worse than waiting for a phone to ring. My memory of phone calls wasn't good. I would always think of Neal: "Why would they mess Mom up?"

When her contact failed to call back, Tami called him, and called him, and called him.

The odyssey continued.

If the shootings of August 31, 1984, initiated the hundred-year drive, the earthquake of January 12, 2010, inflicted the hundred-year wait. The unifying theme: suspended in limbo awaiting terrible news.

We prayed. Tami called. I paced.

And I kept pacing, walking around the house, out to feed the horses, clean the pool, anything to keep busy, sweep the patio so clean you could scrub yourself with the bricks. And then I'd return to the house and just sit there.

I stared into the rooms we'd arranged for the kids. The rooms we'd planned, set up, altered, and rearranged dozens of times in the years since the adoptions began.

And sometimes I'd flash back, to empty beds from another time. "Stop it," I'd command. But I didn't listen. I couldn't stop. Those other beds, children's beds flashed, jagged, angular, sharp colors, dark red, bodies trapped in blankets, forever frozen in sleep. "No," I barked. Those beds were different, soaked in blood, final, fatal, graves of the departed. These were different, clean, empty, but clean, clean awaiting new arrivals.

"Hope," my light side beckoned, "arrivals soon to come. Hope."

But the dark side, far stronger, crushed it. "You never really arrive, won't you learn. Every arrival begets heartbreak. Give up. Clean beds, yes," the dark side continued, "but only because the blood runs elsewhere."

"Stop it," I started, before I was interrupted.

Ringing. Well, one ring. It couldn't finish.

Tami grabbed the phone before the first ring was through. "Hello." Then silence.

She fell to the ground in tears.

———

According to his attorneys, as a child Tiequon's cognitive and emotional capacities were overwhelmed. "Children typically manifest PTSD symptoms somewhat differently than do adults," the psychologist, Lisak, wrote. "They may become jumpy, agitated and restless and be unable to sit still or concentrate for very long." "Traumatized children often desensitize themselves to protect themselves from the overwhelming emotions induced by the trauma."

And Tiequon manifested these symptoms, the psychologist argued, with friends and relatives describing him as "empty" and "numb." Cox said he figured out how to "block out thoughts." As a child, he was described by those around him as "shy and kind of withdrawn," "alert, careful, and always looking around," "quiet and watchful."

The psychologist concluded his assessment by linking Tiequon's hypervigilance with changes in his nervous system, and how these changes affected his ability to thrive and learn. "Tiequon, like many children who are forced to live under such chronic hyper-vigilance," the report stated, "showed other signs of his hyper-aroused nervous system: he could not sit still for long, showed repeated signs of psychomotor agitation and could not concentrate. His hyper-reactive nervous system was constantly being activated by stimuli which he could not screen out, for his life had taught him that all stimuli could signal danger. Not surprisingly, Tiequon had tremendous difficulties in school, where sitting still, concentrating, and screening out noise and distractions are mandatory for precision learning."

———

It sounded like a low chant, as words from a trance. It was other-worldly. It was a voice I had never heard come from her before. As she hung up the phone, she cradled it in her hands, repeating: "They're alive. . . . They're alive. . . . They're alive."

A path through the woods. Morning light slants across the Valley. Shadows ebb. The sun through the windows is electric.

We embrace, a moment of bliss. But only a moment, then hurled back into the world of planning and calculation.

"They're alive."

Now all we had to do was figure out how to get them out of there, something we had failed to do for the last six years.

I returned to the TV, but now with a fresh sense of hope. Tami got back on the phone.

We learned that following the earthquake, U.S. Secretary of Homeland Security Janet Napolitano announced that humanitarian parole would be granted to children already in the process of adoption.

We again returned our attention to the TV, continued scenes of devastation and relief efforts, devastation and relief. But for both of us, we felt an incredible personal relief. We saw immediate hope on a micro level. Everything Clinton, the UN secretary-general, the foreign ministers were speaking of, we would be part of. For the moment, it was good to be part of an international story.

But I had come not to trust the moment. It seemed all too often to turn into another moment, and then something else altogether.

But no matter what, we would do all in our power to bring immediate relief to five orphans as soon as we could. And we pledged in that moment that once the immediate chaos subsided, we would redouble our efforts to bring clean energy, which would mean clean water, to the people of Haiti.

As soon as we could we filled out paperwork to get all five kids on the federal list. We then engaged in a constant back-and-forth with the State Department, and then finally, with the dedicated efforts of a volunteer from a local radio station, were able to get the paperwork resubmitted and through the proper channels.

The major remaining snag was that the Haitian government, concerned with illicit adoptions and exploitation of the chaos following the earthquake, put a halt to most adoptions.

————

Finally, twelve days after the earthquake, and six years since we had started the adoption proceedings, we were told that the children would be on a plane to Florida.

Following another round of delays and misplaced documents, the State Department notified Tami. The news: the four children were on their way to Florida.

"Four, what do you mean four?" Tami said. "There's five."

"Five?" A pause. "Hold on, actually, we'll call you back."

After rounds of additional calls, Tami learned that Clifton's travel documents were missing. Clifton's paperwork had a hold placed upon it in an effort to prevent child trafficking, which was rampant in the disaster's wake. Clifton could not leave, because the government planned to restrict all traffic out of Haiti.

Calling an emergency number with a contact at the Department of Homeland Security, Tami learned that four of the children would arrive in Miami on January 25, 2010. But her contact said he would need several more days before he would know anything about Clifton.

As we continued our vigil, the news out of Haiti deteriorated. Strong aftershocks, routinely hitting 6.0, brought down more damaged and ill-constructed housing. Fears of an impending cholera epidemic spread as the desperate relied upon, and were surrounded by, only badly contaminated water. International aid agencies were trying to get as many children out of Haiti as they could, despite the restrictions.

Fearing that Clifton would be forever trapped in Haiti, Tami arranged for me to meet the other four kids in Florida, while she hired a pilot she knew to fly her to the Dominican Republic. From there she would have to travel west to the border, cross through the mountains, and then make her way across Haiti to the coast.

———

The habeas corpus petition shows a young man failed by society. Raised in a brutal home with an abusive, drug-addicted mother, he never stood a chance. Add to the lessons of the home—that random violence was the way of the world—the horrors of the schools and streets, the violence of gangs and police. The youth faced a life of kill or be killed. With no father, an out-of-control mother, and a war zone of a neighborhood, joining the gang was a survival strategy of last resort, a place of belonging, acceptance, and protection. Always moved between homes, with different rules, at best he had his great-grandmother, who was far from a loving, nurturing influence. She was overly restricting and controlling, only fostering rebellious tendencies in the confused youngster. And in the gang he was taken under the wing of older members who made him feel worthwhile and important, but in exchange, used him to do their dirty deeds. And thus on August 31, 1984, Tiequon Cox acted at the behest of the older OG, Darren Charles Williams.

He was an inevitable symptom of a racist society. Centuries of historical mistreatment created him: slavery, Jim Crow, separate and unequal, broken homes, degraded schools, abandoned neighborhoods, poor health care, and an abusive police department. Tiequon and thousands like him are what you get. He simply became what was unloaded upon him. He reflected what he saw. What right does his maker have to destroy him?

———

A guard looking at his prison photo shakes his head. "Evil," he says. "The guy is just plain evil." "He's a stone-cold killer." In the picture stands 240 pounds of pure muscle, scowling. The file through which the guard thumbs tells a story bare of redeeming qualities.

The psychological analysis: "Antisocial Personality Disorder." Cox is a sociopath, one who refuses to live by societal norms. The sociopath is an outlaw, seeing the law as something for others to follow. He knows what he is doing, and knows it's wrong. But he does it anyway. He doesn't care. He has no remorse, and feels no guilt. Others are merely a means to his ends. He is an assassin. He makes his name in blood. Even in the violent world of gangs he is an outlier.

———

As Tami hurried to catch her plane to the Dominican, the phone rang. It was the State Department again. Now we were told that all five kids were on their way to Orlando, Florida, four on a transport plane and one on a cargo plane.

Another switch in plans. Cancel Tami's flight to the DR. Pack, rush, move, get this thing done before there's another riot, coup, or sudden change of policy.

Soon both of us were on a red-eye to Orlando. In the early morning hours of January 26, 2010, we went through Homeland Security clearance. The vetting process was tight, due to constant rumors of human traffickers rushing Haitian refugees out of the country under the cover of confusion.

We were with Homeland Security for six hours. When we were released we found ourselves in a customs office with a hundred other people.

We kept looking over the crowd for a familiar face.

The room was loud, chaotic, filled with refugees, a din of French, Creole, English, crowded with disheveled adults, crying children, heaps of dirty makeshift luggage.

"Dad!" someone yelled. "Dad!" Then some pushing and jostling.

And then I was swarmed. One tried to jump on my back, two little ones hung on my legs. "Get down, get down," one said. On my knees now, five pairs of arms and legs pummeled me. I was drowning in a sea of children.

I couldn't stop crying.

They mauled me. They mauled Tami. It was heavenly.

After we finally peeled them off, we walked out of the hangar,

Tami in the lead, with the five kids trailing behind like ducklings. I pulled up the rear, proud as could be. Every few seconds I conducted a head count—one, two, three, four, five.

All here, in the United States, for good.

By the grace of God the ways of fate had changed.

42

THIRTY YEARS AFTER

"Dad, we're home," Clifton said, looking at me, as the plane landed in California.

None of them could get over the flight on a commercial airline. How could it be—a toilet on an airplane? They'd open the door, look inside, then look at us. There must be some mistake.

In their first night in an American hotel it took hours for them to shower. We couldn't get them out from under the hot water.

When they first set foot in their new home, they could not stop asking in disbelief, "Is this really ours?"

Full cupboards? And the refrigerator, stocked with food? They kept opening and shutting the door, as if the next time they did so, the food would somehow be gone. This couldn't be real.

Next cause of astonishment: the beds. They were amazed. They would actually get to sleep on a mattress. And each one gets their own bed? They would poke the bed, jump on it, pretend to sleep, then peek from a squinted eye, look at the others, grin, and begin to laugh. It was as if somehow a great joke were at play.

None of them could stop exploring their new home. Endlessly opening and shutting closet doors, going to the front door, ringing the doorbell, having others let them in, then doing it all again. "Hi," the kid outside the door would say. "I'm home." Then gales of laughter.

And the swimming pool—beyond belief. They would peer in, dip their feet, skim their hands across the water, and then one, two, three, everyone was in, kicking, splashing, squealing. If we thought it was hard to get them out of the shower . . . "No, come on Dad," they'd say, "just five more minutes." Hours later we'd pull them out, fingers wrinkled like prunes.

It is one of the magical memories of my life. Tami and I would just follow them around the house, the yard, trying to see all that we took for granted, through their eyes.

As we settled into our new lives in Riverside, the kids gradually let us into more of life in Haiti and the impact of the earthquake.

After the quake they slept outside, terrified of the violent aftershocks. They went two weeks without a bath or shower.

Jameson and Zachary were shooting baskets outside when it hit, confused as to why the court rippled like the sea. Semfia ate a bowl of rice, flustered as she couldn't get the spoon to her mouth. Manoucheka, working in the nursery, ran outside carrying infants in her arms.

Once in the States for several months, their nutrition and health quickly improved, and so did their height. Within a couple of months it seemed all of them had grown several inches. We have the markings, now dozens of them on our kitchen doorway. And while everyone continues to shoot up, the initial year was the most amazing.

With improved health, they all became obsessed with sports: soccer for Semfia, volleyball for Manoucheka, basketball for Jameson and Clifton, football for Zachary.

And if we thought it was hard getting them out of the pool, getting the kids off the dirt basketball court out back was next to impossible. "Time to come in," we'd say, which was met with a chorus of "No." When we finally corralled them, it was as if some great hardship had been imposed.

———

Every morning I rise by dawn. I fall to my knees and thank the Lord, and thank Madee. Her presence is strong, her voice loud. She led me to this outcome. She was right all along: little steps produce big results.

Once I healed, I could finally tell this story. Once again, I enjoy motivational speaking. I want everyone to know how important they are, that every day, life has meaning, that they can do something to make a difference. But it is a long process, a struggle. Nothing comes easy. No one should expect it to.

I speak of the benefits of sports, of my efforts with the NFL Players Association to make the game of football safer and more fair for the players. I talk of the need to get into the depths of our cities and continue to fight for their future, to make sure they do not slip back into their dark ages. I urge kids to stay in school, grow their minds, and stay out of gangs. I tell of my ordeal and pray we prevent the next Tiequon Cox, get him young, really young, before he has a chance to become a killer, before we as society pay the price. I detail our work in Haiti, of improved energy and infrastructure. There is no reason Haiti cannot follow in the footsteps of South Korea or recently Rwanda, war-torn countries that quickly Built Back Better.

But as I learned, one can't just talk, one must act. Each moment is a powerful, elusive, unpredictable opportunity. And as in football, you have to have a plan, be prepared ahead of time, see it coming, and then seize it. In a moment you can change or ruin lives, lead and inspire, or fire fatal shots.

———

On July 22, 2010, the Ninth Circuit Court of Appeals denied Tiequon Cox's claims of ineffective assistance of counsel, finding Cook's decisions tactical given the overwhelming evidence of guilt. On October 3, 2011, the United States Supreme Court denied Cox's certiorari petition, declining to review his case. Cox was SCOTUS cleared, all of his appeals exhausted.

Two years later, on May 2, 2012, Los Angeles County District Attorney Steve Cooley filed a motion with the Los Angeles Superior Court to order the execution of Tiequon Cox.

Cooley said it was time Cox paid for his crimes, and that the state must "hold these killers responsible for the innocent lives they took so many years ago." In the motion, the Los Angeles County District Attorney's Office, represented by Deputy District Attorney Michele

Hanisee, pled that the executions be ordered using a single-drug method now used in Washington State, Ohio, and Texas. "This is about getting our system back on track," Cooley stated. "It's time the state carry out the death sentences that have been returned by juries, imposed by trial judges, and affirmed by our appellate court system."

As the election neared, Tiequon Cox became the face of California's death penalty wars.

Since his release from the Adjustment Center in 2010, Cox "programmed." He was now housed on the fifth tier of East Block, Condemned. He took his yard time and otherwise stayed in his "house," a four-by-nine cell. He got phone time. An old push-button model attached to a sandwich board on wheels was brought to his cell. He talked to his "little homies" back in Hyde Park.

On the streets, he remained a legend. He didn't snitch. Even on death row, he didn't bow down. He was "reputable." As Donald Bakeer noted, back in the neighborhood children were named after him, and the "Fee" progeny extended into the "baby," "tiny," and "infant" generations.

On the streets, in hushed tones, the kids said, "They going to kill big homey."

In his cell, Cox kept a TV tucked under his bed. During the summer of 2012 he pulled it out to watch the London Olympic Games.

Prison staff described him as respectful, but hypersensitive to any signs of disrespect. He never complained. He requested nothing. Unlike most inmates, he refused medications, never taking so much as an aspirin.

While staff preferred his new attitude, they remained on guard, lest he lull them into a sense of false security, just waiting for that moment when they "slip," providing the opportunity to "get loose."

Throughout the fall of 2012, the polls showed continued support for capital punishment. In the weeks leading up to the election, I addressed the California Assembly in Sacramento, and later took the stage with former governors George Deukmejian, Pete Wilson, and Gray Davis to oppose the proposition seeking to abolish the death penalty.

As the election neared, and prosecutors sought Cox's execution, his lawyers maneuvered to save his life.

I received phone calls from Jesse Jackson and actor-activist Mike Farrell, who working with Cox's attorneys sought my support for clemency. I was curious what they would say and whether Cox would finally apologize. But efforts at scheduling a meeting became frustrating, and neither Jackson nor Farrell seemed to know anything about the case. In fact, Farrell, a champion of Tookie Williams, whom he termed a "dear friend," was unaware that Cox had stabbed Williams in prison. Furthermore, the Cox defense team sought total control of the meeting. When we agreed to speak with them at a friend's house in Santa Ana, they canceled. We haven't heard from them since.

On November 6, 2012, Proposition 34, the "Savings, Accountability, and Full Enforcement for California Act," or SAFE, was defeated, voters choosing to retain the death penalty in California.

In declaring victory, "No on 34" stated: "Now that the people have re-affirmed their support for the death penalty, we are committed to coming back to the voters with a reform proposition to streamline and expedite the death penalty in California."

When Jerry Brown ran for governor in 2010, he promised to uphold the law if elected.

Now Cox's name has been called, only the hour and date are unknown.

I've spent endless hours trying to understand him. I get anger. I get rage. But I don't get the callous slaughter of innocents. I don't get the lack of remorse.

Were there any doubt, it would be so different. The last thing I could take is the execution of an innocent. I don't need any more guilt.

I've been told he committed the crime to "prove himself," that he took PCP before the act, to pump himself up. For Cox it was nothing personal, just easy victims and sure success, business as usual, the deaths collateral damage. He killed for reputation. A young man filled with potential chose not to make his name through hard work on the field, instead seeking instant stardom on the streets.

All who cross Cox's path acknowledge his presence. He is talented, strong, intense. But he is ultimately tragic. Instead of channeling his influence for good, he uses it only to destroy. As Judge Boren reflected upon the case, he quoted the movie *A Bronx Tale*: "There's nothing worse than wasted talent."

I must forgive internally, as a means of survival, a way of dulling my rage so that I may go on, channel my energy, try to do some good. For me to obsess over him is to sentence myself to life. I will always have regrets, I will always ask "what if" about Tiequon Cox. But it is not just about me, and he did not victimize only my family. The crime was against the neighborhood, the community of South Central, the city of Los Angeles, this country and its values, against humanity.

True forgiveness does not come easy. It must be earned, created. It comes from reflection, long spells of guilt and suffering, followed by atonement through acts.

For thirty years my family has endured. Neal and Ivan have never recovered. We still await an apology.

―――――

As to the other two defendants, Horace Burns continues to serve his sentence of life without parole, shuttled from one maximum-security prison to another. Sometimes he is housed in the general population, at others placed in protective custody as a snitch. To this day, Burns insists he was not an active participant, and that being along for the ride should not have sent him to prison for the rest of his life.

Darren Charles Williams, with his death sentence commuted, serves a term of one hundred years. Like Burns, he has been moved from institution to institution. Williams has a website, freedarren .com, where he contends he was improperly sentenced, that his confession was coerced, and that his behavior at the time was dictated by his addiction to crack cocaine. On the site, one can view Williams's accomplishments, including his work with children, schools, and animals. Williams appears on the site wearing a short-sleeved shirt in front of a tropical island backdrop, and crouching in front of a virtual Bentley.

———

As to Ossie "Diamond Jack" Jackson, rumors floated throughout the neighborhood. The prosecutor's office said that without CW's cooperation they simply were never able to gather enough evidence to prosecute Jackson. When I searched for him, years ago, I was told all types of tales, and for a time believed that he had disappeared somewhere in the Caribbean. Today, a man in his eighties with the name of Ossie Jackson still resides in South Central Los Angeles. There is no statute of limitations on murder, and he isn't talking.

———

The club itself, where it all started, is gone. On Vermont and Gage one now finds a row of small businesses, a nail salon, a corner store.

———

Valarie Taylor still lives in the neighborhood, not far from the old site of the club. She remains in a wheelchair, still traumatized by the events of thirty years before.

"Oh no, honey, we've put that behind us," her mother says, expressing Valarie's unwillingness to revisit the events. "She's not talking about that." Her mother adds that familiar spots from long ago still trigger breakdowns and panic attacks. Valarie, her mother reminds us, was at the center, the paralyzed victim of the tavern shooting, and the intended victim of the home invasion. From what we have been told, after the shooting the lawsuit was dropped.

———

Back on the streets of Los Angeles, crime continues an unprecedented twenty-year drop.

Many Angelenos credit the work of Chief of Police William Bratton, who brought to Los Angeles the successful techniques of the "New York Miracle," where murder rates fell by nearly 90 percent in just twenty years. Under his successor in L.A., Charlie Beck, crime further declined. Beck has enhanced police-community efforts, and since 2007, gang murders have dropped again by 50 percent. Such programs include "Summer Night Lights," held in Lou Costello Park, a onetime gang hotbed. They are held from the Fourth of July through Labor Day, a period once referred to as "the killing season." The police message has gone from military to service, from occupying army to partners. The message to the community is "how can we help you." We are here to intervene, to halt retaliation, to put a lid on dangerous and violence-inducing gossip.

At Mayor Bradley's request, I served as an advisor to the Christopher Commission, which in the wake of the Rodney King incident sought to improve police conduct and community relations. Above all we stressed the need for increased accountability of both citizens and cops. The results are encouraging.

One of the best examples is in my old home, Watts, which has the greatest concentration of public housing in the West. In Watts, a program known as Community Safety Partnership has been implemented. More officers have been assigned, and community residents known as the Watts Gang Task Force have teamed up with the LAPD. Since the program's implementation, violent crime in Watts's public housing has fallen by more than 60 percent, and drive-bys have become almost a thing of the past. Key is that the police now have an aura of legitimacy in the community, a major goal of our Christopher Commission.

Recent polling shows that more than 80 percent of L.A. residents say the department is doing a good job, and majorities of every ethnicity report the department treats them with respect.

Gang violence and street crime in general will rise to the level of community tolerance: The more it is excused and the more that citizens turn the other way, the greater its contagion. The more you allow, the more you get. It is the duty of society to place restraints on its residents' worst tendencies. Such intolerance for wrongdoing provides the best opportunities for citizens to thrive. The approach of the LAPD today also fosters more community trust and encourages the kind of informal guidance and social control so influential during the time of my childhood and central to Madee's vision of a neighborhood.

Today, the tragedy of August 31, 1984, stands as a kind of period piece, a dark reminder of a bygone era. The crime was random. It could have been anyone. But it was a sign of the times, when emboldened gangsters felt confident they could dope up, invade a home, kill its residents, and walk away free. Sad, but Horace Burns spoke for these times when he dismissed the death of sleeping children as "just something that happened." Thankfully, a cultural change has occurred, with that way of thinking ever more distant.

Each year we hold the Alexander family picnic somewhere in the old neighborhood. Each year the community Madee fought to save feels a little bit better. Each year more people choose to return to the city. Now, people aren't just trying to flee the old hood, they're trying to fix it. Things are different. The dream is within reach.

43

A FULL HOUSE

It is a warm autumn evening, and family members gather at our home in Riverside. I sit at one head of the long dining room table, Tami at the other. In between are my sisters Joan and Mary, and my brother Gordon. We drink sweet tea from tall glasses.

Outside, dusk sets in. Tami turns on the overhead light above the table. The family is reflected in the sliding glass door.

As we reminisce, everyone is pleased at how well the kids are doing. There are certainly struggles, drama. Raising five kids in your seventies is a challenge. It's exhausting. It's energizing. They wear me out. They keep me young.

When four are calm, one flares up. When three comply, two rebel. Rarely are all five in line at the same time. But this is no surprise. And overall they thrive. They have been in California for several years now. They are the next generation of the dream, come out west to find their futures.

In the yard outside the dining room, the boys, Jameson, Clifton, and Zachary, play basketball in the fading light. Their yells and cheers create a reassuring backdrop to our conversation. Before me, in the living room, Manoucheka braids Semfia's hair, a ritual that will go on for hours. Before them, a Nancy Drew mystery plays on the TV. The pug, Mr. Goodman, and a mutt named Checkers sleep sprawled at the girls' feet.

At the table, my sister Joan looks through a series of family photographs. She wears a white T-shirt with a green design. The shirt says ALEXANDER FAMILY REUNION: 2010. It has a large tree with the boughs named after southern kin going back to the nineteenth century. Her expression changes as she comes to the pictures of the departed, the yearbook photos of Damon and Damani, the portrait of Dietra. She lifts her index and middle fingers to her lips and kisses them, then places the kissed fingers on each of the photographs and whispers, "Angels."

Behind Joan, the sliding door opens and the three boys come inside, panting, their deep Haitian voices filling the room. "Tacos," Clifton says hopefully. "No," Jameson counters. "Rice and beans." "No," says Zachary. "Pizza."

The door closes. The din of a dozen voices fills the dining area. Themes of dinner plans, rides to football games, and delivery of gift baskets compete. The front doorbell rings. Tami's daughter and granddaughter join the fray.

"How many people can we fit in this house?" I ask.

"One more." Tami laughs.

I recline, and smile. Years ago, Tami and I flew to Haiti to save the children. But it worked out the other way around.

Outside, the breeze rustles the high palms. A loosened frond drifts into the swimming pool. Beyond the pool, my Arabian horse swishes its tail to shoo flies.

Inside, on the dining room wall, a painting of Madee, wearing a Bruin-blue dress and matching earrings, watches over the scene. As she gazes down, she is pleased. The Alexander home is once again full, vibrant, wonderfully chaotic.

Madee always said, "There's nothing worse than an empty house."

My Family

(l to r: Jameson, Zachary, Manoucheka, Tami, me, Courtney Alexander-Shrieve, Clifton, Semfia)

Photograph courtesy of Dayna Perry

ACKNOWLEDGMENTS

Kermit would like to thank:

His parents, Ebora and Kermit Sr., who suffered unthinkable hardships to give their children the hopes of a better life, a greater education, and a relationship with God; his aunts, Eldora and Bertha, for their love and support during their own time of grief; his wife, Tami, for helping him find his way out of a deep darkness and regain a sense of purpose; his children, Kelton, Courtney, Candice, Manoucheka, Jameson, Clifton, Zachary, Semfia, and Cyauna, for reminding him how precious life is and how deep love can be; his brothers and sisters, Barbara, Mary Ann, Neal, Geraldine, Crystal, Joan, Gordon, Daphine, Kirk, Stacey, Troy, and Robin, who gave him strength to continue the battle for law and order; a preacher man named Tom, who prayed him back to the fold; and his friends Alex and Jeff for taking what was in his heart and putting it onto paper.

Alex and Jeff would like to thank:

Their family members for their ongoing patience and support during the writing of this book. Alex would especially like to thank his wife, Teresa, for her inspiration and invaluable editorial input.

All the authors would like to thank the following people for their contributions, without which this book would not have been possible: Alex Alonso, Donald Bakeer, George Bargainier III, Pete Bollinger,

Roger Boren, Wayne Caffee, Kelly Carroll, Mario Cavanola, Morgan Chappell, Edward Cook, Vernell Crittenden, Michelle Hannesee, Tricia McCarthy, Hal Miller, Tony Moreno, Eric Patao, Sam Robinson, Jeff Russell, David Sofaer, Willie Stokes, Dalida Vartanian, and Josh Williams.

The authors would also like to thank their agent, Scott Mendel, and editor, Todd Hunter, for their continued suggestions and support.

NOTE ON SOURCES

In addition to Kermit Alexander's personal recollections, this section lists the major sources used by the authors in each chapter. For books referenced, full citations are provided in the bibliography below.

1. An Empty House
The details of the interior of Ebora Alexander's house in the late summer and fall of 1984 utilize the crime scene photographs of the Los Angeles Police Department, as well as the trial testimony of the homicide detectives and criminalists.

2. There Were No Strangers
Ebora Alexander's regular routine, as well as her thoughts and concerns on the morning of August 31, 1984, are based on extensive personal conversations with members of the Alexander family. The section on the Los Angeles Olympics uses information from *Tom Bradley: The Impossible Dream*, by J. Gregory Payne and Scott C. Ratzan, as well as the ABC Sports Presents video *1984 Summer Olympic Highlights*. The scene set inside the 1975 Chevy van is based upon trial testimony of involved participants, personal discussions, and drives through the neighborhood with LAPD gang detectives and gang scholar Alex Alonso, as well as maps and photographs of South Central L.A. and National Weather Service data.

3. From Jim Crow to Mudtown
The history and culture of New Iberia come from the City of New Iberia home page online, as well as the authors' personal visit. *The Marines of Montford Point: America's First Black Marines* is used regarding Kermit Sr.'s

military service. The section on the Great Migration and the statistics of blacks entering Los Angeles utilizes Josh Sides's book *L.A. City Limits*. R. J. Smith's *The Great Black Way* contains information on post–World War II Los Angeles.

4. Charcoal Alley

Information on African Americans and UCLA is from "Reclaiming UCLA: the Education Crisis in Black Los Angeles," by Ana-Christina Ramon and Darnell Hunt, in *Black Los Angeles*. The scene involving Sondra Holt is based upon signed declarations from members of her family, found in the Excerpt of Record in the habeas corpus petition of Tiequon Cox filed in the Ninth Circuit Court of Appeals.

5. Mama, Go Get 'Em

The scene depicting Kermit's brother Neal and nephew Ivan is drawn from personal communications as well as their trial testimony. Details of the scene around 126 West Fifty-Ninth Street are taken from the *Los Angeles Herald Examiner* of September 1, 1984, and the *Los Angeles Times* of September 1, 1984.

6. Our Family Isn't Like That

The information on the criteria of the Robbery Homicide Division is from the LAPD website. The information on the murder of prostitutes in South Central is from the *Los Angeles Times*, October 3, 1985. The words of Kermit's sisters in the interrogation with detectives at the Newton Police Station come from personal discussions as well as from Tom Friend's article "Kermit's Song," for ESPN's *Outside the Lines*. Details of the crime scene are taken from the trial testimony of LAPD crime technicians. The information regarding the bodies of the deceased is from the trial testimony of the medical examiner from the Los Angeles County Coroner's Office.

7. The Hundred-Year Drive

The quotes regarding the crime are from the *Los Angeles Herald Examiner* of September 1, 1984, as well as from the *Los Angeles Times* of September 1, 1984. The quote from Jesse Jackson is from the *Chicago Sun-Times* of November 29, 1993. The words of Councilman Farrell are from the *Los Angeles Sentinel* on September 6, 1984. For other information on Farrell and his fight against crime, see the *Los Angeles Times*, February 14, 1981.

8. I Need to Go to the Hospital
The descriptions of the suspects and the findings of the LAPD fingerprint technician are taken from the trial testimony. The reconstruction of the crime by the homicide detectives is based upon their trial testimony and upon an article by Paul Ciotti in the *Los Angeles Times Magazine* on August 2, 1987.

9. The Lost Litter
The scene of the Alexander family in Kermit's sister Daphine's house is based upon personal communications with family members who were present as well as Paul Ciotti's *Los Angeles Times Magazine* article of August 2, 1987. Tom Friend's ESPN article, mentioned above, is also referenced in this chapter.

10. Black Tommy, Sweet Daddy
The police outreach to the community for leads in the case is from the *Los Angeles Sentinel* of September 6, 1984. The information regarding all of the false leads that were investigated is from the trial testimony of various detectives of the LAPD. The quote from John Hadl is from the *Los Angeles Herald Examiner* of September 1, 1984.

11. Eternal Rest Grant unto Them
The memorial brochure provided by the church is here referenced. Information on the funeral service is from newspaper accounts from the *Los Angeles Times* of September 8, 1984, and *Los Angeles Sentinel* of September 13, 1984. On the history of Holy Cross Cemetery see "Here Lies the History of Holy Cross Cemetery," in the *Culver City Patch* online, by Catherine Cloutier.

12. Alone
Josh Sides's *L.A. City Limits* is a source for the industrial history of South Central Los Angeles. For the lack of progress by the police in solving the case, the *Los Angeles Sentinel* from September 13, 1984, is referenced. The television movie *Brian's Song* is mentioned regarding Kermit's hit on Gale Sayers and his season-ending injury of 1968.

13. The Mayor Wants to See You
The words of Los Angeles's district attorney, Ira Reiner, are taken from the Reporter's Transcript on Appeal, from the case of *People v. Horace Burns*.

References to the Manson case refer to *Helter Skelter*, written by Vincent
Bugliosi with Curt Gentry. Truman Capote's *In Cold Blood* is referenced for
the Holcomb, Kansas, murders of 1959. The series of newspaper references
are from the *Los Angeles Times* of September 20, 1984.

14. I'm Afraid He'll Turn Into One
Tom Bradley: The Impossible Dream, by J. Gregory Payne and Scott C. Ratzan,
is the source of certain details regarding Mayor Bradley and his office. Information on Chief Daryl Gates comes from *Chief: My Life in the LAPD*, by
Daryl Gates and Diane K. Shah. Information on Chief William Parker is
found in John Buntin's *L.A. Noir*. For information on Pop Warner coaching
at the Carlisle School, see Lars Anderson's *Carlisle v. Army*. For analysis of
Chief Gates and the LAPD, see Mike Davis's *City of Quartz*. For critics of
Chief Gates's tactics in the 1984 Olympics, see George Barganier III's Ph.D.
dissertation, "Fanon's Children." Newspapers consulted for this section
include the *Los Angeles Sentinel* of November 8, 1984.

15. An Epidemic of Violence
General information on the violence of football and the history of the
NFL comes from Kevin Cook's *The Last Headbangers*, John Miller's *The
Big Scrum*, Lew Freeman's *Clouds Over the Goalpost*, and Daniel Flynn's *The
War on Football*. The 1951 University of San Francisco football program is
covered in the ESPN documentary *'51 Dons*. Information on Los Angeles
homicide rates in the days of the Wild West are found in Kevin Starr's *Cal-
ifornia*. More recent data comes from *Homicide in California 1981–2008*, by
George Tita and Allan Abrahamse, for the Governor's Office of Gang and
Youth Violence Policy, April 2010. Words of David Cunningham are found
in "Donna Murch Tells the Unknown Story of the Crack Epidemic's Effect
on Black and Brown People," from *Nommomagazine*, online.

16. Hyde Park
Information on the police raid is from the Reporter's Transcript from the
case of *People v. Tiequon Cox*. The section on the railroad monopoly is from
the *Elusive Eden* by Richard Rice et al. Demographics on Hyde Park are
from the *Los Angeles Times*, "Mapping L.A." The details of Hyde Park come
from photographs and the authors' personal trips through the neighborhood. Information on crack cocaine derives from declarations in the Excerpt
of Record in the habeas corpus petition of Tiequon Cox, as well as from

testimony found in the Reporter's Transcript in the case of the *People v. Darren Charles Williams*. Information on crack also comes from *Science Online*: How Stuff Works, by Stephanie Watson. The tactics employed by LAPD in assaulting the rock houses is from *Chief*, by Daryl Gates and Diane K. Shah, as well as Mike Davis, *City of Quartz*. Information on James Kennedy and the firearm is from the Reporter's Transcript of the trial of *People v. Tiequon Cox*. The name "Tony Anderson" is used in place of the real name of the juvenile detention officer who contacted Kermit.

17. Gladiators, Panthers, and Tales from the Crypt

Information on the history of black gangs in Los Angeles comes from Alex Alonso's article, "Out of the Void: Street Gangs in Black Los Angeles," in *Black Los Angeles*, as well as from his master's thesis, "Territoriality Among African-American Street Gangs in Los Angeles." On the Watts Riots, Gerald Horne's *The Fire Next Time* was useful. For varying opinions on the nature of the Black Panthers and the transition into the Crips, see George Barganier III's Ph.D. thesis, "Fanon's Children," Tookie Williams's *Blue Rage, Black Redemption*, and Daryl Gates and Diane Shah's *Chief*. For details of gang life and the gang identity, see Sanyika Shakur's *Monster*, Colton Simpson and Ann Pearlman's *Inside the Crips*, and Deshaun Morris's *War of the Bloods in My Veins*. Information also comes from personal communications with LAPD gang detectives, Alex Alonso, and George Barganier III.

18. Little Cat Man

Information on the Rolling Sixties is from personal interviews with LAPD gang detectives. Information on the M-1 carbine comes from the trial testimony of the firearms expert Jimmy Trahin. The interrogation of James Kennedy is drawn from the Reporter's Transcript in the case of the *People v. Tiequon Cox*. Descriptions of PCP users are taken from Spencer and Boren, *Residual Effects of Abused Drugs on Behavior*.

19. He Took a Wrong Turn

The fingerprint examiner's analysis is from the Reporter's Transcript in the case of the *People v. Tiequon Cox*. The updates on the arrest in the case are from the *Los Angeles Times* of October 24, 1984, and the *Los Angeles Sentinel* of October 25, 1984. Descriptions of Tiequon Cox are from personal communications with LAPD, San Quentin correctional officers, a Los Angeles County district attorney, and the Eight Tray Gangster Crip Monster Cody, in his memoir *Monster*. Accounts of Cox while incarcerated are from the Excerpt of Record in the habeas corpus petition. Cox's own words are likewise from the habeas corpus petition. Accounts of Detective Crews's search of Cox's great-grandmother's house are taken from the *Los Angeles Times* of October 24 and October 25, 1984.

20. It Went to My Heart
The account of Linda Lewis is taken from the Reporter's Transcript in the trial of *People v. Tiequon Cox*. The arrest of Horace Burns is based upon a personal interview with Tony Moreno. The words of Daryl Gates are from *Los Angeles Sentinel* on November 8, 1984. Information on Sterling Norris is from Paul Ciotti's article in the *Los Angeles Times Magazine* for August 2, 1987. Information on Horace Burns is from the Reporter's Transcript of the trial of *People v. Horace Burns*.

21. The Third Man Faces Death
Information on the history of the death penalty can be found in Robert J. Lifton and Greg Mitchell's *Who Owns Death?* Other specifics on the death penalty in California are from personal communications with San Quentin correctional officers. Information on the arrest of Williams is from the Reporter's Transcript of the trial of the *People v. Darren Charles Williams*. Information on the search for the money in Burns's backyard is from the Reporter's Transcript in the trial of *People v. Horace Burns*.

22. Horace vs. Horse
Details of the procedures of a capital case are taken from the Reporter's Transcript for the trials of *People v. Tiequon Cox* and *People v. Horace Burns*. Insights into the defense of Horace Burns were provided in a personal communication with defense counsel Hal Miller. The specifics of the jailhouse kite written by Burns are taken from a photocopy of Burns's letter included in the trial transcript.

23. Nothin' About Nothin'
The description of the early morning hours of August 31, 1984, is taken from the testimony of Ida Moore and Delisa Brown, as recorded in the Reporter's Transcript for both the cases of the *People v. Tiequon Cox* and the *People v. Horace Burns*. Likewise, Horace Burns's trial testimony is from the Reporter's Transcript.

24. Kill Them All

The closing argument of the district attorney and the defense counsel is from the Reporter's Transcript in the case of *People v. Horace Burns*. The procedures regarding Burns's conviction come from the Clerk's Transcript in the case of *People v. Horace Burns*. The editorial comment on the Burns case is from the *Los Angeles Sentinel*, June 20, 1985.

25. Do You Know Who That Is?

Information regarding the atmosphere entering the Cox trial, as well as the alleged threats, comes from personal communications with Judge Roger Boren and defense attorney Cook. The courtroom sequence between Judge Boren and attorney Cook is from the Reporter's Transcript for the trial of *People v. Tiequon Cox*. Tiequon Cox's own words are from the Excerpt of Record in the habeas corpus petition. Donald Bakeer's words are from the Excerpt of Record, as well as from his personal communication with the authors. Juror statements regarding Cox's demeanor at trial come from the Excerpt of Record.

27. Born of the South

The family history of Tiequon Cox is taken from the declarations set forth in the Excerpt of Record in the habeas corpus petition. The psychiatric testimony is likewise taken from the Excerpt of Record. The full scholastic and disciplinary record of Tiequon Cox is further provided in the Excerpt, as are the declarations of classmates and teacher Donald Bakeer.

28. So Drive

Procedures of the trial are provided in the Clerk's Transcript in the case of *People v. Tiequon Cox*, while the details of the van ride come from Ida Moore's and Delisa Brown's trial testimony as recorded in the Reporter's Transcript. Kennedy's testimony and the prosecutor's argument likewise come from the Reporter's Transcript. The incidents from Tiequon Cox's childhood are from the Excerpt of Record. The hearing between Judge Boren and Cox is from the Reporter's Transcript. The section about hardened gangsters breaking down over their mothers comes from João H. Costa Vargas, *Catching Hell in the City of Angels*.

29. Don't Cry
Information on the history of the Rolling Sixties comes from personal communications with LAPD gang detectives, San Quentin correctional officers, and gang scholar Alex Alonso. As to the origin of the nickname "Little Fee," this is based on personal communications with Alex Alonso as well as a personal conversation with a San Quentin correctional officer. Cox's words are taken from the Excerpt of Record. The words of attorney Ned Cook are from a personal communication. Cox's prior incidents are from the Reporter's Transcript of the trial, while the details of his time at CYA are taken from declarations found in the Excerpt of Record. The testimony in support of Cox during the penalty phase of the trial is recorded in the Reporter's Transcript.

30. Let Him Die on the Rocks
The closing arguments of the attorneys are found in the Reporter's Transcript of the trial. The words of Judge Boren in condemning Cox to death are found in the Clerk's Transcript.

31. The Gray Goose to the AC
The details of Cox's bus ride and admission to San Quentin are provided by San Quentin correctional officers. The information on San Quentin's history and architectural details are taken from trips inside San Quentin Prison and discussions with prison personnel. Accounts of the 1986 election are taken from the *Los Angeles Times* of November 5, 1986. The disciplinary incident involving Tiequon Cox is taken from interviews with prison personnel.

32. An American Tragedy
The information regarding Darren Charles Williams is taken from the Reporter's Transcript of his trial, as well as from a printed transcript of his interrogation. The details of the lawsuit involving Jack's Vermont Club are taken directly from the complaint and answer in the civil proceeding. The scene inside Jack's Vermont Club is based upon the contents of the lawsuit, testimony in the trial of Darren Charles Williams, as well as personal interviews with patrons of the bar who detailed the interior, the atmosphere, and the music that was played in the bar during the mid-1980s. The remainder of the testimony, as well as the comments of Ira Reiner, is found in the Reporter's Transcript.

33. To Reign in Hell
The information on California's prison gangs comes from personal communications with San Quentin correctional staff, as well as an interview with Willie Stokes. Books providing information on prison gangs include Chris Blatchford's *Black Hand*, Willie Stokes's *The Testimony of a Black Sheep*, and Colton Simpson and Ann Pearlman's *Inside the Crips*. The details of death row are from the authors' personal visits to East Block Condemned. The incident in which Tiequon Cox stabbed Tookie Williams is from the personal communications with San Quentin personnel, and from the *Los Angeles Times* of June 11, 1989.

34. I Cannot Forgive the Choice
The denial of Tiequon Cox's appeal is from the opinion of the California Supreme Court. The account of the execution of Robert Alton Harris is from the *St. Petersburg Times* of April 22, 1992.

36. A Superhero
The denial of Darren Charles Williams's lawsuit is taken from the decision of the Ninth Circuit Court of Appeal. The account of the execution of William Bonin is taken from the *Orange County Register* of February 24, 1996. The reversal of Darren Charles Williams's verdict of death is from the opinion of the California Supreme Court. The escape attempt of Tiequon Cox is based upon a personal communication with members of San Quentin staff as well as the *San Francisco Chronicle* of July 27, 2000. Information on Roscoe Tuilaepa and Noel Jackson is taken from personal communications with prison staff as well as from the court opinions in their cases in the California Supreme Court.

38. The Land of High Mountains
On the history of Haiti see Philippe Girard, *Haiti*; Laurent Dubois, *Haiti: The Aftershocks of History*; and Graham Greene's novel *The Comedians*. For Kermit's relationship with Tami Clark and their trips to Haiti see Tom Friend's article and the video "Kermit's Song" on ESPN's *Outside the Lines*.

39. We Can't Do This
For the execution of Tookie Williams, see the *San Francisco Chronicle* of December 13, 2005, the *New York Times* of December 14, as well as Williams's book *Blue Rage, Black Redemption*. Authors' personal communications with

San Quentin correctional officers also informed the material on Williams's execution. Likewise, information regarding Tiequon Cox's routine in the Adjustment Center is based upon such personal interviews.

40. We Take Them All
Opinion of Judge Fogel in *Morales v. Tilton* (2006).

41. News That Demands a Chair
Information on many aspects of the Haitian earthquake of January 2010 comes from Paul Farmer's *Haiti After the Earthquake*. The symptoms and diagnosis of post-traumatic stress disorder are from the *Diagnostic and Statistical Manual of Mental Disorders, Fourth Edition*. Information on the Clintons' efforts in Haiti are taken from Philip Rucker, "Haiti Holds a Special Place in the Hearts of Bill and Hillary Clinton," *Washington Post*, January 16, 2010. On California's petition to abolish capital punishment, sources included personal communication with members of victims' rights groups, district attorneys, members of the ACLU, and various other interested parties. On Cox's appeal and assertion of PTSD, sources include the legal briefs filed by his attorneys as well as the psychiatrist's report included in the Excerpt of Record for the habeas corpus petition.

42. Thirty Years After
For information on Cox's appeal, see the opinion of the Ninth Circuit Court of Appeals. Information on Cox in prison is from San Quentin staff. Judge Boren's words are from a personal interview. Information on District Attorney Steve Cooley's motion to execute Cox is found in the *San Francisco Chronicle* for August 12, 2012. Darren Charles Williams's website, FreeDarren.com, was accessible at the time of this writing. Information on the present whereabouts of Burns, Williams, and Ossie Jackson is provided by Alex Alonso. The information on Valarie Taylor comes through a personal communication with her mother and Alex Alonso's contact with her sister. Information on the crime drop in Los Angeles is from John Buntin, "What Does It Take to Stop Crips and Bloods from Killing Each Other?," *New York Times Magazine*, July 10, 2013.

BIBLIOGRAPHY

Alonso, Alex. "Territoriality Among African-American Street Gangs in Los Angeles." Master's thesis, University of Southern California, 1999.

American Psychiatric Association. *Diagnostic and Statistical Manual of Mental Disorders*. 4th ed. Washington, DC: American Psychiatric Association, 1994.

Anderson, Lars. *Carlisle vs. Army: Jim Thorpe, Dwight Eisenhower, Pop Warner, and the Forgotten Story of Football's Greatest Battle*. New York: Random House, 2008.

Asbury, Herbert. *The Gangs of New York: An Informal History of the Underworld*. 1928, reprint, New York: Vintage, 2008.

Bakeer, Donald. *South Central L.A. Crips: The Story of the South Central L.A. Street Gang from 1971–1985*. Los Angeles: Precocious, 1987.

Barganier, George Percy, III. "Fanon's Children: The Black Panther Party and the Rise of the Crips and Bloods in Los Angeles." Ph.D. diss., University of California, Berkeley, 2011.

Bennett, Lerone, Jr. *Before the Mayflower: A History of Black America*. 6th revised ed. New York: Penguin Books, 1988.

Bentley, Brian S. *One Time: The Story of a South Central Los Angeles Police Officer*. Los Angeles: Cool Jack, 1997.

Bing, Leon. *Do or Die*. New York: HarperCollins, 1991.

Blatchford, Chris. *The Black Hand: The Bloody Rise and Redemption of "Boxer" Enriquez, a Mexican Mob Killer*. New York: Harper, 2008.

Brands, H. W. *American Dreams: The United States Since 1945*. New York: Penguin, 2010.

Brook, John Lee. *Blood In, Blood Out: The Violent Empire of the Aryan Brotherhood*. London: Headpress, 2001.

Bugliosi, Vincent, with Curt Gentry. *Helter Skelter*. New York: Bantam, 1974.

Buntin, John. *L.A. Noir: The Struggle for the Soul of America's Most Seductive City*. New York: Three Rivers Press, 2009.

Cannon, Lou. *Official Negligence: How Rodney King and the Riots Changed Los Angeles and the LAPD*. Boulder, CO: Westview Press, 1999.

Capote, Truman. *In Cold Blood*. New York: Random House, 1965.

Cook, Kevin. *The Last Headbangers: NFL Football in the Rowdy, Reckless '70s*. New York: Norton, 2012.

Corwin, Miles. *Homicide Special: A Year with the LAPD's Elite Detective Unit*. New York: Owl Books, 2003.

———. *The Killing Season: A Summer Inside an LAPD Homicide Division*. New York: Simon & Schuster, 1997.

Cureton, Steven R. *Hoover Crips: When Cripin' Becomes a Way of Life*. Lanham, MD: University Press of America, 2008.

Davis, Deborah. *Guest of Honor: Booker T. Washington, Theodore Roosevelt, and the White House Dinner That Shocked a Nation*. New York: Atria Books, 2012.

Davis, Mike. *City of Quartz: Excavating the Future in Los Angeles*. New York: Vintage Books, 1990.

Dubois, Laurent. *Haiti: The Aftershocks of History*. New York: Picador, 2012.

Dunn, William. *Boot: An LAPD Officer's Rookie Year in South Central Los Angeles*. New York: iUniverse, 2008.

———. *The Gangs of Los Angeles*. New York: iUniverse, 2007.

Engel, Howard. *Lord High Executioner: An Unashamed Look at Hangmen, Headsmen, and Their Kind*. Buffalo, NY: Firefly Books, 1996.

Farmer, Paul. *Haiti: After the Earthquake*. New York: PublicAffairs, 2011.

Flynn, Daniel J. *The War on Football: Saving America's Game*. Washington, DC: Regnery, 2013.

Frady, Marshall. *Martin Luther King, Jr.: A Life*. New York: Penguin, 2002.

Freedman, Lew. *Clouds Over the Goalpost: Gambling, Assassination, and the NFL in 1963*. New York: Sports Publishing, 2013.

Gates, Daryl, with Diane K. Shah. *Chief: My Life in the LAPD*. New York: Bantam, 1992.

Gentry, Curt. *J. Edgar Hoover: The Man and the Secrets*. New York: Norton, 1991.

Girard, Philippe. *Haiti: The Tumultuous History—From Pearl of the Caribbean to Broken Nation*. New York: Palgrave Macmillan, 2005.

Greene, Graham. *The Comedians*. New York: Penguin, 1967.

Griffin, John Howard. *Black Like Me*. New York: Signet, 1962.

Hagedorn, John M. *A World of Gangs: Armed Young Men and Gangsta Culture*. Minneapolis: University of Minnesota Press, 2008.

Harris, Joseph E. *Africans and Their History*. New York: Meridan, 1972.

Hobsbawm, E. J. *Primitive Rebels: Studies in Archaic Forms of Social Movement in the 19th and 20th Centuries*. New York: Norton, 1959.

Horne, Gerald. *Fire This Time: The Watts Uprising and the 1960s*. Charlottesville: University Press of Virginia, 1995.

Hunt, Darnell, and Ana-Christina Ramon, eds. *Black Los Angeles: American Dreams and Racial Realities*. New York: New York University Press, 2010.

Hurston, Zora Neale. *Tell My Horse: Voodoo and Life in Haiti and Jamaica*. 1938; reprint, New York: Harper Perennial, 2009.

Irwin, John. *Lifers: Seeking Redemption in Prison*. New York: Routledge, 2009.

Lieberman, Paul. *Gangster Squad: Covert Cops, the Mob, and the Battle for Los Angeles*. New York: Thomas Dunn Books, 2012.

Lifton, Robert J., and Greg Mitchell. *Who Owns Death? Capital Punishment, the American Conscience, and the End of Executions*. New York: HarperCollins, 2000.

McLaurin, Melton A. *The Marines of Montford Point: America's First Black Marines*. Chapel Hill: University of North Carolina Press, 2007.

Mailer, Norman. *Executioner's Song*. 1979; reprint, New York: Grand Central, 2012.

Miller, John J. *The Big Scrum: How Teddy Roosevelt Saved Football*. New York: HarperCollins, 2011.

Moore, Joan W. *Going Down to the Barrio: Homeboys and Homegirls in Change*. Philadelphia: Temple University Press, 1991.

Moreno, Tony. *Lessons from a Gang Cop*. Los Angeles: Moreno, 2003.

Morris, Dashaun "Jiwe." *War of the Bloods in My Veins: A Secret Soldier's March Toward Redemption*. New York: Scribner, 2008.

Parson, Dan. *Making a Better World: Public Housing, the Red Scare, and the Direction of Modern Los Angeles*. Minneapolis: University of Minnesota Press, 2005.

Patterson, James T. *The Eve of Destruction: How 1965 Transformed America*. New York: Basic Books, 2012.

Payne, J. Gregory, and Scott C. Ratzan. *Tom Bradley: The Impossible Dream*. Santa Monica, CA: Round Table, 1986.

Perkins, Useni Eugene. *Explosion of Chicago's Black Street Gangs 1900 to Present*. Chicago: Third World Press, 1987.

Rice, Richard B., William A. Bullough, and Richard J. Orsi. *The Elusive Eden: A New History of California*. New York: McGraw-Hill, 2002.

Robinson, Eugene. *Disintegration: The Splintering of Black America*. New York: Anchor Books, 2010.

Ross, Jeffrey Ian, and Stephen C. Richards. *Behind Bars: Surviving Prison*. Indianapolis: Alpha Books, 2002.

Sarat, Austin. *When the State Kills: Capital Punishment and the American Condition*. Princeton, NJ: Princeton University Press, 2001.

Shakur, Sanyika. *Monster: The Autobiography of an L.A. Gang Member*. New York: Grove Press, 1993.

Sides, Hampton. *Hellhound on his Trail: The Electrifying Account of the Largest Manhunt in American History*. New York: Anchor Books, 2010.

Sides, Josh. *L.A. City Limits: African American Los Angeles from the Great Depression to the Present*. Berkeley: University of California Press, 2003.

Simpson, Colton, with Ann Pearlman. *Inside the Crips: Life Inside L.A.'s Most Notorious Gang*. New York: St. Martin's Griffin, 2005.

Smith, R. J. *The Great Black Way: L.A. in the 1940s and the Lost African-American Renaissance*. New York: PublicAffairs, 2006.

Spencer, John, and John Boren, eds. *Residual Effects of Abused Drugs on Behavior*. National Institute of Drug Abuse, Research Monograph 101. Rockville, MD: U.S. Department of Health and Human Services, 1990.

Starr, Kevin. *California: A History*. New York: Modern Library, 2005.

Steele, Shelby. *The Content of Our Character: A New Vision of Race in America*. New York: Harper Perennial, 1991.

Stokes, Willie R. *The Testimony of a Black Sheep*. Salinas, CA: Author, 2009.

Vargas, João H. Costa. *Catching Hell in the City of Angels: Life and Meaning of Blackness in South Central Los Angeles*. Minneapolis: University of Minnesota Press, 2006.

Vigil, James Diego. *A Rainbow of Gangs: Street Cultures in the Mega City*. Austin: University of Texas Press, 2002.

Wald, Elijah. *The Dozens: A History of Rap's Mama*. New York: Oxford University Press, 2012.

Walker, Lee H. *Rediscovering Black Conservatism*. Chicago: Heartland Institute, 2009.

Wilkerson, Isabel. *The Warmth of Other Sons: The Epic Story of America's Great Migration*. New York: Vintage, 2010.

Williams, Stanley Tookie. *Blue Rage, Black Redemption*. New York: Touchstone, 2004.

INDEX

Police Department, L.A. (LAPD) (*cont.*)
Alexander family funeral and, 74
Alexander murders investigated by, 3, 39, 42–44, 46–49, 54–56, 58–62, 69–73, 81, 85, 88, 94, 98–99, 101–3, 127–36, 138–39, 142–43, 147, 151–52, 226–27, 229–31, 234
Alexander murders reconstructed by, 59–61
Alexander's arrest by, 94–95
Alexanders interrogated by, 42–43, 46, 55–56
Bradley and, 11, 13, 96–98, 101
Burns's trial and, 159, 174
Central Division of, 142
City Hall and, 96
Community Resources Against Street Hoodlums (CRASH) Unit of, 100, 102, 109, 142
and Cox's childhood and adolescence, 302
Cox's criminal record and, 210–11, 213
Cox's mother and, 191, 202–3
criticisms of, 101
drug raids and, 100, 109–12
Gang Enforcement Unit of, 142
Harris and, 245
high-profile investigations of, 40
Kennedy interrogated by, 126–28, 131–34, 138–39
and killer of black prostitutes, 41
leads pursued by, 70–71
Metropolitan Division of, 49
and motive in Alexander murders, 62, 69, 71
Newton Division of, 41–42, 46, 48–49
Olympics and, 100
relations between community and, 81, 86, 117, 311–12
Robbery and Homicide Division (RHD) of, 40–41, 59, 126, 131, 142, 151, 226
77th Street Division of, 41–42, 100
Southeast Division Patrol Unit of, 210
street gangs and, 99–100, 102
and suspects in Alexander murders, 69–70
and threats to Lewis, 144
and violence in South Central, 8, 52–53, 248
Watts Riots and, 30
Williams interrogated by, 151–52, 226–27, 229–30, 234–36
Williams's trial and, 226, 230–31, 234, 236
Ponce, Fernando, 69
Pop Warner football, 97, 102, 184–87
Port-au-Prince, 264, 270–71, 284, 286
earthquake near, 291–94
post-traumatic stress disorder (PTSD), 293, 296–97, 299
Preston School of Industry, 212
prison gangs, 238–39, 241, 255, 258
Prohibition, 108, 222

Q

Quisenberry, Dan, 93

R

Ramirez, Richard (Night Stalker), 40
Rancho La Ballona, 77–78

Reagan, Ronald, 11, 92, 225

Reconstruction, 26

Reiner, Ira, 90, 147, 236

Retton, Mary Lou, 12

Reynoso, Cruz, 224–25

Robinson, Jackie, 28–29

Rodriguez, Cesar, 231

Rolling Sixties Crips (RSC):

Burns and, 141–42, 147, 160–61,
164, 169–72

Cox and, 136, 160–61, 178, 183,
197, 208–9, 213, 215, 219, 240,
254, 258, 281

intragang wars of, 125

Kennedy and, 112, 126–28

and motive in Alexander murders,
147

origins of, 208

at San Quentin, 240–41, 254, 256

and threats to Lewis, 144

violence and crimes of, 126–27

Williams and, 151–52, 169, 236, 240

Roosevelt, Franklin, 294

Roosevelt, Theodore, 107

Rosenberg, Ethel, 150

Rotstein, Joanne, 182, 215–17

S

St. Columbkille Roman Catholic
Church, 10, 48, 74, 76

St. Eugene's Catholic Church, 74–75

St. Vincent's Hospital, 10, 179

San Francisco, Calif., 9, 14, 32, 40, 63,
84, 98, 151, 221, 292

San Francisco, University of (USF), 106

San Francisco 49ers, 4, 29–30, 32, 37,
87, 97, 106–7

San Mateo Daily Journal, 278

San Quentin State Prison:

Adjustment Center (AC) at, 223–25,
241, 254–58, 280–81, 308

Condemned Unit at, 224,
238–42, 245, 247, 252, 254–56,
281, 308

Cox's imprisonment at, 220,
223–25, 238, 240–42, 247,
254–58, 280–82, 308

Cox's transfer to, 221–23

executions at, 216, 222, 244–47,
252–53, 276, 278, 289, 296

physical appearance of, 221–22

prisoners' takeover attempt at,
256–58

Williams's imprisonment at, 238,
240, 252, 254, 277

Williams's lawsuit against, 252

Santos, Alfredo, 222

Savings, Accountability, and Full
Enforcement for California Act
(SAFE), 309

Sayers, Gale, 87, 266

Schwarzenegger, Arnold, 278

Scott, "Monster" Kody, 122

Shea, Joe, 75–77

Shelley v. Kraemer, 159, 189

Sherry, William, 58

Simpson, O. J., 12, 136, 184

Singletary, Mike, 266

Slauson, J. S., 14

Slauson Avenue, 14–15, 38, 77, 82,
166

Slausons, 116, 119

slaves, slavery, 26–27, 66, 302

Haiti and, 264, 273

Snoop Dogg, 276

Soledad State Prison, 238